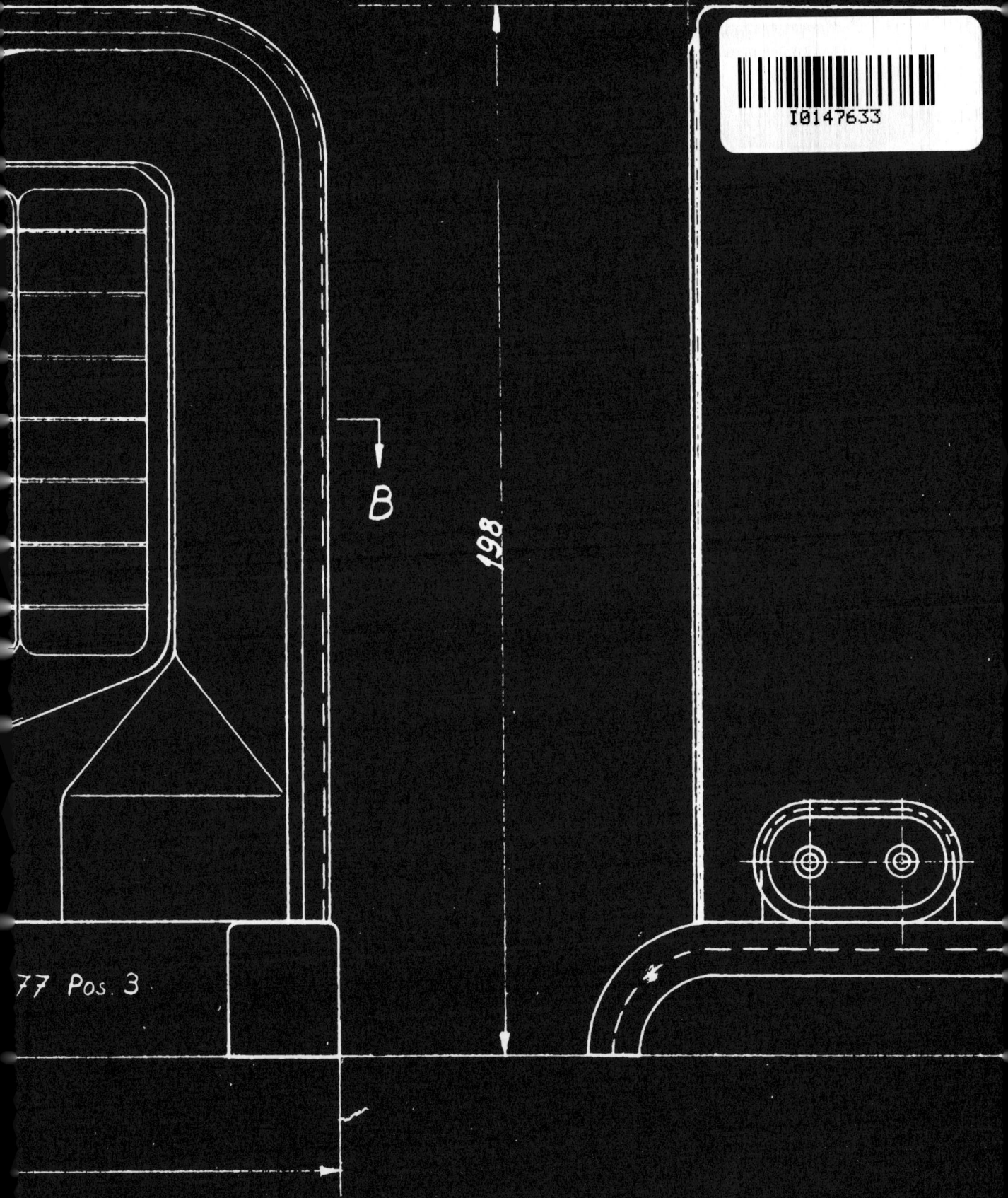

64

198

B

77 Pos. 3

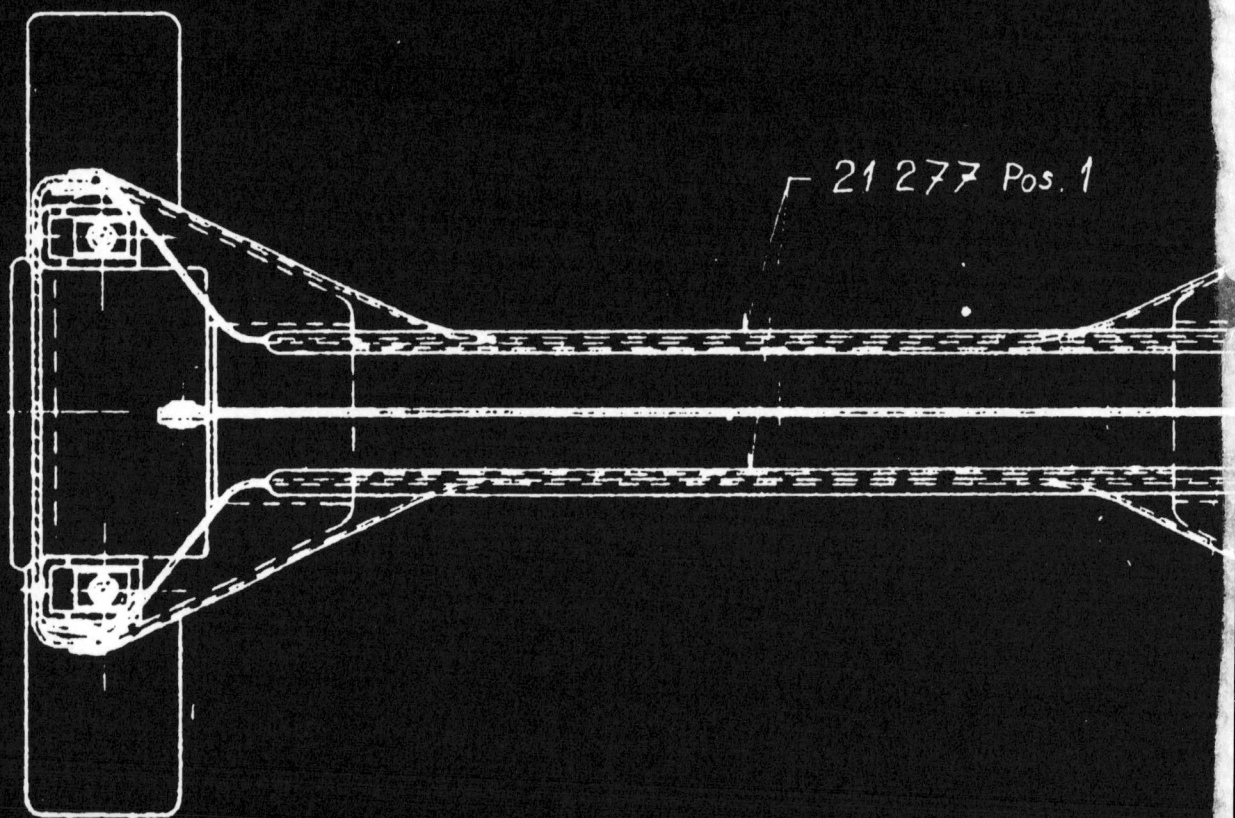

21 277 Pos. 1

Schnitt B-B

Therma Swiss Pioneer of Electric Appliances 1904–1978

Claude Lichtenstein

Lars Müller Publishers

Contents

On the Sources

The archive of Therma's history is held by Stiftung Glarner Wirtschaftsarchiv (Glarus Economic Archives Foundation/GWA) in Schwanden (Glarus South): written documents, printed matter, sources on the history of construction and photographic prints of products and buildings (www.glarnerwirtschaftsarchiv.ch). Six months after starting work on this publication, a surprisingly large collection of photo negatives was added to the project – more than 20,000 glass plates, sheet films and slides in various formats. The selection made after viewing these images has decisively influenced the character of this book. A significant number of the illustrations in this publication stem directly from these negatives. The traces of processing they displayed (retouching, manual color grading) or remnants of chemical decomposition processes have been kept in many cases. The negative numbers were often scratched into the coating of the glass plates and therefore frequently appear as mirror images.

The Question of Dating

Several markers are relevant when dating the development of an industrially manufactured object:

– patent applications
– factory plans
– dated photographs of study models, prototypes, production-ready models or products
– dates within model designations
– initial advertisements in the printed press
– initial presentations at trade fairs
– documentation in dated catalogs
– mentions in the minutes of meetings, in annual reports or in correspondence

Against this backdrop, it is generally not possible to date a specific development project with a high degree of precision.

Most of the negatives in Therma's photo archive are numbered, with the year forming part of the numbering system as a prefix. In most cases, however, more precise information about the specific day and month is missing. Before 1947 it is possible to provide approximate dates, thanks to other established details (such as photographs of letters with a date). It seems fair to assume that the sequential numbering of the negatives each year would be chronological. Some of the Therma prints in the Glarner Wirtschaftsarchiv (although not the negatives) have a date added in handwriting from the period when they were created.

The set of catalogs and brochures available to the author was not complete. In some cases the publications are not dated.

In extant appliances, the date of manufacture can be deduced from the serial number and factory number, but this does not reveal the period during which technical development occurred. The point in time when production of a particular model commenced is only indicated by the first instance of the list number in the manufacturing logbooks.

In some cases the dating of an object is therefore an estimate, although the degree of imprecision should be limited to one or at most two years. That does not affect the publication's division into sections on particular eras (Parts 1 to 6).

Therma Schaulager

The display showroom known as Therma Schaulager has been open to the public since September 2024: a permanent exhibition with over three hundred appliances from the entire period from 1904 to 1978 (cooking stoves and table-top hotplates, heating stoves and radiant heaters, irons, cooking appliances, toasters, coffee machines, refrigerators and much more), as well as documents and excerpts of films. It is housed on the second floor of the former enameling plant, completed in 1931. A local-interest foundation, Stiftung Pro Schwanden und Umgebung, runs and funds the exhibitions.

www.therma-schaulager.ch

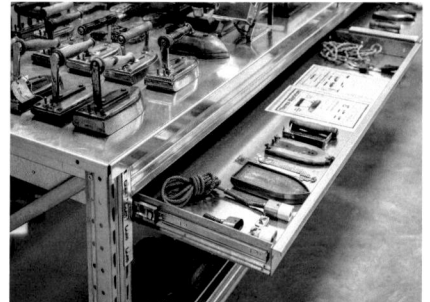

From the Shadow of the Mountain to the World Market

Therma, an electrical appliances manufacturer, numbered among Switzerland's most important industrial firms for decades and was nothing less than a global company in the interwar period, exporting its products to almost every continent. After 1945, its significance dwindled and it primarily became a major player in Switzerland, again working in a spirit and on a scale that was new and groundbreaking for that era. This book traces the company's development from 1904 to 1978.

Founded as a family business in 1904, S. Blumer, Schwanden, Fabrik elektrischer Heiz- und Kochapparate subsequently became Therma, Fabrik für elektrische Heizung A.G., formerly S. Blumer, in 1907. For two decades, until 1954, the name on the letterhead was Therma, Fabrik für elektrische Heizung A.G. In 1954 the company was renamed Therma AG, in conjunction with a change to the articles of association. Although the Electrolux Group absorbed the company in 1978, appliances were still produced in Schwanden until 2015 – including some developed under the Therma brand. Therma remained an active brand name until 2004 and is still protected by Electrolux today. In the interest of simplicity, this book refers to Therma and its parent company in Schwanden.

Over the course of these decades, the parent company gradually became the center of a group with multiple branches (the Therma Group) that encompassed subsidiaries such as Kummler & Matter, Elcalor, Maxim, Sursee, Grossküchen Schlieren and one subsidiary in both Austria (Volta, Bregenz) and Germany (Therma Hergensweiler, Baden-Württemberg). It would be beyond the scope of this book to address the various phases underlying the firm's expansion into a corporate group from the perspective of developments in economic history; that would also blur this publication's primary purpose as a design history. However, these aspects cannot be omitted entirely. We endeavor in this account to weave together the relevant contextual aspects that are mentioned and explained to form a plausible narrative. The spotlight nevertheless remains on Therma and its headquarters in Schwanden.

At certain times as many as 1,200 people worked in this village, the main settlement in the Glarus hinterland, in a factory complex that underwent multiple expansions between 1908 and 1963. For decades, the three hundred meters from the train station to the factory entrance were as crowded as a big city when work began early in the morning. There were even "Therma trains" in the main valley, timed to suit the work schedules of Therma's labor force.

As always in such cases, various factors had to come together before something like this could become reality. Someone had to set the ball rolling, which in this case proved to be a man who was almost still a teenager: Samuel Blumer, who was much more of an enquiring empiricist by nature than a heroic visionary. He took the first step at the turn of the century when he was barely twenty years old. At the time, he did not know that it would be the first of many subsequent steps; he had simply stumbled upon a subject that he found enormously fascinating: electricity. That fascination often prevented him from doing work that would have been more important for his family at the time (chopping wood, clearing snow?); he later made comments along those lines. However, his persistence and gift for asking questions served him well when he bought an iron on the market, examined its inner workings and realized that the heating element was poorly designed. He developed his own and, convinced of its superior design, applied for a patent. That was the first of what were to be many patents. It suggests that he was already thinking about his own manufacturing infrastructure at a very young age. That laid the foundation for Therma's amazing history.

If he had been shown the photograph of the Therma building complex in Schwanden when he was twenty and seen how it would look thirty years later, (→2.5) he probably would have been astonished and incredulous and would probably have been quite shocked at his initial innocence to boot. That should by no means be held against him. The idea of a prophet with an early major project in the pipeline that is vindicated by the course of time does not do justice to Samuel Blumer. Given the importance of the company and indeed the group that developed from the young man's irresistible leanings, he could be seen instead as a phenotype of the sorcerer's apprentice who is just doing his own thing and only realizes afterwards what he has unleashed. Although there is one important difference for, in contrast to the fairy tale, Blumer did not watch helplessly as the porridge boiled over on the stove and spilled out into the world; he instead knew precisely how to help prevent such loss of control in housewives' – yes, housewives' – everyday life in the kitchen with his ingeniously designed appliances.

Therma in Schwanden had long been the major employer in the canton of Glarus. Blumer must have felt the heavy weight of responsibility on his shoulders. Although he relinquished this responsibility formally in 1928 – aged just forty-seven and for health reasons – he remained associated with the company throughout his life and the workforce always remembered him as a fair boss even after his departure. It goes without saying that an industrial company is never a sure-fire success but must hold its own in a competitive environment and react to historical, social, market, domestic and foreign policy constellations, not to mention technological developments. That is easier said than done. Therma provides an impressive example of what it really entails and the demands it places on company management every day around the clock. While this book primarily addresses the history of the products – their development, structural engineering, manufacturing processes and use, i.e. their design in the broadest sense of the term – it is crucial to consider these other factors, too. That involves reflecting on what it means to maintain a pioneering company's status in the long term, to transform a firm with an aptitude for progress into a byword for reliable quality, out of responsibility not only for the shareholders, but also for the employees, who come from the same geographical context and from social milieux you know and recognize.

This all took place in the Swiss canton with the highest level of industrialization relative to its population at the time. In the canton of Glarus, which covers roughly 685 square kilometers and had a population of roughly 33,000 when Therma was founded, the local populace had not been able to earn their living from farming since the late Middle Ages. However, thanks to the steep gradient of the rivers in the Glarus hinterland, the Linth and Sernf, which thus offered a ready source of energy, the topography attracted trade and industry, especially the textile industry (spinning mills, weaving mills, fabric printing plants).[1] Their origins lie in the early eighteenth-century cottage industry, when numerous Glarus families spun yarn from raw cotton for traders in Zurich. Machine spinning displaced this cottage industry after 1750, driving the population into poverty; a few poor harvests around the mid-nineteenth century prompted hundreds from the canton to emigrate to the New World, where they founded New Glarus in rural Wisconsin. Shortly afterwards, however, major weaving mills and fabric printing works were established in Glarus, which rapidly became a major player on the world market. In 1864, Glarus was the first Swiss canton to enact labor legislation; its cantonal Factory Monitoring Act limited the workday to twelve hours, prohibited night work, granted protection to pregnant women, banned factory labor for children under twelve and made factories subject to mandatory inspection.[2] This legislation, along with the Glarus textile companies' international success, secured a sustainable livelihood for the valley for decades. Glarus textiles were successful because they used the fabric printing process primarily for individual pieces of cloth, achieved high-quality results and could reproduce images from all over the world much more cheaply than was possible with woven silk or even silk painting: what were known as *Tüechli*, headscarves of around one square meter, were first printed in panels, before being separated and having their edges rolled. Initially, the Glarus textile printing industry was not really creative in design terms, but was commercially alert – displaying excellent entrepreneurial skills in reacting quickly and being willing to take risks. Its success stemmed from the price advantage afforded by transferring traditional artisanal or small-scale production of a single item to the reproduction-oriented practice made possible by fabric printing. Textile companies in the canton – including weaving mills – were very successful globally for decades, but lost their technological edge over the years.[3] Therma's founding coincided with the first setbacks they experienced and proved to be a stroke of good luck for the canton and the region. Numerous workers from the textile industry earned their living at Therma within a completely different technological framework; it was, however, also rooted in an entrepreneurial spirit (perhaps even an enterprising one) that found a particularly fertile breeding ground in the canton of Glarus thanks to its topography and its political system of direct democracy that aims to be very close to citizens.[4]

1   In 2025, the population of the canton of Glarus is around 41,000.
2   August Rohr, "Die Rolle des Staates im 19. Jahrhundert," in *Industrie-kultur im Kanton Glarus. Streifzüge durch 250 Jahre Geschichte und Architektur*, eds. Rolf von Arx, Jürg Davatz and August Rohr (Chur: Südostschweiz Buchverlag, 2005), pp. 31–32.
3   There is extensive literature on the history of the canton of Glarus; in our context in particular: von Arx, Davatz and Rohr, *Industriekultur im Kanton Glarus*, pp. 12–22.
4   To this day, voting in cantonal referendums is by raised hand of those eligible to vote in the *Landsgemeinde* (cantonal assembly) in the cantonal capital, Glarus.

1

A very early photograph (perhaps even the earliest) depicting manufacturing methods at Therma. It shows numerous women at three large tables, with a few others next to an elongated work surface by the windows. Each is busy with her specific task within the group. The common thread is that they are all involved in producing electrical components: winding wire for heating elements on the wall by the windows, assembly of heating units and switches on the tables, along with fabrication and assembly of cables and plugs. The completed components on the wall shelving and the ceramic housings stacked in layers on the table closest to the camera are meticulously arranged, suggesting that considerable importance was given to this photograph. Industry – in Latin *industria*, meaning diligence – implies multiplication, generating a large number of similar objects and individual components: in other words, industriousness. The shot must have been taken by a respected professional photographer. The special format of the unnumbered glass negative – larger than 13 × 18 cm, smaller than 18 × 24 cm – differs from the standard versions later utilized.

The bright, clean room is flooded with daylight, which suggests that it is lit from above, probably even from three sides. Everything is tidy and looks new: the iron trusses, the ceiling beams, the paneling – painted white throughout – and the still pristine floor. The Therma heater suggests that it may be rather chilly, although the women are not dressed for winter. They are accustomed to rather frugal indoor temperatures.

When and why was the picture taken – and where? One hypothesis: the ceiling construction points to an upper floor, presumably in the factory extension of 1916, which was of course during the war, when many men, including Therma employees, were sent to guard the country's borders. That was a period when electrical energy was also being vigorously promoted by politicians in response to wartime imperatives, with a view to counteracting what was dubbed the coal crisis: the shortage and rising prices for firewood and coal. And so it was also a period when Therma could scarcely keep up with demand. At the same time, it was becoming increasingly difficult to obtain the raw materials and semi-finished products it needed both within Switzerland and on markets abroad. A number of challenges coincided, but the recompense for overcoming them was also huge: In the 1916/17 financial year, orders more than doubled compared to the previous year, shooting up from just under 100,000 appliances to over 200,000, and a year later hitting over 300,000 – almost 1,000 per day!

The photograph must have been taken in this context. It is undated but it seems likely that is fall 1916 or spring 1917. Is it also a kind of advertising image? Was Therma trying to convince the young women's parents that factory work was not necessarily noisy and dirty? And that you can sit down while working and even have a backrest? Some of the twenty-plus women shown are very young, barely adult, and had perhaps only recently completed compulsory schooling. What might they have earned per hour – 20, 30, 35 centimes? What other options would they have had? Perhaps a comparable or lower-paid job in a nearby textile factory? And if it was piecework, who counted the units they produced? There must have been higher-ranking employees in this room, overseers (perhaps the woman standing by the window with her back to us). None of the names of these workers are recorded. That holds true for virtually all the many thousands depicted in the Therma archive, with just a few exceptions. Mostly the staff simply appear in photographs. However, even when directors, vice directors, authorized signatories or plant managers are depicted, they mostly remain anonymous throughout the decades in Therma's archive of photo negatives – a visual thesaurus for posterity. After all, people were well aware of who they were in daily working life in the company. I suspect that one of the young women pictured here – the one at the middle table looking into the camera – appears again in a group photo forty-three years later, when she retired in 1959, along with other workers or employees. – Is it really her? And does negative 59182 really show the firm saying farewell to long-serving workers? That's all speculation.

This photograph does not even have a reference number. Yet looking at it raises questions about how the firm was organized and pushes us to hunt for plausible explanations for its meaning, the underlying reasons. For the motivation behind the motif.

1904–1924

New Life,
New Attitude:
Heat from
Electricity

How S. Blumer,
Schwanden
Became Therma,
Fabrik für
elektrische
Heizung A.G.

1.1

1.2

1.3

1.1 The father: Samuel Blumer (1847–1897).
1.2 His son, company founder Samuel Blumer (1881–1959), as a young man.
1.3 Blumer family house and workshop "In der Herren," on the edge of Schwanden village.

Before Therma AG was founded, the young Samuel Blumer had managed to support himself and his family thanks to his fascination with electricity's mysteries, although initially he had been secretive about pursuing that seemingly abstruse interest, long viewed as suspect by his relatives. In 1904, he had Therma's predecessor entered in the commercial register as the simplest form of Swiss company, an ordinary partnership: *S. Blumer, Fabrik für elektr. Heiz- & Kochapparate Schwanden (Schweiz) (S. Blumer, Electrical Heating and Cooking Appliances Factory Schwanden (Switzerland))*. The establishment of the firm had been preceded by difficult years following his father's early death. He had been an inventor and designer, as technically gifted as he was inexperienced in business, and had manufactured sewing machines of his own design in his workshop. As a young man, Samuel's father had even shown his work at the Vienna World's Fair in 1873. With his striking countenance, as seen in his photograph, he could easily have been mistaken for a Scottish scientist or New England poet.[1] He was only fifty when he died in 1897, leaving behind a family of five. His eldest child, Samuel Blumer (1881–1959), then just seventeen, took on his share of responsibility for ensuring a livelihood for his widowed mother and three siblings. He did his best to offer repair and maintenance services for his father's sewing machines throughout the valley around Schwanden. Meanwhile, his long-nurtured dream of studying at the engineering college in Winterthur faded into a mere illusion. And anyway, he would not have been eligible to attend the Federal Polytechnic School – later to become ETH – as financial reasons meant he had only completed compulsory education.

Despite all these unfavorable circumstances, Samuel Blumer's technical flair proved to be a considerable asset. Over and above his grasp of how mechanical systems function, he also developed an interest in the problems and options arising from electrical engineering's laws and challenges. In his eyes, this discipline offered the promise of a new world, in an era when electricity had only recently progressed from the realm of entertaining party tricks to become a credible pledge of progress. As a material resource that offered a promising alternative to wood, coal and gas, it attracted particular attention and support from Swiss politicians. Switzerland, a country short on commodities, unexpectedly discovered it had a natural resource at its fingertips in the form of hydroelectricity – an up-and-coming sustainable form of energy that could reduce, if not end, reliance on imported fuels like coal. Replacing those imports would admittedly take some time and Switzerland's dependence on them would have a widespread impact, particularly during the First World War, in the form of the "coal shortages." That crisis, however, also pointed to the means of overcoming it: widespread electrification. The political decision to electrify the entire Swiss rail network after the First World War conveyed a powerful signal in that spirit.

Reservoirs were being created and power stations built in ever greater numbers throughout the Alps and their foothills. A small power station near Schwanden – almost literally on the Blumer family's doorstep – had already begun operating in 1899 and the young Samuel Blumer found it irresistibly captivating. It was Blumer's fascination with the phenomenon of electricity that led him to set up *S. Blumer, Schwanden* in 1904, which three years later – in 1907 – developed into *Therma, Fabrik für elektrische Heizung A.G.*, rapidly developing an international reputation and ultimately operating globally for decades.

First of all, though, let's look back to the original impetus. At the outset, this whole business, germinated in secret between sewing machines and bicycles, sparked strong pangs of conscience in Samuel Blumer. Decades later, in 1932, he recalled his irresistible fascination with and "longing for this new land," which was the underpinning of all that followed.[2] [→A] In those early days, Blumer generated his own electricity for lighting and used the surplus to produce heat, constructing a primitive stove. However, he soon realized

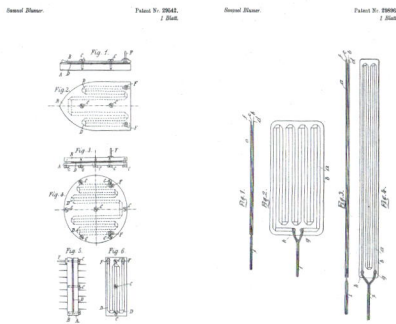

1.4

* ELEKTRO- *
THERMOSTAT

NACH DR. MED. G. WÜTHRICH

PATENTE A.

S. BLUMER, SCHWANDEN
FABRIK ELEKTRISCHER HEIZAPPARATE

1.5

[→A]
"As a fourteen-year-old boy in Zurich, I saw the first electrically powered trams running effortlessly up the Zürichberg alongside the Rössli-tram [horse-drawn streetcar], and later the construction and operation of Schwanden power station (1898/99) familiarized me with this mysterious force. Back then, a machine operator at the power station lent me a book on electrical engineering, which further heightened my longing for this new territory. As a result, I often constructed electrical bell and doorbell systems and attempted to build a small dynamo and other electrical devices in our workshop for my own use. And when Marconi reported on his first successes with wireless telegraphy, I did not rest until I had managed to transmit characters wirelessly over a distance of twenty meters. While this tinkering and enquiring was often more of a gimmick than serious work at that time, that changed completely when I acquired an old dynamo machine for a reasonable price in 1902. The water power available to operate our workshop was just enough to set this generator in motion and so I had my own source of electricity at my disposal, which opened up new pathways and possibilities for me." (2)

1.4   Samuel Blumer's first two patents:
       "Electric radiator" (filed December 1903)
       and "Flexible electric heating plate"
       (filed January 1904).
1.5   Advertising brochure for the electric
       thermostat with copies of medical refer-
       ences, front page, 1904. The electric
       current is still obtained via the ceiling
       lamp's socket.

that "I did not know enough to manufacture irons and cooking appliances."[3] He therefore purchased an electric iron and a Prometheus electric kettle to examine their technical construction. During this investigation, he spotted the lack of stability in the devices' wafer-thin vapor-deposited metal layer on a grainy mica substrate. Blumer remedied this shortcoming with his first technical development, a design for a heating element, which was much improved technically and in manufacturing terms, as was emphasized in the early company catalogs; it took pride of place in his concept as the "Blumer system."[4] [→B] His brainwave entailed introducing a thin, narrow nickel strip as the conducting element, which was wound back and forth to form the heating surface. In 1904 Blumer received the first Swiss patent for this invention in the category of "Electric heating element," more precisely specified as a "Strip heating element with adjacent windings pressed between mica" for use in irons and hotplates.[5] Mica, a finely stratified non-conductive silicate, was an ideal insulation material. Blumer's design principle offered the advantage of greater resistance to short-term excess voltages in the grid, a common problem at the time. That was the Achilles' heel in heating elements based on conventional designs.

Blumer's uncle Niklaus Zweifel, a restaurateur, convinced that Blumer's system was a dramatic improvement, encouraged him to found a company and provided most of the necessary working capital to the tune of 20,000 CHF. That made him a partner in Therma's predecessor, S. Blumer, Schwanden, Fabrik elektrischer Heiz- und Kochapparate, which began trading in early 1904, shortly after Blumer turned twenty-three.

[← B]
"To date, either wire resistors or a granular resistor mass have been used, or precious metals have been dissolved chemically and this metal solution has been applied in a liquid state to insulating material and subsequently baked on. The wire resistors were either used as they were (for heating stoves or ovens) or as braiding between asbestos, or they were laid or pressed between highly refractory insulating material (chamotte, glass beads, enamel, asbestos wool, etc.) and thus formed in heating appliances. This process requires a more or less homogeneous fusion between the insulating material and the surface to be heated, which makes any necessary replacement of the heating appliance very costly, if not impossible. [...] The Therma system differs completely from the above-mentioned constructions, as neither wire nor metal surface resistors are used. Therma heating appliances have surface resistances in wide strips of thinly rolled metal of a special alloy, which has a high specific resistance and can durably withstand relatively high temperatures without oxidizing. Using these metal strips primarily offers the option of accommodating an extremely large cross-section, the resistance strips also have excellent adaptability and finally it is possible to press the flat strips against the surface to be heated at high pressure without having to fear damaging deformation." (4)

[→ C]
"For six weeks I have been using two of your electric thermostats no. 205 in the nursery of the Swiss Nursing School. I am happy to testify that I am extremely satisfied with them. During this time I nursed two premature babies of minimal birth weight using the Blumer thermostat in a normal cot rather than an infant incubator, with excellent results in both cases. The constant, steady warmth supplied by this method, which does not require any monitoring, can be advantageously used to replace care in an infant incubator – especially with untrained nursing staff. Moreover, with its very low power consumption, it offers a significant economic advantage over the incubator and can also be used for nursing care in private households wherever electric lighting is available." (8)

The first product developed for market launch by S. Blumer, Schwanden was known as the electric thermostat: a heating pad available as either a flat surface or wrap-around strips, both covered with cotton fabric. The front page of the brochure advertising it, published in spring 1904, proclaimed "Based on Dr. med. G. Wüthrich's method" and "Patents pending." Realizing that Blumer's innovative, reliable design, incorporating a flexible, coilable heating element, would be suited to medical applications, Gottfried Wüthrich, Schwanden's young village doctor, had encouraged Blumer to contact various clinics to run in-practice tests with the device, which could also be used to preheat an operating table. The patent specification for the device was entitled "Electrically heatable, flexible heating plate."[6] The first advertising material, printed in Schwanden, included a testimonial letter, dated March 25, 1904, from a doctor, Marie Heim-Vögtlin. Having been the first female medical student in Switzerland, she subsequently became the first female doctor in the country practicing independently, founded the Swiss Nursing School in Zurich (1899), and is also recognized as an important champion of equal rights for women in Switzerland.[7] She reported to Schwanden that she was completely satisfied with the "Blumer thermostat," having tested it "with excellent results" on two premature babies.[8] [→ C] A little later, Professor Kocher, director of a clinic in Bern, and Professor Eichhorst from the University of Zurich also expressed their appreciation of Blumer's appliance.[9]

Dr. Wüthrich was an important mentor for Blumer in the early days. He was convinced of the potential offered by the thermoelectric industry and made astute use of his scientific contacts, continuing to do so subsequently as a long-standing member of Therma's Board of Directors (serving in this role until 1952!). The company's history thus began with a remarkable alliance – albeit not initiated for strategic reasons – between an academic and an impecunious inventor. Perhaps a village community was better suited to bringing the two together than a large city would have been. Nonetheless, it is also fair to assume that the Blumers were anyway well-known in the valley as a family of bright sparks.[10]

In 1906, "List III" from S. Blumer, Schwanden, already enumerated over thirty products, some available in varying models and sizes. The catalog, while still rather thin, included an electric heater, advertised as "portable." Fitted with a handle, it was much lighter than conventional potbelly stoves and did not need to be positioned in a specific spot, as, being powered by electricity, it did not have a flue! The really innovative aspect was its convenient format as heat could now be provided just where people needed it, in contrast to previous systems. Four sizes of this basic heater were available. Its design was simple: heating elements ran horizontally between the two narrow sides, which were screwed to the perforated plate cladding, which was bent to form a semicircle at the top. It employed a straightforward structural frame without the conventional distinction between front and rear. One of the narrow sides contained only the contact pins in the simplest version, while the more sophisticated model also had an on/off switch, although it did not yet incorporate a stepping switch. This basic heater type remained part of the product range for many years, even after more modern designs were developed.[11]

Irons for household and commercial use formed an important category at S. Blumer, Schwanden from the outset. From today's perspective, it is astonishing to note the widely differentiated types of irons produced. Blumer's "1906 List" offered laundry irons (light, standard or heavy), heavy irons for off-the-peg clothing, tailoring irons, polishing irons (i.e. for starched collars), millinery irons and even children's irons. Now that the Blumer heating element was proving its worth in operation, its reputation spread. As it was less expensive to manufacture than other heating elements, it could be sold at a competitive price. The range also included cooking appliances:

1.6a

1.6b

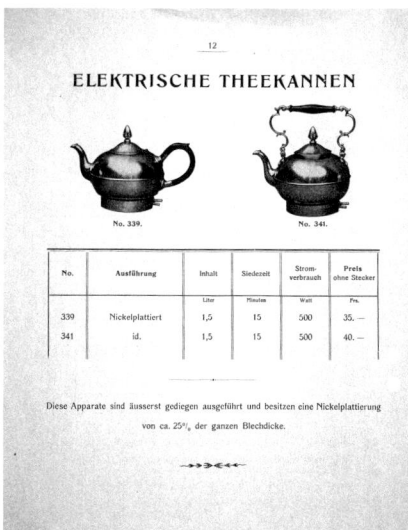

1.6c

1.6 Three excerpts from the S. Blumer, Schwanden catalog, 1906: this heater model was portable, a clear practical advantage; page with differentiated iron models (one part cut out); two electric teapots with the heating element in the cylindrical base.

kettles to boil water and make tea, a table-top cooking stove (single hot-plate) and two mini-stoves (both for table-top use), each with two hotplates, the simpler version in cast iron ("polished hotplate") and the more expensive version ("polished hotplate, nickel-plated fittings, black enameled infill").[12] The largest product was a 160-kilogram cooking range "for 10 to 20 people," an example of a format midway between domestic and professional appliances.

Even at the time, the design for Blumer's irons was unusually functional and devoid of decorative elements – in contrast to slightly older models from the competing brand, Elektra Wädenswil – while the shape, finish, materials and ornamentation of other appliances, such as some electric teapots or the large cooking range mentioned above, reveal that they were aimed at an upmarket clientele. The same applies to the cigar lighter ("nickel-plated, black polished wooden handle with push-button switch and cord").[13] That reflects the advance of electrification during this period; the middle classes had embraced its advantages earlier than landlords in working-class neighborhoods. Odor-free electrical appliances helped boost cultural interest and were thus a sign of an individual or company's open-mindedness and contemporary spirit.

Samuel Blumer's company found a receptive market. Its products were soon in such great demand that the company had to pull out all the stops to fill the orders. No one would have guessed from the catalog that this wealth of objects came from the Blumer family's inconspicuous home, often cast into shade by the mountains. One indicator of the unusual circumstances probably went unnoticed in the throes of this pioneering era. The sixteen pages of the 1906 S. Blumer, Schwanden catalog feature a medley of typographic elements that now appears bewilderingly heterogeneous; it combines a range of fonts and writing styles as well as Jugendstil-like decorative elements, which, however, do not appear consistently, suggesting that print templates from several sources were assembled to form a single booklet, with page numbering added later.

An iron is not highly complex, yet the question of how to manufacture these devices remains. How can safe and durable insulation be provided for the heating element? Where and how is the nickel plating applied to the iron soles and housings – and by whom? A manufacturer could not avoid such questions. Samuel Blumer found answers to all of them. His appliances proved their worth and most electricity companies in Switzerland included them in their range. As household electrification gathered pace, the number of orders grew accordingly. Blumer's start-up came under increasing pressure. 4,000 orders had to be filled in the very first year and the figure was even higher in 1905 and 1906. There was a pressing need to set up a proper factory in a suitable building and to convert the S. Blumer, Schwanden ordinary partnership into a public limited company with better capitalization. In fall 1906, the prospectus inviting stock subscription explained this step by referring to the inconvenient working conditions. It notes, "The previous operations of the small business, with a total capital of only around 20,000 CHF, were essentially limited to manufacturing electrical heating elements, while other firms were contracted to complete the locksmith, tinsmith, grinding, polishing and nickel-plating work. It has nevertheless proved impossible to satisfy the growing demand over the last six months."[14]

As the prospectus pointed out, the company needed 250,000 CHF capital to improve its market opportunities after its expansion. 100,000 CHF was earmarked "for construction of a factory for thirty to fifty workers including technical facilities [and] located near the railroad station." Published in January 1907 with this declaration of intent, the prospectus achieved its goal. The requisite capital was raised and the constituent general meeting was held on February 16, 1907; the application for building permission for the

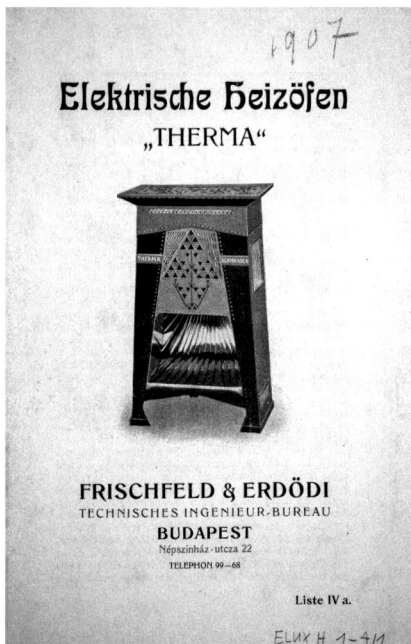

factory bears the same date. The plot of land "near the railroad station" had already been identified in late 1906 and the municipal assembly approved its sale, apparently "guided by a desire to raise their district's industry to a new level."[15] Even back then, Schwanden was no longer a farming village and the local populace was well disposed toward industry. The land in question was outside the village at the start of the small valley with the Sernf River, which branched off at this point. That was a farsighted choice of location, encompassing as it did scope for potential future expansion.[16] Hans Böniger, a local Reformed Church pastor, suggested the company name, based on the Greek word for heat (thermē): Therma.

1.7   Electric heater for stationary use sporting the new Therma brand, 1907. The imprinted name of Therma's outlet in Budapest testifies to an astonishingly broad network of dealers and agents in the year the company was founded.

[→ D]
"The war year 1915/16 brought us a boom that far exceeded our expectations. Orders were placed for 98,187 appliances, compared with 43,725 in the same period of the previous year. Goods worth 1,531,806 CHF were delivered and invoiced, compared to 681,268 CHF in the previous year. [...] On the one hand, the fuel shortage prevailing everywhere led to increased demand for electric cooking and heating appliances, and on the other hand, the lack of German competition on the foreign market meant more orders were placed with us." (18)

Less than a year later, the factory had made its mark on this location. It was made up of two flat-roofed sections; an imposing three-story main building, with a south-westerly orientation and facing out of the valley, held the management and administration (initially even with an apartment for the director's family), while adjacent to it stood the two-story workshop wing, seven windows set along its length, which was entered from the courtyard side. Séquin & Knobel, an architectural firm with international experience specialized in industrial construction, was in charge of the design and execution.[17] Construction began in March 1907 and production was already underway in October. For the fledgling company Therma, formerly S. Blumer, Schwanden, this was the beginning of a trajectory that would make it a global player for many years to come.

The timing could not have been better. Manufacturing of electrical apparatus was a trailblazing sector with few competitors in Switzerland or even internationally. The founding of the Electrotechnical Institute at the Swiss Federal Polytechnic (today: ETH Zurich) in 1912 was a clear signal of the field's significance. Electrical engineering had previously only been taught at the university as a subdiscipline of physics (electromagnetism). Now, however, it was about to start affecting daily life.

In Therma's early days, incoming orders and turnover doubled from year to year. Growth was even more pronounced during the First World War.[18] [→ D] Being a cutting-edge industry means venturing out into the open, into the realm of what is possible but not yet definite. Although there was scant certainty, the promise that the industry held dispelled skepticism. Many developments were linked to confidence that progress really was on their side: a clean new energy source obtained from hydropower – no more hauling coal! At the same time, it is important to bear in mind that the emergence of the electrical appliance industry was inextricably linked to the advent of the electricity generation industry, both mutually influencing each other. There was an urgent need for end users to purchase the electricity produced by the power plants. The Therma factory was per se a major electricity consumer; it never had a smoking factory chimney as a symbol of "industry." Given the systemic coupling of electricity generation and consumption, the entire sector also called for a new type of electrical engineering infrastructure; with a view to maintaining a balance, control devices were needed to help manage the relationship between centralized generation and decentralized consumption of electricity. As part of this process, electricity companies also gradually came together to form a grid, first regionally, then nationally, nowadays across Europe and internationally, and perhaps intercontinentally in the future. Electrification was a major epoch-defining project for politics, technology, business and society alike; Therma was founded in the sector's early days, when some still found the field rather volatile. Convinced of the potential of electrification, Therma contributed to and benefited from its success in equal measure.

In all of this, it is important to bear in mind that a network of representatives also had to be established abroad. Important target countries for the company at the time were the Netherlands, Norway, Italy, Spain, Argentina, Mexico and Uruguay (where the Casa Suiza, owned by the trading company Finsterwald y Schaich in Montevideo, had the name Therma written in large letters on display in its shop window).

Three years after Therma was founded, the 1910/11 catalog already listed 120 different products, four times as many as Blumer's company had offered in 1906. The range now included fourteen heating stove models, sixteen irons, forty-five cooking appliances of various types, ranging from kettles and hot water pots in various sizes, along with the product family related to stoves (comprising hotplates, table-top stoves, bains-marie, baking and roasting ovens, flat frying and baking pans, egg boilers, milk stoves,

1.8a

"Therma" Fabrik elektr. Heizapparate, Schwanden

1.8b

1.8   The new factory building shortly after its
       completion, view from the northeast
       (top) and from the west (bottom), 1908.
1.9   Public brochure for 1910/11: title page
       and three double pages. The wide variety
       of products and models conveys a sense
       of how energetically electrification of
       familiar applications was pursued.

1.9a

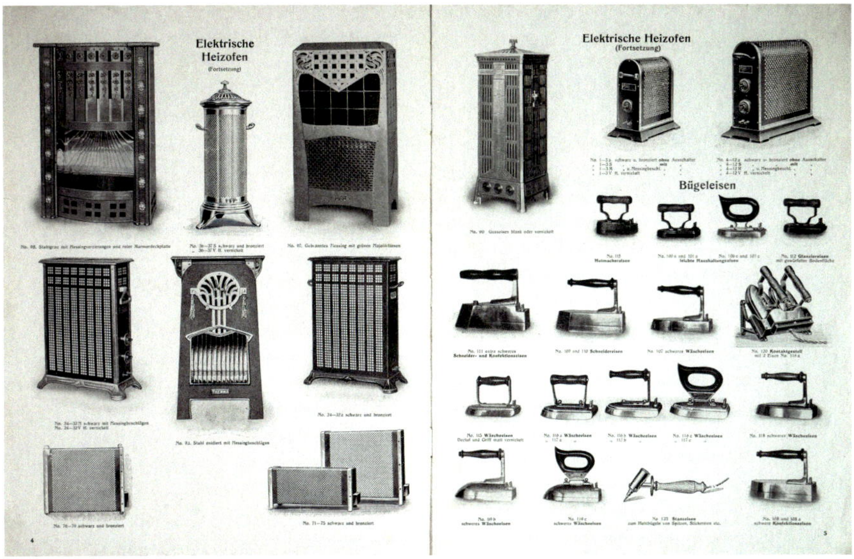

1.9b

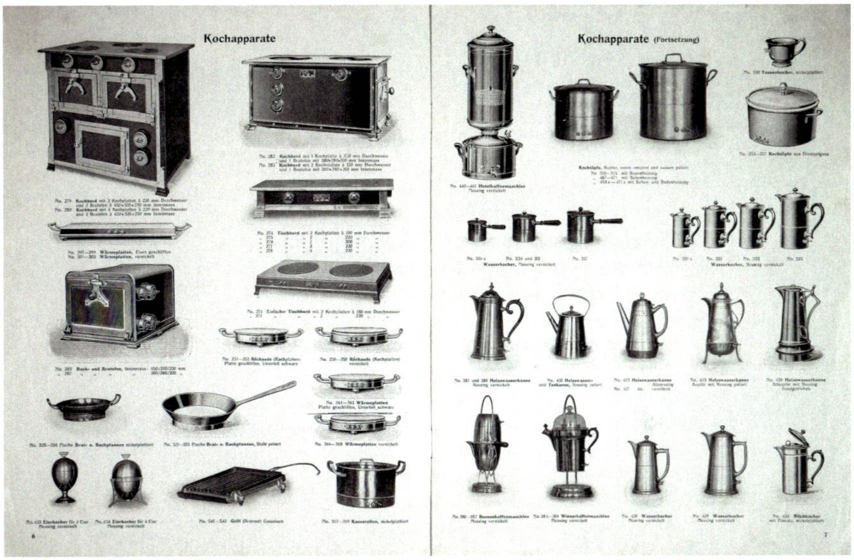

1.9c

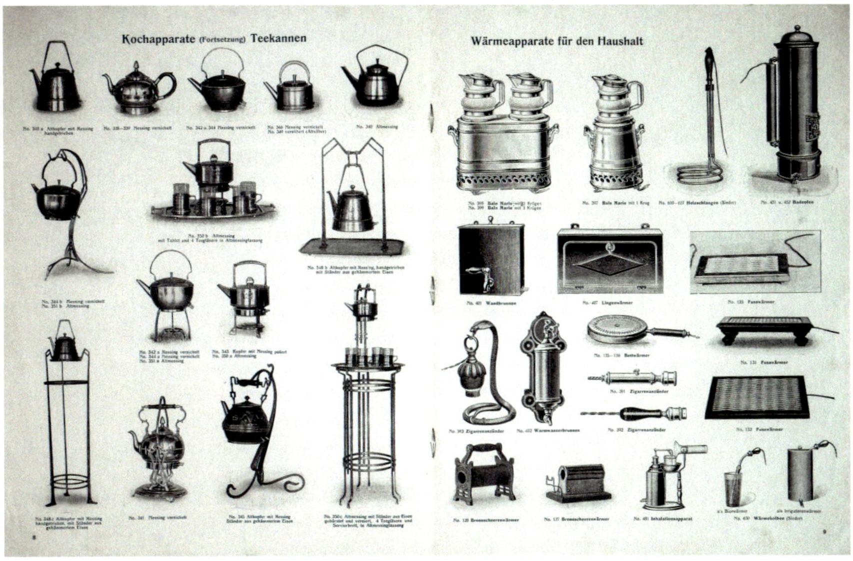

1.9d

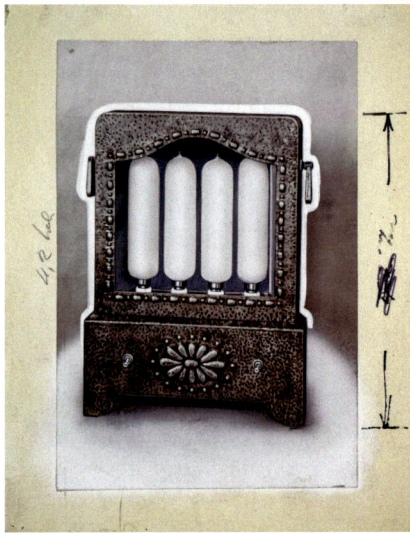

1.10

grills, casserole dishes, hotel coffee machines, saucepans with integrated heating elements), as well as bed warming devices, laundry warmers, foot warmers, curling iron warmers, sealing wax warmers, glue stoves, drying cabinets, waffle irons and host tongs. 170 prices were indicated for these 120 items, as the "esteemed customers" had a choice between a number of surface treatments for the kettles and electric teapots or coffeepots. Would they like the appliance in polished copper with a tin-plated interior? Nickel-plated? Fine silver-plated? Nickel-plated brass? Recycled brass? Recycled copper with brass? This range of options for finishes references traditional craftsmanship and reveals its continuing sociocultural influence on this modern industry of electrical appliances. There was not yet any socially mediated concept of "industrial design." In the early days, the Therma range was aimed in part at the innovation-friendly middle class, adopting a vaguely industrial Jugendstil-inspired design language. That did not apply so much to the irons or the aforementioned portable heaters, but was more relevant for the larger heating appliances, which from 1907 were also sold with infrared lamps intended to evoke open fires. Teapots and related accessories (including curious hanging devices in wrought iron) also had a distinctive design imprimatur. Other product categories with more functional designs, in particular cooking stoves, are discussed below.

At this point, it seems fair to wonder whether this astonishing range of products had actually become possible as the fruit of the plan to construct a proper factory to do more than just assemble heating elements, as announced in Samuel Blumer's 1906 plan. The answer to that question: it would still have been impossible. These enormously diverse product types and variants could not have been manufactured on the few hundred square meters of floor space available, even if – as must have happened frequently – some appliances were only made to order by a specialist store or an electricity company, rather than being kept in stock. That assessment is also underpinned by the specific telegram code assigned to each appliance and variant in the catalogs, for example terms starting with O, as in the German term *Ofen*, for the stoves (such as olga, oluk, olmu and thirty others in the same category), whereas the irons were given codes beginning with B, again in keeping with the initial letter of their name in German (bali, bara, bino ...). The manufacturing resources for this range were not yet available in Schwanden, be it space for the requisite range of tools, the technical know-how or the wide spectrum of assorted material stocks. Blumer's comment about the early years and the justification he gave for building a factory remained applicable to Therma until the late 1920s; Therma's product range was inconceivable without a systematic, orderly division of labor with other industrial companies. In his later recollections of the period between 1907 and the First World War, the company founder mentioned this in passing: "At that time, I often had to make trips to our suppliers, to Klus, Turgi or wherever else."[19] Klus refers to Eisenwerke Klus, i.e. Von Roll, and Turgi probably indicates the BAG bronze goods factory in Turgi (formerly Eisenwarenfabrik W. Egloff). Blumer's wording, "or wherever else," suggests that there were a number of other suppliers of workpieces or semi-finished products, such as Stöckli in Netstal. The Klus ironworks (Von Roll) probably supplied the hotplates with the spiral groove on the underside for the heating element (Therma patent) and perhaps also the small cast-iron table-top stoves. BAG supplied the feet for cooking stoves, covers for irons and reflectors for parabolic radiators, while the stove factory in Sursee cast parts for hotel cooking stoves, such as oven doors with latches and decorative edges to cover screw heads. It is important to note that in most cases the technical developments originated in Therma; patented elements or components, which Therma invented and developed to market maturity, were manufactured elsewhere before being installed or assembled in Schwanden. There are strong indications of a systematic division of labor between industrial companies, sometimes even extending across national borders.

1.10   Lamp heater, ca. 1910: hammered surface, industrial Jugendstil and hand-crafted appearance.
1.11   Price list for dealers: Teapots, blueprint from March 1910.
1.12   An electric kettle, disassembled: The cylindrical bulge of the water-containing section is visible; the flexible heating element is attached to it on the outside (winding tape). The ceramic elements threaded onto the wires manually prevent short circuits.

1.11

1.12

A veritable series of factory expansions in rapid succession in 1912, 1914, 1916 and 1918, including extensions, always involved expanding the tool and machine park, too, and thus extending manufacturing expertise, although the step toward in-depth in-house production was not taken until after 1925. (→ Part 2)

That brings us back to Samuel Blumer's explanation in the founding prospectus that his company essentially only manufactured heating elements and installed them in components supplied by external firms. The public limited company was founded in 1907 with the argument that this practice should change. However, it actually took years for manufacturing to become established in Schwanden for the full product range. Metal goods production began in 1908; machines to work sheet metal were purchased on an ongoing basis after that date. The shift from buying-in to in-house production was gradual and continuous. Numerous metalworking machines for sheet metal are, however, already visible in a photo album with original prints produced for the twentieth anniversary in 1927.

A more detailed consideration of manufacturing in Schwanden emerges if a particular appliance is examined, for example, an electric coffeepot from Therma's early years (around 1910).[20] All types and models of electric tea- or coffeepots and kettles comprise a section to hold water combined with a base that houses the heating element. The two are divided by a horizontal joint. The receptacles for water in these devices have an interior cylindrical recess at the bottom, into which the heating element is coiled – within the base and invisible from the exterior – and connected by wiring to the plug contacts in the base. Blumer's design for the heating element, which was made of flexible, thinly rolled nickel, was compatible for various cylinder radii, including the narrower base cylinder of a small mocha pot. In an electric coffeepot in the Therma storage and display unit, known as the *Schaulager*, the receptacle that holds the ground coffee is stamped with the logo of F+R Fischer in Göppingen (Württemberg), making it likely that the coffeepot's two main sections are from the same firm. (cf. 1.13) However, the heating element was produced in Schwanden, where it was attached to the appliance, and the two coffeepot sections were also assembled there. It is classed as a Therma product (list numbers 358 to 361). This is therefore a case of close cooperation between two companies, Therma and an outside supplier, in this case even from another country, that produced the body of the coffeepot. There must have been close cooperation, as the coffeepot's structural design forms a specific whole that was developed under Schwanden's leadership, manufactured with a division of labor and assembled into a finished product at Schwanden; it is not about subsequent electrification of an existing product. The space under the body of the coffeepot, between its three feet, is a void, which held a canister of methylated spirits in F+R Fischer's version. In the model here, the space could be used to store a demitasse cup – and perhaps it was kept in the design to preserve the coffeepot's typical flair. Another Therma model, this time for Viennese coffee, contains a similar design for the heating element; in this case, the body of the coffeepot is suspended from a support bracket that allows it to pivot and is set on a round base, which had been the fuel canister in the model from Württembergische Metallwarenfabrik WMF that was the forerunner for this design. Both examples demonstrate that Therma worked closely with other manufacturers in its production practice.

These explanations do not yet address the question of the source of the designs that determined the form of all these objects – at a time when industrial design did not exist even in a rudimentary form, while the decorative arts (or, more precisely, the applied arts in the context of industrial production) were a pragmatic hybrid that melded craftsmanship and a functional or conventional iconography of everyday objects that formed part of social traditions. The answer to the question is unsatisfying, for we

1.13

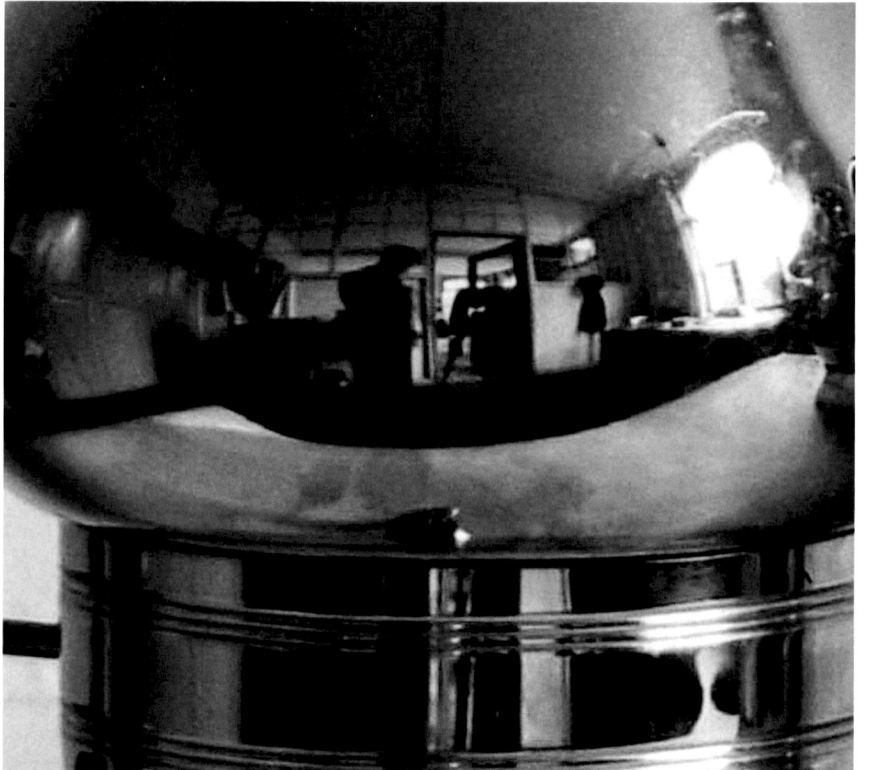

1.13a

1.14a

1.13 Electric tea- and coffeepots: With its square base and diagonally positioned handle, the tea-making device is probably a study. This surprisingly radical model does not appear in any catalog.

1.13a The unknown photographer and his location: We do not know who took the many thousands of photographic plates (and after 1945 also sheet films) that depict Therma equipment over the years and decades. For almost half a century, there is no information about the photographers, how many of them were on the team or how long they worked for the company. Therma commissioned well-known photo studios, especially Schönwetter in Glarus, to take photos of the buildings, and probably also early staged photos with people. But what about the products? It was only in the 1960s, when Friedrich Engesser and the Halpern agency's designers and employees became involved, that the outside world was given any indication of authorship by specific individuals. And even then, it was not always mentioned.

At times, though, the photographer and his workspace appear as a shadowy side effect in an inverted mirror image. The nickel-plated coffee machine on the table (cf. 1.13) testifies to the photographer's presence in the room, next to the camera on the tripod. While there is pronounced distortion of the space, which also seems to be extended into the depths, it is clearly recognizable as a room in the factory thanks to the windows. In all these cases, we know that the camera shutter was opened by pressing the cable release. That is well-established. What's so special about it? That we see this precise moment.

1.14 Teapots, ca. 1910 (cf. 1.11).

1.14b

1.15

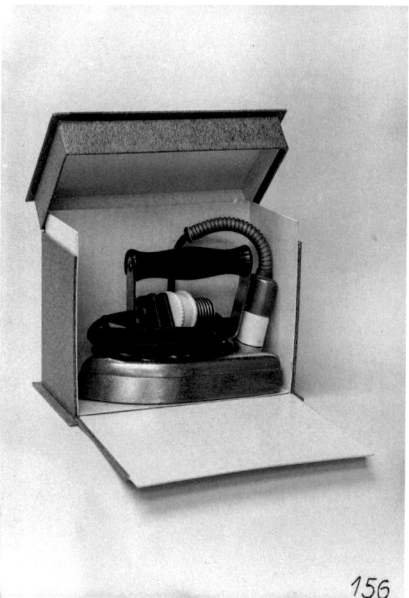

156

1.16

1.15　Radiant heater made of cast iron, nickel-plated, ca. 1912. The new logo with the lightning bolts appeared around this time.

1.16　Travel iron in its packaging: The cable with plug has an additional adapter for lamp sockets. The appliance was packed into the hinged box for transport.

1.17　A page from the 1912 general catalog: iron with the three handle types a, b and c.

don't know; perhaps at best we don't know yet. Some of Therma's electric teapots resemble designs by Peter Behrens, others suggest Henry van de Velde, Bruno Paul or other figures from the Deutscher Werkbund. Some are bizarre, others are quite coherent in the context of their time or even surprising, such as the study for a teapot or kettle with a square base that turns into a truncated cone further up, although it probably never went into production. How might this photograph have come about? There are no clues available. Although there is no evidence that Samuel Blumer sought contact with the Technical College for Metalwork, founded in 1908, and its director Martin Vermeulen at Zurich's School of Trade, he may well have done so. [→ 1.13/1.14]

It is only for the period after 1925 that cautious answers can be given to these questions about Therma. We need to bear in mind that a consistent product culture did not exist in Therma's early years and only began to develop after the First World War. There are various reasons to believe that professional appliances, such as catering ovens, tilting cooking pots, general-use ovens, bakery ovens and patisserie ovens – i.e. back-end appliances – made a substantial contribution to the evolution of function-oriented design. [→ Part 2]

Stylistically, much of the range still simply complied with the conventions of the day. That makes it all the more astonishing that another part of the firm's manufacturing was already hinting at functional design and aimed to bring progressive technology closer to its application, without drawing on socially mediated design idioms. In the early years, a persistent notion of what constituted a prestigious appearance was still most apparent in some of the indoor heating appliances – the stationary models – whereas such influences were already more discreet in electric teapots and coffeepots, and even less apparent in irons, kettles, boilers and cooking stoves.

Samuel Blumer described the years up to around 1913 as a period of intense personal involvement with his company. "At that time, I had a particularly heavy workload. I was a design engineer, plant manager, salesman and buyer rolled into one and in addition often had to assist our accounts department. Our workforce was very small back then, with only one young technician available for both design engineering and operations." [21]

Somewhat later, however, from 1918 on and for about two years, Blumer's staff included a scientific luminary who appears all too briefly in Blumer's memoirs. That was the eminent engineer F. Paul Habicht (1884–1948), whose work is acknowledged in an obituary as endeavoring to develop "a new, mathematically based method for sizing electric radiators to replace the previously widespread primitive empirical methods." [22] Although Therma's Swiss patent for the Therma rotary switch for cooking stoves does not mention Habicht as the designer, the United States Patent Office's patent certificate no. 1458484, "Electric Rotary Switch," filed on August 25, 1921, does name him in this role. [23]

Despite his workload, with hindsight Blumer also judged the first seven years of Therma as the densest, most stimulating phase. He commented, "The period from 1907 to the outbreak of the World War in 1914 was the happiest and most productive for me during all my years at Therma. It was a time of pioneering work for our company and to some degree for the industry in general. The following products were created in those years, and to some extent even earlier in my company: strip heater units for irons, cookers and flat pipes; carriage heating appliances for trains; hot water boilers for kitchens and bathrooms; electric cooking stoves with a completely new, convenient design; grooved hotplates, in which the heating coils were pressed directly into the hotplate's spiral grooves thanks to the use of insulating stone mass [mica] – and much more. All of these were new

„THERMA"-BÜGELEISEN

MIT

DAUERHEIZ-KÖRPER C. L.

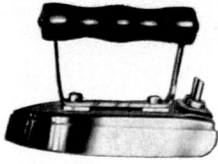

No. 100 a	No. 101 a
„ 1100 a	„ 1101 a
„ 2100 a	„ 2101 a

No. 100 c	No. 101 c
„ 1100 c	„ 1101 c
„ 2100 c	„ 2101 c

No. 116 a
„ 1116 a
„ 2116 a

No. 116 b
„ 1116 b
„ 2116 b

No. 116 c
„ 1116 c
„ 2116 c

No. 117 a	No. 118 a
„ 1117 a	„ 1118 a
„ 2117 a	„ 2118 a

No. 117 b	No. 118 b
„ 1117 b	„ 1118 b
„ 2117 b	„ 2118 b

No. 117 c	No. 118 c
„ 1117 c	„ 1118 c
„ 2117 c	„ 2118 c

No. 119 b

No. 112

No. 119 c

1.17

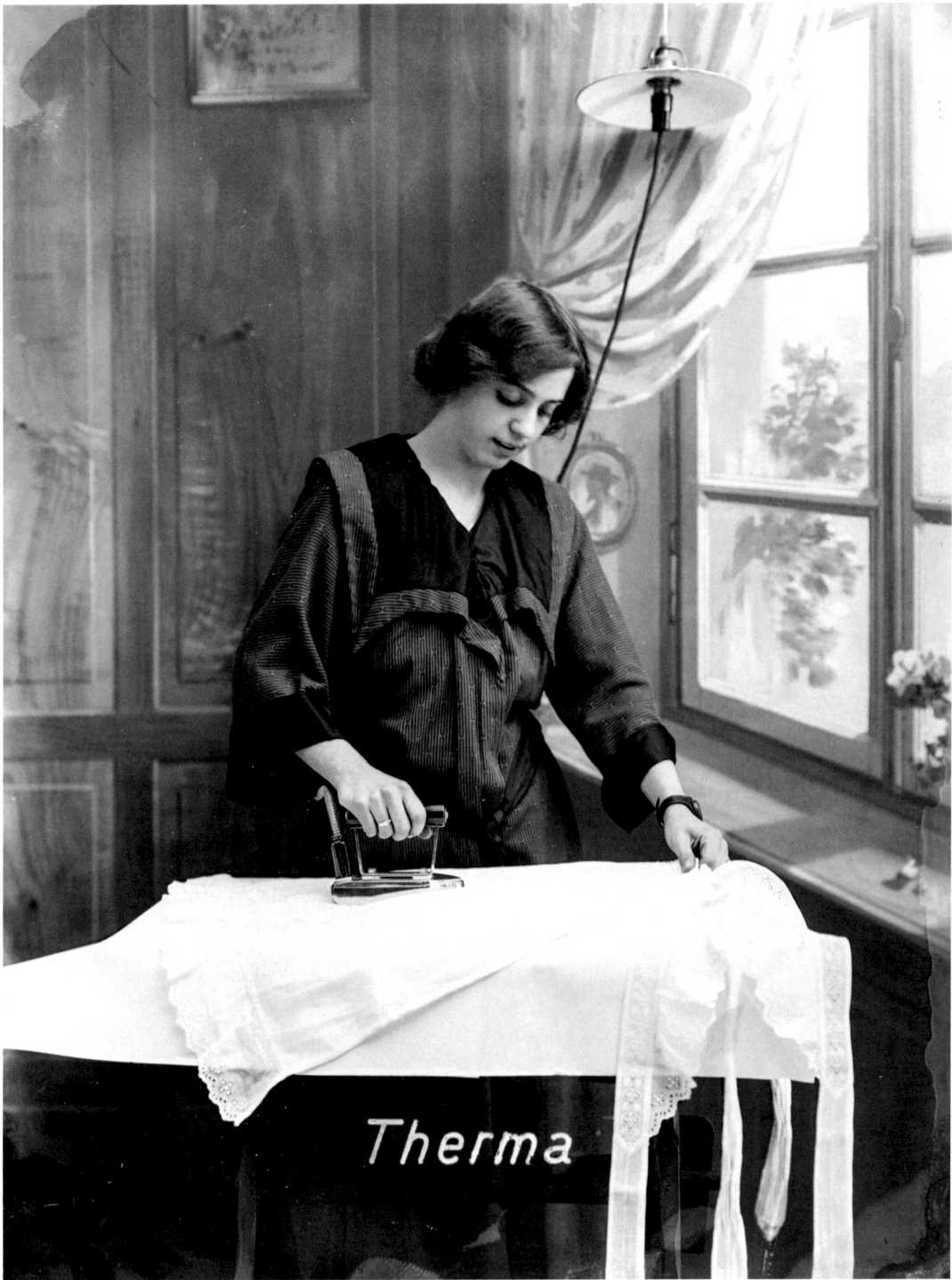

1.18

1.19

N. V. Electriciteits Maatschappy Electrostoom
Postbus 301   ROTTERDAM   Postbus 301

Elektrische Heizöfen «Therma»

Modell
1916

Modell
1916

Elegante
Form

Billiger
Preis

Geringes
Gewicht

Höchste
Heizwirkung

Bei Bestellung ist stets die Spannung (Volt) anzugeben.

Strom-verbrauch	schwarz und bronziert		ff. vernickelt		Mehrpreis mit Regulierschaltern	Gewicht
	List.-Nr.	Preis ohne Zuleitung	List.-Nr.	Preis ohne Zuleitung		
Watt		Fr.		Fr.	Fr.	kg
700	4061	20. —	4261	28. —	unregulierbar	4,0
1200	4062	25. —	4262	35. —	8. —	5,0
2000	4064	32. —	4264	44. —	10. —	7,5

Die angegebenen listenmässigen Wattzahlen stellen die Maximalwerte dar, für welche die betreffenden Ofengrössen geliefert werden. Auf Wunsch wird jeder Ofen zum gleichen Preise auch für eine beliebig kleinere Wattzahl, und zwar bis zum Wert seiner nächst kleinern Nummer geliefert. Ohne besondern Bestellungsvermerk werden die Oefen stets ohne Regulierschalter geliefert.

Aufsatz zu obigen Oefen.

Nr. 4061/4062 schwarz und bronziert Fr. 2. —
„ 4261/4262 vernickelt „ 3. 50
„ 4064 schwarz und bronziert „ 2. 40
„ 4264 vernickelt „ 4. 20

Preise der Zuleitungsschnüre, 2 m lang mit Kontaktstöpseln.
zu Nr. 4061/4261 Fr. 2. 40.
„ „ „ 4062/4262 „ 3. — für Oefen mit Schalterregulierung.
„ „ „ 4062/4262 „ 4. 50 für Oefen mit Stiftregulierung.
„ „ „ 4064/4264 „ 3. 50 für Oefen mit Schalterregulierung.
„ „ „ 4064/4264 „ 5. 25 für Oefen mit Stiftregulierung.

76 D — 1916

1.20

1.18   Young woman ironing, ca. 1915. Her clothing suggests she is a young wife rather
than a domestic servant. The power
supply from the rear via the lamp socket
appears to have been retouched. In
those days, electricity often came into
households with lighting, but the ceiling
lamp in this staging is set in an implau-
sible position.
1.19   Advertising flyer for iron, ca. 1923.
1.20   Leaflet for an electric heater, with printed
text for the Netherlands, 1916.

[→E]

Some figures: In the 1908/09 financial year, 7,000 appliances were ordered, 11,000 in the following year, then more each year: 17,000 – 22,000 – 27,000 – 41,000 – 44,000 in the 1914/15 financial year, and subsequently such growth rates during the war: 1915/16: 98,000, 1916/17: 205,000, 1917/18: 280,000 – that means a forty-fold rise in demand in ten years! During this period, output rose from 175,000 to almost 5.7 million CHF. 1919/20 was another strong year: orders for 210,000 appliances, then the figures fell until 1924: between 100,000 and 125,000 annually. The year with the lowest figures was 1921/22: 90,000 orders. Various factory expansions – extensions, additions, new buildings (1912, 1914, 1916, 1918) – required several increases in share capital to 1,500,000 CHF (after 1918/19). The workforce in 1908 initially comprised 26 blue-collar workers and white-collar employees, grew to 320 in 1919/20, had to be reduced to 200 in 1921/22 and subsequently rose again; in 1926/27, twenty years after the company was founded, there was a 400-strong workforce. (25)

creations that were a source of inspiration for our company for many years and some of which still form the manufacturing basis for their appliance categories today."[24]

That is the way an inventor speaks, rather than someone who is solely an entrepreneur or manager. Blumer remembers taking delight in being creative and having a growing following, building up a reputation and a clientele, pointing the way to progress, and doing his bit to improve the world: energy from electricity, clean, combustion-free and without soot, offering immediate power, efficiently and economically, without consuming oxygen; energy for cooking, hot water, comfort.

The First World War put the brakes on this original creativity, which was engaged in a quest to determine what to produce, and instead gave precedence to the performance principle, specifically the question of how to boost output through organizational creativity in manufacturing. That had become essential for survival, as demand doubled from year to year during the war.[25] [→E] The groundbreaking era of electrification affected the world of work as well as private households, the office as well as the factory itself.

1.21

1.22

1.23

1.21 Cast-iron compact table-top cooking stove with two hotplates and a cable with a metal sheath around the ceramic connections.
1.22 Compact table-top cooking stove made of enameled sheet metal surfaces and angled profiles screwed together, from ca. 1913.
1.23 The same table-top cooking stove as in 1.22, but with an oven placed on the hob.

In those years, Blumer was engaged in disagreeable competition with Elektra, a company in Wädenswil founded by Vorarlberg industrialist Friedrich Wilhelm Schindler-Jenny.[26] Grand Burgher Schindler, also a native of Glarus, resided in Bregenz and had caused a sensation at the 1893 World's Fair in Chicago when Elektra displayed the first fully electrified kitchen; in his eyes he had paved the way and Blumer, almost a generation younger, was now the one benefiting from that. In the young Blumer he faced a capable, even technologically superior competitor, who repeatedly made life difficult for Elektra, especially in 1915 when Therma won a copyright dispute over church heaters that went all the way to Switzerland's Supreme Court. Technically speaking, Therma's designs far outstripped Elektra, not least thanks to the Blumer heating element.

Using chromium-nickel as a new hard-wearing material was an important step for Therma. The nichrome alloy, developed shortly before in the USA in 1911, performed better than the nickel previously used due to its higher temperature resistance and rapidly became established in the metalworking industry. Therma secured a batch immediately and promptly became familiar with its traits. By late 1911, the heating elements in Therma irons and hotplates were already made from nichrome. New, relatively light cooking stove models were launched in late 1912, breaking with the previous heavy design derived from the Elektra (Wädenswil) model. "The new Therma cooking stoves were light, easy to handle and cheap," Blumer wrote on the company's twentieth anniversary.[27] At around the same time, the company introduced the first wall-mounted boilers with a capacity of 10, 20 or 40 liters, followed in 1913/1914 by the pioneering grooved hotplate, which soon became the reference model.

Looking at photos from around 1914, it is easy to understand why Blumer referred to "cooking stoves with a completely new, convenient design." The innovation lay in replacing the solid cast iron previously used for small-scale or table-top stoves with a box-like housing made by screwing together white or black enameled metal sheets; from a manufacturing point of view, the same basic assembly method could be used for the various different models. There were cooking stoves of this kind with two, three or four hotplates; others were compact table-top models or had table-height legs; the range included versions with or without a back wall, with or without an oven ("roasting oven"), and soon also variants that combined hotplates with cooking boxes (an energy-saving setup with low-grade heating to finish cooking food, which was placed in recessed containers insulated with grated cork).[28] Only the cover panels with their perforations were still made of cast iron until around 1930, after which they were deep-drawn. Pressure to reduce transportation costs during the Great Depression led to them being replaced around 1930 by laterally canted sheet metal panels.[→ Part 2] The range of cooking stove models was essentially structured like a modular construction kit. Suppliers provided pre-enameled individual sheets (prepared in keeping with the order specifications). Therma only gradually introduced sheet metal forming and working. Photographs of the test room with assembled housings record the early phase of development around 1915. The series of Therma stoves from these early years reveals that the electric cooking stove did not yet exist as a formal archetype; its development in the collective consciousness was still in its infancy. It was not until around 1935 that developments associated with the domestic cooking stove culminated in the consolidated concept of the stand-alone range-style stove with the oven/roasting oven "in the plinth" (as it was initially somewhat confusingly called) below the hotplates.

In cooking stoves from this era, vertical edges made of hollow profiles partially concealed the screw connections. There was also the option of a model with a baking and roasting oven as well as other add-on elements, such as an enameled back wall and shelving trays. This design concept

1.24

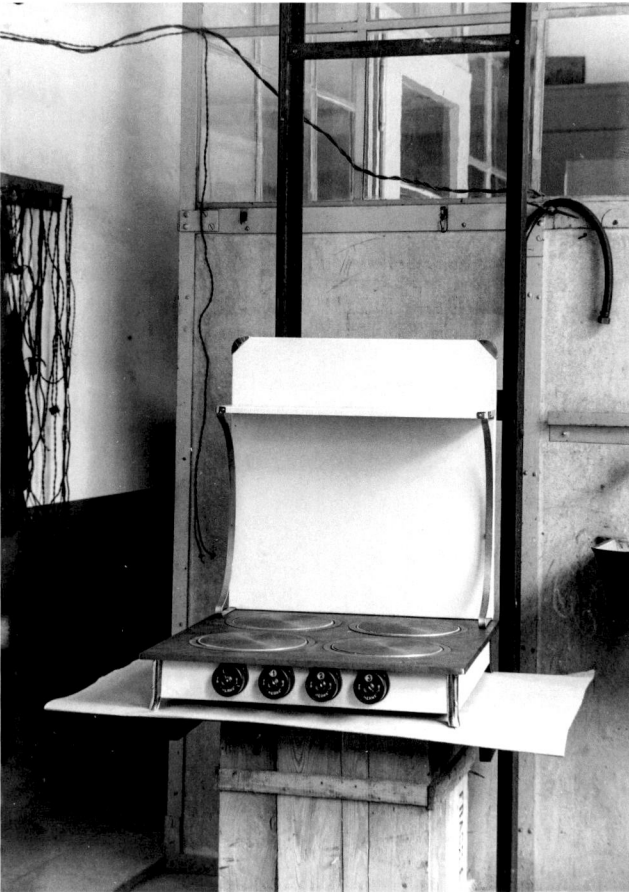

1.25

1.26

1.24 Stove with table legs and two hotplates,
ca. 1914.
1.25 Stove with four hotplates and back wall
with shelf, ca. 1914.
1.26 Stove with four hotplates, oven, back
panel and shelf, ca. 1914.

1.27

1.27 Assembled stovetops before the hotplates
were inserted, ca. 1915.
1.28 Stoves in the test room, ready for delivery
after final inspection, ca. 1915.
1.29 Stove model with the oven "in the base,"
ca. 1912/1913.

1.28

1.29

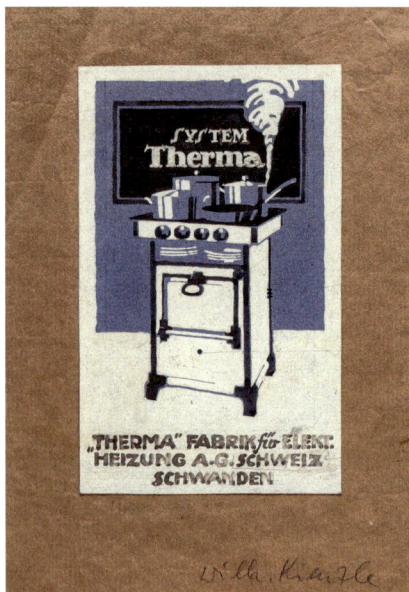

1.30

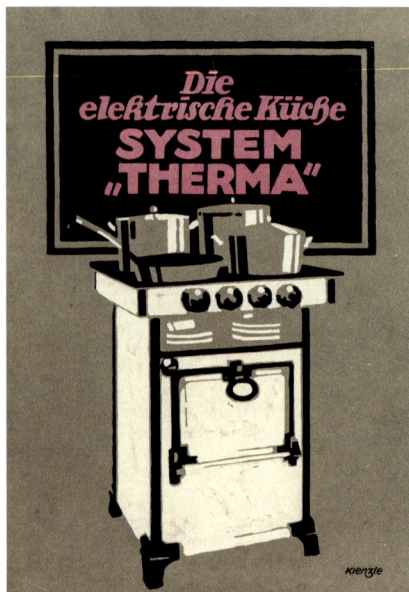

1.31

based on flat elements allowed for a modular, additive construction method, making very different models possible with just a few design variants. Cast iron, on the other hand, basically presupposes the principle of integrally formed pieces and therefore of clearly predefined use. One striking detail is that the feet were turned slightly outwards and curved at the base in all models. Until the early 1930s, that was an almost obsessive aesthetic convention, intended to express the object's self-contained unity and emphasize the appliance's autonomous status. Placed in the kitchen, the cooking stove was for years not viewed as part of the house, in the sense of being part of the architecture, but was seen instead as part of the fittings. At the same time, photographs reveal that individual components, such as the sink, draining board and cooking stove could be viewed together from the perspective of utilization thanks to additional (optional) surfaces to the sides, creating the fitted kitchen in its embryonic stage, so to speak.

Therma's pioneering years came to an abrupt end with the First World War. For a decade, Blumer had successfully endeavored to improve the quality of its products through specific inventions and continuing technical development. Now, however, all efforts were directed toward increasing production – between 1914/15 and 1916/17, turnover grew fivefold – which meant that the manufacturing facilities had to be expanded several times and equipped with additional tools and machines. At the same time, many workers and employees were not available for work in the factory, having been called up to help secure the country's borders. Procuring raw materials and semi-finished products was a source of great concern during the war years. Shortages were so severe that Therma was even forced to melt down nickel cookware it had bought from household goods stores in order to manufacture heating elements in the large quantities needed.[29] Further technical development of the products could only be considered again shortly after the end of the war when economic overheating turned into a bitter recession. The aim at that point was to significantly increase the volume of semi-finished products manufactured in-house. In his memoirs, Samuel Blumer described this developmental step in terms that mark the advance into a new era. "Whereas Therma had previously purchased cast and sheet metal components mostly finished or pre-machined from subcontractors and had only manufactured the electrical components and assembled the appliances, in the future the entire manufacturing process, from untreated sheet metal plates and untreated castings on, was to occur within the company's own workshops. Implementing this program required extensive purchases of equipment, operational changes and also structural extensions."[30]

Implemented in hectic succession, in 1925, 1926, 1928 and 1931, these building extensions, signified something akin to a new start after the difficult economic period in the wake of the First World War. They also made Therma an important producer of electrical appliances on international markets and a major protagonist in industrial and design history, given its now considerably expanded vertical manufacturing range.

1.30   Wilhelm Kienzle, design for an advertising poster, gouache, 21.5 × 13.5 cm, mounted on a signed, brown backing, ca. 1913.
1.31   Wilhelm Kienzle, the finished version of the small poster, 29.5 × 21 cm, ca. 1913.

1   Fig. in *Schweizer Pioniere der Wirtschaft und Technik* 11 (Zurich: Verein für wirtschaftshistorische Studien, 1960), 78.
2   Samuel Blumer, "Lebenserinnerungen," typescript, 1942, p. 9. – GWA Elux B 1–1
3   Ibid., p. 10.
4   "Das System Blumer," in: Therma catalog 1908/09. – GWA Elux H 1–11/1
5   CH patent no. 29542: "Elektrischer Heizkörper," filed on December 4, 1903.
6   CH patent no. 29896: "Elektrisch heizbare, biegsame Wärmeplatte," filed on January 19, 1904.
7   Anna Heer co-founded the nursing school together with Marie Heim-Vögtlin.
8   Marie Heim-Vögtlin, quoted in the first brochure for the electric thermostat by S. Blumer, Schwanden 1904. – GWA Elux H 1–11/1
9   Cf. catalog S. Blumer, Schwanden, List III, 1906. – GWA Elux H 1–11/1
10 Anna Katharina "Didi" Blumer was the author of the very successful book *222 Rezepte. Kochbuch für die einfache Küche* (with Christine Zulauf, 25 editions from 1908 to the present day).
11 There were also simply constructed and very functional stove variants for floor and wall mounting.
12 Catalog S. Blumer, Schwanden 1906.
13 Ibid.
14 Prospectus for the issue of 250,000 CHF shares in Therma Fabrik für elektrische Heizung A.G., formerly S. Blumer, Schwanden, quoted in Samuel Blumer, "Bericht des Delegierten an den Verwaltungsrat der Therma AG über das Geschäftsjahr 1926–27," p. 2. – GWA Elux B 2–3/2
15 S. Blumer, "Bericht des Delegierten an den Verwaltungsrat der Therma AG über das Geschäftsjahr 1926–27," p. 2. – GWA Elux B 2–3/2
16 Ibid.
17 Files in the Cantonal Archives of the Canton of Glarus.
18 9. Jahresbericht (1915/16) des Verwaltungsrats an die Generalversammlung der Aktionäre [Ninth Annual Report of the Board of Directors to the General Assembly of Shareholders], October 23, 1916, p. 2. – GWA Elux B 4–1
19 Blumer 1942, p. 26.
20 Disassembled brass kettle in the Therma Schaulager in Schwanden.
21 Blumer 1942, pp. 27–28.
22 M. Russenberger, "F. Paul Habicht als Ingenieur und Wissenschafter" (obituary), in *Mitteilungen der Naturforschenden Gesellschaft Schaffhausen* 23 (1949/1950): 302.
23 CH patent no. 85638: "Elektrischer Drehschalter," filed on March 27, 1919.
24 Blumer 1942, pp. 25–26.
25 Annual reports from Therma between 1908 and 1927. – GWA Elux B 4–1
26 Friedrich Wilhelm Schindler-Jenny (born in 1856 in Mollis, Canton Glarus, died in 1920 in Kennelbach, Austria), manufacturer and pioneer in the electrical appliance industry, founder of the Elektra company in Wädenswil, also took legal action against Samuel Blumer, but lost the case.
27 Samuel Blumer, "Bericht des Delegierten an den Verwaltungsrat der Therma AG über das Geschäftsjahr 1926–27," p. 7. – GWA Elux B 2–3/2
28 CH patent 69302: "Elektrischer Kochherd," filed on November 7, 1914.
29 The USA and Great Britain had imposed a nickel embargo on Switzerland because of Switzerland's policy of neutrality. See Blumer 1942, p. 30.
30 Ibid., p. 36.

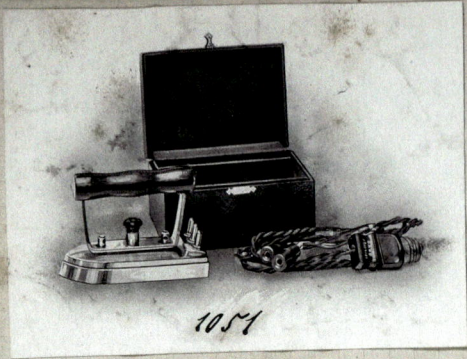

1051

1052 / 1082

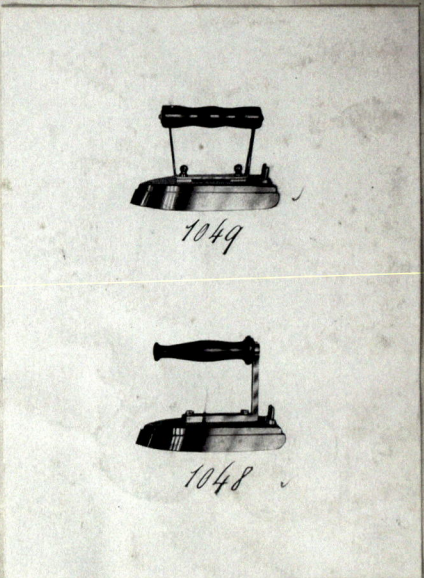

1049

1048

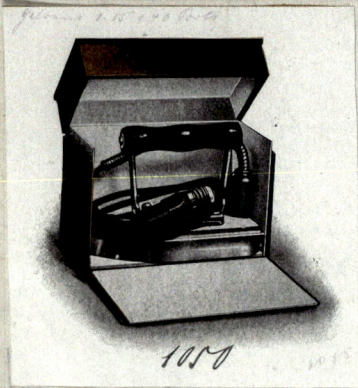

1050

1047

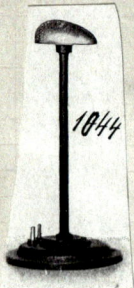

1044

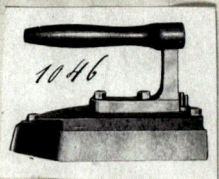

1046

1045

1043

Nr. 124 b

1042

1041

1039

Bügeleisenstecker II

1039

1040

Bügeleisenstecker I

1446

1053

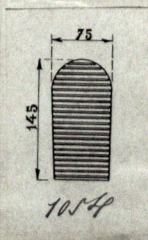

75

145

1054

1.32

36

211

1.33

AT. ART. HENRY WIEMKEN, BÂLE.

„THERMA"
FABRIQUE D'APPAREILS DE CHAUFFAGE ÉLECTRIQUE
SOCIÉTÉ ANONYME
SCHWANDEN (SUISSE)

1.34

166

1.35

1.32   Page from a book, designated as "check
        for photos from photographic plates,"
        ca. 1913.
1.33   Heating appliance with circular footprint.
1.34   Advertising card, painted with a stylized
        contrast between the imaginary moun-
        tain panorama and the imagined artificial
        surroundings.
1.35   Parabolic radiant heater, first version
        with pivoting reflector in the bracket,
        ca. 1921. Therma only manufactured the
        heating element; all the other parts
        came from external suppliers.

1.36

Therma
ELECTRIC HEATING AND COOKING APPARATUS

★ Unsurpassed for quality.
More than 1½ million in use. ★

The most important works for such articles
on the continent of Europe.
Catalogues on application

"Therma"
Electric Heating Manufacturing Co Ltd.
Schwanden
(Switzerland)

Plancha eléctrica Therma
Nuevo modelo

incomparable
en
calidad
y
elegancia

Solamente son legítimos los aparatos
marcados con el nombre
»Therma«

De venta en todos
los mas importantes
almacenes y
establecimientos de
material eléctrico de España

"THERMA" REFLECTOR-KACHEL

Ongeëvenaard in kwaliteit.
Stroomverbruik 500-700 Watt.
Alom verkrygbaar.

Vraagt Uwen electrischen Installateur.

N.V.E.M. ELECTROSTOOM
Rotterdam

„THERMA"

ELEKTRISKE VARME- OG KOKEAPPARATER
FAAES HOS ELEKTRICITETSVERKER OG ELEKTRISKE
FORRETNINGER
STORM & BULL, LTD.
GENERALREPRÆSENTANTER FOR NORGE
KRISTIANIA

THERMA
Fabrica d'apparelhos de aquecimento electrico
Sociedade anonyma
SCHWANDEN SUISSA

1.36   Therma's international reach, with sales
outlets in numerous countries, was
reflected in its advertisements in many
languages; these included not only
German, French and Italian, but also
English, Spanish, Portuguese, Danish,
Dutch, Norwegian, Swedish and
Serbian. Ca. 1920.

„THERMA" FABRIK FÜR ELEKTRISCHE HEIZUNG A.G. vorm. S. BLUMER
SCHWANDEN, 25. August 1919
SCHWEIZ

UM VERZÖGERUNGEN ZU VERMEIDEN, BITTEN WIR, BESTELLUNGEN UND REPARATUREN
STETS GETRENNT VON DEN ÜBRIGEN KORRESPONDENZEN ZU BEHANDELN.

BRIEF- & TELEGRAMM-ADRESSE:
„THERMA" SCHWANDEN
POSTCHECK-KONTO Nº IXb 22 GLARUS
BANK-KONTO:
SCHWEIZERISCHE KREDITANSTALT GLARUS
ABC CODE 5TE EDITION · TELEPHON Nº 54
GOLDENE MEDAILLEN:
MAILAND 1906 · MARSEILLE 1908 · BERN 1914
PERMANENTE AUSSTELLUNG IM HAUPTBAHNHOF ZÜRICH

Nr. U/St.
IN DER ANTWORT
GEFL. WIEDERHOLEN

P.P.

In der Anlage übermitteln wir Ihnen unsere neue Preiskarte über elektrische Heisswasserapparate, deren Preise sich
ab heute wie folgt stellen:

    Nr. 877, 15 Liter Inhalt, = Fr. 170.--
    Nr. 878, 30 Liter Inhalt, = Fr. 220.--
    Nr. 879, 50 Liter Inhalt, = Fr. ███.--.
                                       345.-

Der Preis des automatischen Temperaturschalters beläuft sich für
die beiden Apparate Nr. 877 und 878 nunmehr auf Fr. 36.-- und
für den Apparat Nr. 879 auf Fr. 45.--.

Bei dieser Gelegenheit möchten wir nicht unterlassen, auch
auf unsern Dörrapparat hinzuweisen, über den wir Ihnen kürzlich
eine neue Preiskarte zustellten, wonach dessen Preis nunmehr
Fr. 100.-- beträgt.

Sämtliche obenerwähnten Notierungen verstehen sich inkl.
Teuerungszuschlag, mit Ihrem gewohnten Rabatt. Die Apparate werden, im Gegensatz zu früher, nunmehr ebenfalls in den Abschluss
eingeschlossen.

Wir hoffen gerne, dass die vorstehenden, reduzierten Preise
zur Neu-Belebung des Geschäftes beitragen werden und indem wir
Ihren belangreichen Orders mit grossem Interesse entgegensehen,
zeichnen wir

                            hochachtungsvoll:

                            "THERMA"
                      Fabrik für elektrische Heizung A.-G

Beilage: 1 Preiskarte Nr. 97 D.

FORM Nº 258 D 2.19.

1.38

1.37   Appliances in the expanded test area.
        Small appliances on the left: kettle, elec-
        tric tea- and coffeepots, irons in the
        back. The white appliances were porce-
        lain enameled, the black ones painted.
        The glazed area and the fan (with pipe)
        were used for ventilation. Ca. 1917.
1.38   Letterhead from 1919: The elaborate
        typographical design was emblematic
        of pride in what had been achieved
        during the previous fifteen years. Graphic
        designer unknown.

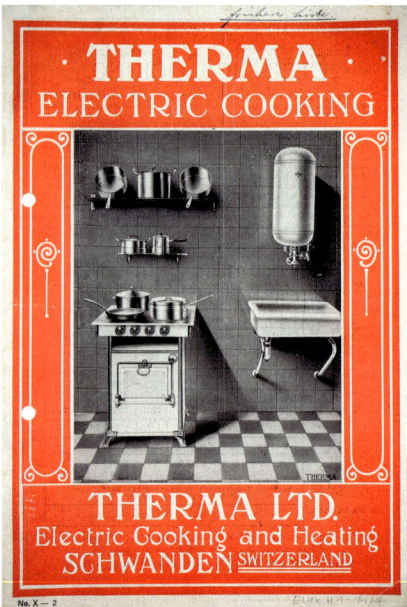

1.39

1.41

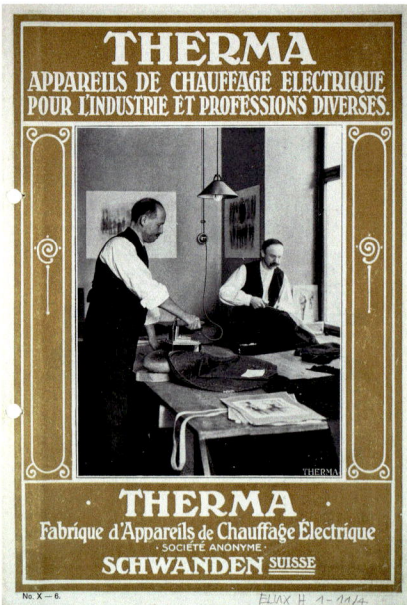

1.40

1.42

1.43

1.44

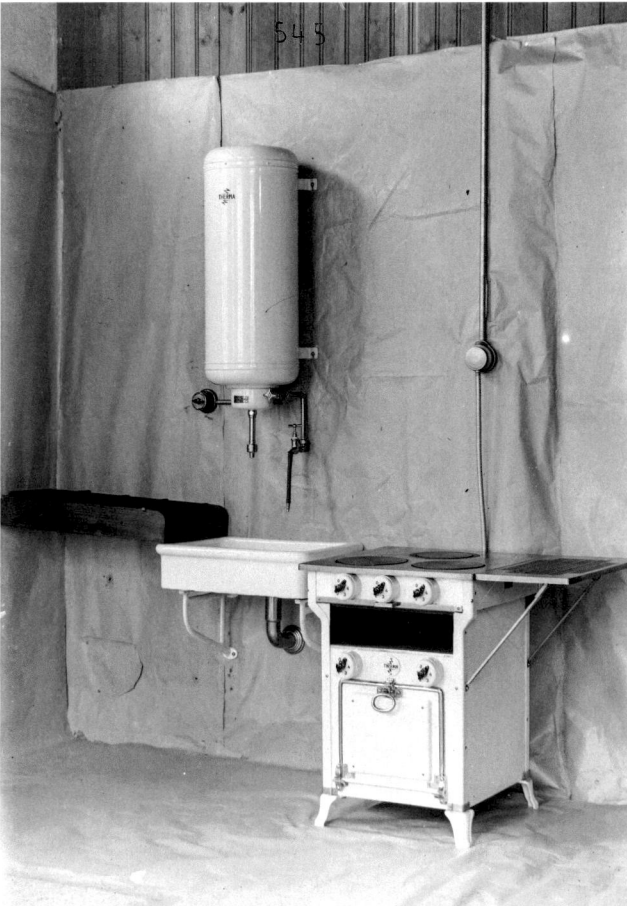

1.45

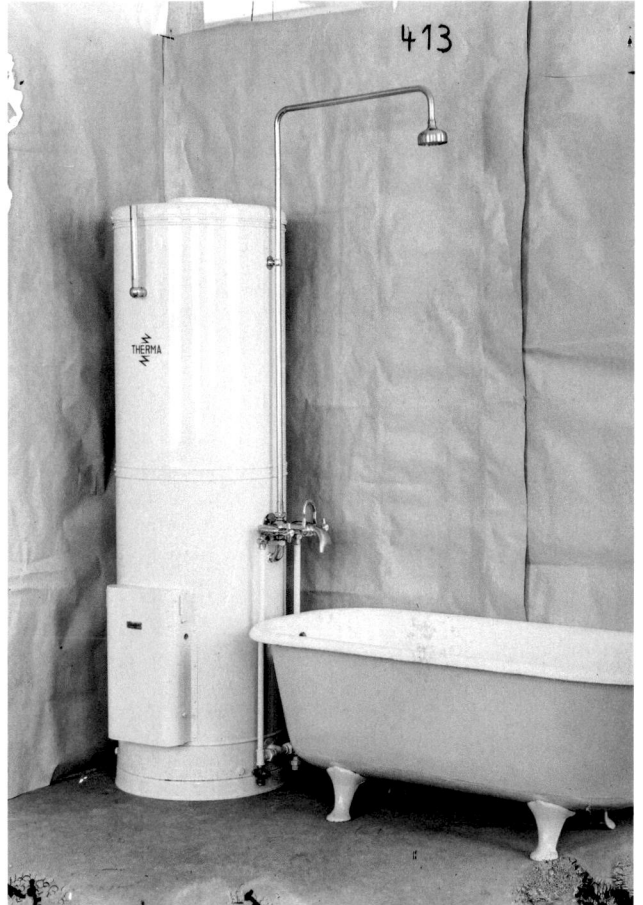

1.46

1.47

1.44 Advertising card: The delights of hot
water straight from the tap.
1.45 Early ensemble: stove with additional
shelf, wall-mounted boiler, ceramic draining board and an inclined wooden drip
tray. The hot water tap is located on the
boiler, ca. 1923/1924.
1.46 Floor-standing boiler and bathtub,
ca. 1912.
1.47 The trademark from ca. 1912 to 1926.

1.48 Therma exhibition stand, presumably at the Fiera Campionaria (Sample Fair) in Milan in 1925. By the wall are a tilting caldron and a catering stove: commercial appliances would soon make a significant contribution to Therma's reputation.

2

The effort that clearly goes into what appears to be an insignificant production step may seem remarkably disproportionate to casual onlookers. That, however, is simply how things work in the world of industry. Even traditional craftsmanship entails a series of steps to produce an object; in industrial production, that becomes a sequence of operations involving specialized machinery. This flanging machine for commercial-grade cookware plays a crucial role in manufacturing tilting, floor-standing caldrons or steam caldrons and catering-size frying pans. The rounded stainless steel hollow body is already formed, the seam welded, the base convex, as stipulated in the Therma patent specification, and welded to the caldron wall. The next step is bending and folding the rim, in order to make the vessel more rigid and ensure a tight fit for the autoclave lid.

The caldron is centered and clamped into place on the inclined plane and the workman uses the upper handwheel to adjust the height of the tool that carries out the flanging, the roller with a circumferential groove to the right of the workpiece. The electric motor driving it is concealed behind the machine. The lower feed wheel is used to tilt the work platform by means of a worm gear. The machine is set on a concrete base and appears to have been installed shortly before the photograph was taken. The photograph is not dated but is, however, from before the Second World War. Autoclaves like this (tilting, floor-standing or steam caldrons), a standard part of the equipment in professional kitchens, were not manufactured in large quantities, but in small batches and only to order. From the late 1920s, these large-scale professional appliances made a significant contribution to Therma's sales figures and played a crucial part in building the company's international reputation.

The young worker's posture conveys great concentration and care. The tool is set on a concrete plinth, photographed in situ in the production hall. The background offers revealing evidence of photographic practices at the time. Behind the tool, two employees, out of sight on trestle ladders, are holding up a light-colored cloth, which has clearly moved back and forth slightly during the lengthy exposure. This method provided a calmer background to facilitate the retoucher's work. What was this photograph's original purpose? Although the process appears deceptively inconspicuous, company management obviously attached importance to having it depicted in a photograph to highlight the company's design excellence and professional standards. Was the tool purchased? Or was it perhaps even developed in-house at Therma?

2.0　Worker at a flanging machine during production of a tilting caldron, undated photo (ca. 1930).

That is a distinct possibility. While there is a tightly knit connection in industry between the finished product and the machines, tools and manufacturing methods utilized, that link is also dynamic and variable.

The photograph documents a phase in Therma's development in which the firm's in-house production expanded significantly, as a consequence in particular of the extensions to the factory in 1926 and 1928. During that period of economic success and impressive expansion, the management pursued the strategic goal of greater self-sufficiency, even though an industry based on true autarchy could not and would not ever exist – for "supply chain" is one of the key terms in the manufacturing industry's vocabulary.

1925–1939

Inventiveness and the Path to Industrial Design

Therma Becomes a Global Company

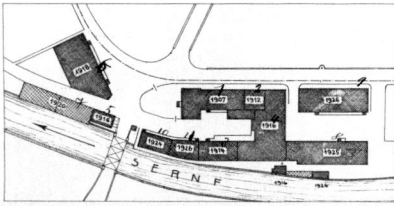
2.1

2.2a

2.2b

2.3

A schematic site plan from July 1927 produced for the Board of Directors and business associates illustrates Therma AG's rapid successive growth phases in its first twenty years: 1907 – 1912 – 1916 – 1918 – 1925 – 1926.[1] Two distinct types of window figure in the building's various sections. Pre-1924, tall rectangular window openings with segmental arches in the wall were used; from 1925, there were considerably larger glazed areas between narrower struts, with the ceilings no longer supported by trusses but in reinforced concrete instead. In other words, pragmatic, modern industrial architecture entered the scene at Therma in 1925. The last two extensions mentioned above – initially single-story, although additional floors were soon added to them, too! – underpinned plans to increase the range of machines on site, with the overarching goal of boosting in-house component production to make Therma less dependent on suppliers.

A diagram produced by Zurich's municipal energy utility, Elektrizitätswerk der Stadt Zürich (EWZ), visualizes electrical energy supplied from 1905 to 1930.[2] Differentiating between domestic supplies, high-voltage current and electricity for the lighting network, it shows electricity generation shooting up in this quarter-century from less than 10 million kWh (1905) to 250 million kWh (1930). Electricity generated rose steadily and rapidly, almost doubling between 1924 and 1930, except during the crisis-stricken years from 1920 to 1923. Economic conditions favorable to construction during those years, along with targeted campaigns promoting use of electricity for cooking, also from other large electricity generators, fueled business success for both Therma and the electrical sector more generally. This growth took place against the backdrop of fierce competition with the gasworks, which produced town gas from coking coal and, like the electricity firms, also sought support from political circles.

Parallel to these two factors – the steady expansion of Therma's premises, reflecting this business success, and rising output from the major electricity generators during the fifteen years from 1925 to 1939 – Therma grew strikingly more mature and professional on several levels. That included greater technical expertise in research and development, manufacturing, operational safety and appliance reliability – and, last but not least, in the products' appearance. The combined impact of all these developments bolstered the company's reputation. During these years, Therma became a global brand that exported to the most important European markets, the Middle East, South Africa ("Transvaal") and Latin America. At certain periods, over seventy percent of all electrical appliances in Switzerland were produced by Therma.

In the fifteen years from 1925 to 1939, the firm's product developments gradually attained a new level of design quality. By that, I do not mean a stylistic imprimatur, but rather an assurance about the structural design that the public perceived as an expression of a technical culture, also conveyed through the material and attention to detail. That holds true for household appliances such as irons, cooking stoves, radiant heaters and convection ovens, as well as to a growing number of professional appliances for the catering sector: hotel and restaurant stoves, grills, tilting and floor-standing caldrons, frying pans, steam cooker cabinets, patisserie and bread ovens, hotel coffee machines and devices for keeping food warm (bains-marie). Before 1932, Therma stood only for heat production: warming rooms, liquids or solids. From 1932, cooling was added to its repertoire: domestic refrigerators and cooling systems for businesses, including scientific laboratories. The commemorative publication for the firm's twenty-fifth anniversary in 1932 proudly documents the international dissemination of Therma appliances. They were used, for example, in the legendary Karstadt restaurant in Berlin – the world's largest department store boasted a spacious restaurant and an extensive open terrace on the top floor – as well as in Rotterdam in the De Bijenkorf department store, with its stunning architecture by

[→ A]
A leaflet from 1930 lists the orders/deliveries of Therma professional appliances, inter alia from and to the following international customers (selection):

1925
- Cologne: Hotel Ewige Lampe: five cooking stoves, plus holding cabinets, grill, tilting caldron

1926
- Düsseldorf: New hospital: five professional cooking stoves, three fifty-liter tilting caldrons, one professional baking oven
- Osaka: Nichizui Trading Ltd.: a six-hotplate stove

1927
- Berlin: Siemens-Schuckert Schaltwerk highrise (architect Hans Hertlein): five ten-hotplate stoves, one six-hotplate stove, five tilting caldrons
- Elberfeld: Hotel Kaiserhof: three large cooking stoves
- Frankfurt/M: Siemens-Schuckert employee restaurant: a professional stove
- Granada: Hotel Sierra Nevada: a ten-hotplate stove
- Trieste: Italian shipyards for submarines: four fifty-liter tilting caldrons

1928
- Cologne: Restaurant Rheinpark-Terrassen: thirty-three appliances (eleven cooking stoves, eleven tilting caldrons, three grills, etc.)
- Montevideo (Uruguay): Bar Pedemonte: a pastry oven
- Paris: Restaurant Langer, Champs-Élysées: one ten-hotplate stove, pastry oven, grill, tilting caldron

1929
  Berlin: Karstadt department store: thirty-three appliances; one unit each of a cooking stove with six, eighteen or twenty-six hotplates, eleven holding cabinets, seven bains-marie, five 100-liter tilting caldrons, three with a 200-liter capacity, one 300-liter tilting caldron (4)

Willem Marinus Dudok, and in Helsinki (Stockmann department store). The twenty-fifth anniversary publication also contained photographs of Therma appliances in the galley of the flying boat Do X, on Navigazione Generale Italiana's giant ocean liner *Augustus* and in the Mitropa dining cars on the Rhaetian Railway.[3]

This book can only touch on some facets of the extremely important topic of professional catering appliances. This product category was, however, included in the annual reports from 1927 on, developing into an important source of income for the company in just a few years thanks to the volume of orders, even in politically and economically challenging periods. More and more renowned restaurant and hotel kitchens were equipped with Therma appliances.[4] [→ A] They had to prove their technological maturity and reliability in demanding daily operation. These commercial appliances are also relevant to this account as technical developments in this range benefited appliances for private households, too. Kitchens in hotels, restaurants and hospitals are generally not concerned with looking attractive, but optimum ease of use and maximum functionality are essential in these settings. That means specifically that they must offer excellent functionality in practical operation, sophisticated movement sequences, simple cleaning, good hygienic performance, and ease of repair if there is a breakdown. These functionality-oriented criteria break free from outdated formulaic notions about how prestige is conveyed in such appliances. As standards alter under the impact of real-world considerations, the evolution of a novel design language can also be observed at Therma, with a new sense of how a high-end product should look, That involves an awareness of the outstanding finesse in the products' structural design. (How does it feel to open the door on a roasting oven, operate a tilting caldron or close the lock on a ham steamer cabinet?) Therma is a good example of when and how these kind of haptic and acoustic signs of technological maturity also began to appear in consumer goods. Numerous Therma patents mention the growing technical awareness of the design engineer teams working on household appliances, as seen, for example, in the decision to deploy a technically sophisticated lever ratio to provide an agreeable contact pressure when closing the door of an oven. Determining the right spring pressure on the new drum switch also involved ensuring a pleasant haptic experience.[5] [→ B] Such considerations make it easy to understand, even decades later, why existing customers, potential clients and streams of trade fair visitors associated the name Therma with a promise of all-around quality.

The captions for the objects depicted in the following double-page spreads illustrate this point and explore it in greater depth, as a complement to this broad-brushstroke account.

2.1   Overview plan of the factory expansions with the relevant years up to 1926. Annex to Samuel Blumer's report to the Board of Directors concerning the company's twentieth anniversary, 1926/1927.
2.2   De Bijenkorf department store, Rotterdam (architect Willem Marinus Dudok, 1930): exterior and restaurant kitchen with large Therma cooking stove, destroyed in 1940.
2.3   Collage with the famous means of transport equipped by Therma: the flying boat Do X (Dornier) and its galley, as well as the Italian transatlantic steamer *Augustus*. From the anniversary publication *Therma Schwanden 1907–1932*.

2.4

2.4 *Metropolis*-style visualization of Therma Schwanden before the enameling plant was built, ca. 1929.

2.5 The Therma factory complex shortly after completion of the enameling plant, photo from 1932.

2.6 The diagram shows the standard cooking stove's wiring, here with three hotplates, depicted from the rear, 1927.

2.7 Front page of the cooking stove brochure from 1927/1928: The export model is shown under the name Eutherme, referencing the dealer in Cape Town.

2.8 The new design concept: domestic stove with step switches moved to the back; only the handles remain on the front for operation, 1926/1927. The stove's top cover is still made of cast iron; the metal panels are painted black.

2.9 Cooking stove with the foldaway top panel opened up: simplified construction of the feet, top panel pressed from sheet metal and enameled in black, sides and front in colored enamel, from ca. 1930.

2.5

54

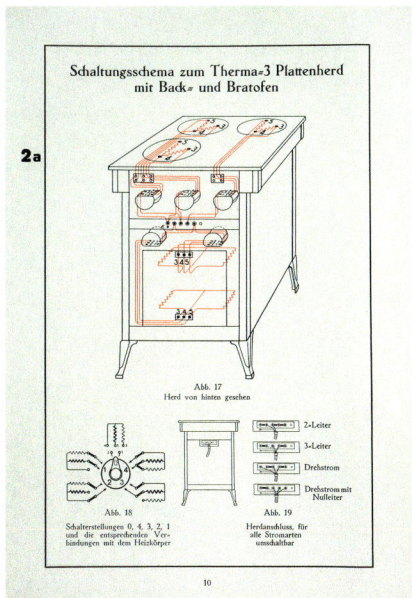

Schaltungsschema zum Therma=3 Plattenherd
mit Back= und Bratofen

2a

Abb. 17
Herd von hinten gesehen

Abb. 18
Schalterstellungen 0, 4, 3, 2, 1
und die entsprechenden Ver-
bindungen mit dem Heizkörper

Abb. 19
Herdanschluss, für
alle Stromarten
umschaltbar

2=Leiter
3=Leiter
Drehstrom
Drehstrom mit
Nulleiter

10

2.6

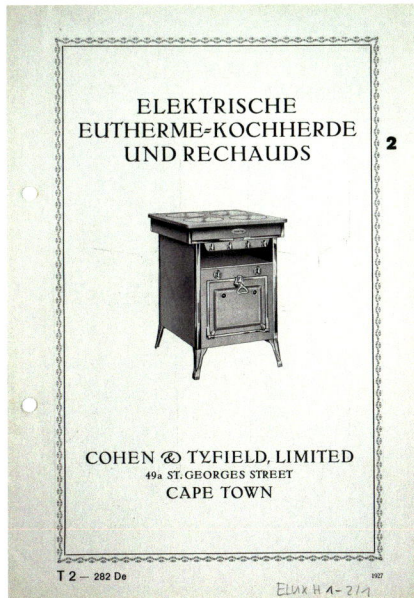

ELEKTRISCHE
EUTHERME=KOCHHERDE
UND RECHAUDS

2

COHEN & TYFIELD, LIMITED
49a ST. GEORGES STREET
CAPE TOWN

T 2 — 282 De   1927

ELUX H 1-2/1

2.7

599

2.8

811

2.9

Drive device for electric turn-and-hold rotary switches, CH patent no. 119311 (March 30, 1926 / May 2, 1927): "The object of the present invention is a drive device for electrical turn-and-hold rotary switches, in which a flat spring is installed between the drive shaft and the rotatable member carrying the contacts, which by rotation about its longitudinal axis on the one hand exerts an accelerating effect on the said rotatable member and on the other hand decelerates a recoil of the latter on the drive shaft. This protects the entire switch, ensuring a very long service life, while also ensuring that anyone operating the switch does not feel a shock." (5)

[→C]

"Demand for Therma appliances is increasing constantly and the excess strain on production in the last six-eight months has forced us to overshoot delivery dates in both the export and Swiss business, [the extent of] which is absolutely irresponsible in management's view. [...] In order to maintain Therma's good name, it is absolutely vital to begin construction of a new building. [...] It would be possible to discontinue in-house production and source semi-finished products from outside. This would undoubtedly be detrimental not only to profitability, but also to the quality and reputation of Therma products. There is no doubt that our customers' confidence in our goods would diminish as soon as they heard that we were once again having our semi-finished products manufactured externally and were now mainly engaged in the production and installation of electric heating appliances. For these reasons, the construction of a new building seems to me to be unavoidable, despite the relatively high capital outlay." (6)

In the period preceding the outbreak of the Second World War, the defining development for Therma was the construction of two further buildings: the production hall in 1928 and the enameling plant in 1931. The new Technical Director, engineer Hans Dietler, came up with recommendations and ideas for both projects. He resolutely advocated that the firm should move consistently to more in-house production.[6] [→C] Putting forward arguments to the Board of Directors to justify building the production hall, he urged the firm to implement up-to-date production methods based on the American model. "The decisive ground that led me to propose a hall construction for the new building was scope to introduce modern working methods such as assembly-line work, concentrating similar activities in one room or in adjacent rooms to achieve minimal transportation and minimizing non-productive paid labor through a clear arrangement of the workshops. The project is based on a work plan and work schedule in keeping with modern principles. [...] A rational working method requires the passage of the material from the truck through the warehouses and other rooms to be as smooth as possible, avoiding any unnecessary storage or intermediate transportation. That is why I devised the solution of building a hall, which would require a flat roof with skylights."[7] Once again, implementation was rapid; the production hall was built shortly after this recommendation was made in late October 1927 and was already operational in September 1928. That was certainly partly thanks to Therma's booming business at the time.

The general thrust of the new developments that were already becoming apparent can be illustrated by the novel design for a domestic cooking stove, with the initial in-house designation "Model 1926." "Demand for our new cooking stove model was particularly brisk," the company reported to shareholders in the 1926/27 annual report.[8] The electrical switch was shifted from the front to the back of the device, a key feature that involved a more fundamental development step than simply altering the appliance's appearance. The electrical technology was thus separated from the means of operation, the handle, which was connected to the switch at the back by a square shaft. That switch, known as a roller switch, was technically ingenious and patented. Engineer F. Paul Habicht had developed the technical principle around 1920.[9] [→ 2.10] From that point on, the switches, previously purchased from various external suppliers, were developed in Schwanden and manufactured in-house. Changing the position of the switch element improved the users' experience, as explained in the patent specification under the heading "Electric cooking stove." "As a result, the supply wires to the rotary switches and hotplates et cetera no longer need to be routed to the front of the cooking stove [...]. Locating the switch arrangement to the rear means no live metal components are required at the front of the stove, which is important for operating safety. Furthermore, any sparking at the switches can be made completely invisible and a switch cap can be avoided."[10] The drip tray to catch spills is no longer in the immediate vicinity of the switch. There is a spatial separation between utilization in practice and the underlying technical setup.

A surprising variant of this can be found in the kettle, in this case with the power cable plugged into the recessed one-pin plug at the end of the wooden handle – sufficiently distant from the boiling water. The disadvantage was that the handle could not be unscrewed because of the wiring, which meant this design could not be used in a compact travel version. The alternative that was devised, a metal cover (a small roof-shaped form) over the plug-in contact, evolved shortly afterwards into Therma's signature oval sleeve, enclosing the appliance plug on all sides. That remained the standard solution for small household appliances for decades – until the 1960s, when the power cables were permanently connected to the appliance (iron, coffee machine, et cetera).

2.10   Back of the household stove with roller switch and wiring. The wires are not yet shielded, but are carefully separated from each other by ceramic insulators (here not visible).

2.10

2.11

2.11   The same stove with the later *Siedlungs-herd* ball handle on the oven door, an optional work surface to the side and with two additional gas burners, probably 1934. The top cover was pressed from sheet metal; the metal surfaces are enameled.

2.12   Kettle with the plug socket still at the end of the handle, ca. 1925.

2.13   Travel kettle with the hallmark Therma oval socket, introduced after 1920, and removable handle in duroplastic, ca. 1934.

2.13a

2.13b

2.12

2.14

2.15

[→ D]
"A total of thirty-one significant new designs were completed in small appliance engineering, in addition to the redesigns occasioned by stricter regulations of the testing agencies in Switzerland and abroad, as well as by harmonization [of electrotechnical components]." (11)

Official bodies such as EMPA (Swiss Federal Laboratories for Materials Science and Technology) and the Swiss Electrotechnical Association (SEV) tested and certified the operational safety of electrical appliances, particularly new models; requirements for the technical configurations gradually grew more stringent in the light of their findings. [11] [→ D]

Does this growing focus on operational safety perhaps explain why the Therma trademark, which had been utilized since 1912, was replaced? [→ 1.47] The new logo first appeared in late 1926 and remained in use for over thirty years, until late 1958. [→ 2.27] Unfortunately, it is not possible to identify or even speculate about who created these brands in the period prior to 1958, when Carlo L. Vivarelli was first involved. In the old version, the name "Therma," in capital letters, was combined with two lightning symbols in a round medallion – well-designed yet with a symbol dating from the era that still highlighted electricity's magical power; after all, it offered to heat water odor-free and to transform raw meat into a tasty roast in the oven. In 1926, that no longer seemed so earth-shattering and a lightning bolt logo was more likely to evoke associations with electric shocks. The new wordmark, on the other hand, referred with a rather placid, cozy flair, to the trustworthiness of the well-known, widely recognized manufacturing plant in Glarus. It drew on a preliminary version that looked more handwritten, but added a more modern touch. The new wordmarks could be scaled up or down very effectively: large on a boiler or a professional tilting caldron, even larger above an exhibition stand, small on a cooking stove, even smaller on a toaster or iron. The wordmarks Eutherme (for Therma export models for Germany and England), Therminox (from 1934 for dishwashers), Megatherma and Prelecta as well as Electral (for cookware) were extensions or variants of the logo in analogous typographic fonts. [12]

The type designations for household cooking stoves were far from uniform. Small cooking stoves to be set on a table were initially called "little stoves." Later these became known as "stand-alone hotplates" when legs were added so that they could quite literally "stand on their own two feet" as independent, compact appliances. The household cooking stove with an oven under the hob, which later became the fundamental version for decades, was described around 1915 as a "cooking stove with oven in the base." In the 1940s and 1950s, the term "stand-alone hotplates" was used to describe a hob-style portion placed on an external base, i.e. what was formerly known as a "little stove." In 1959/1960, the "stand-alone hotplate" had a second lease of life, transformed into a compact "stove with legs" (Kochtisch, free-standing, but without an oven). [→ Part 5] For a long time, the only reliable identifying feature of a Therma product was the order number, probably also due to some extent to the numerous export markets. Evocative, concisely expressive model designations such as express cookers, adjustable irons or rapid heaters only appeared after 1940.

Rational and rapid production quickly became the decisive criterion for manufacturing methods. There were various stages in this development, each influenced by increasingly acute domestic and international competition, coupled with the growing struggle to remain competitive given the significantly higher cost of living in Switzerland compared with neighboring countries. [13] Director Dietler made the following announcement to the Board of Directors, clearly indicating the course adopted by the company, "As a result of the downturn in sales prices and rising exports, we must increasingly abandon cast iron as a material and replace it with enameled sheet metal, allowing us to make greater use of our in-house production." [14]

This process can be demonstrated by comparing the electric fireplace from around 1928 with the octagonal stove from 1925, which has a more modern design. The electric fireplace has a cast-iron casing, while the housing of the stove is in folded sheet metal. There is a clear separation between the

2.16

2.17

front and back in the electric fireplace; the heating element was attached to the housing through the appliance's open back before the cover was screwed on. However, individually drilled and threaded apertures were needed to connect the components. Moving away from cast iron also reduced transportation costs thanks to the lower relative weight of pressed sheet metal.[15]

To a certain extent the octagonal heating stove, launched around 1925, replaced the familiar appearance of previous heating appliances with their perforated grilles and sheet metal housings. It was not very glamorous but was convincing due to its sober effectiveness, which was also a result of the manufacturing method. That meant this design was kept on board until the 1950s. The casing is made from a single sheet of metal, folded into shape with right-angled folds at the top and bottom edges. The heating wires were pressed into plates made of asbestos-containing fiber cement (Eternit), which were inserted into grooved ceramic spacers and screwed to the housing. The perforated sheet metal base and top plates, manufactured with identical methods, were screwed to the casing (with additional feet affixed on the base). Sheet metal housings of various heights placed over the same core structure were an economical way to offer two models with different performance ratings. The model remained part of the range for many years, initially with wooden handles permanently screwed in place, while fold-out handles made of black plastic were introduced around 1935.

In 1925, Therma overcame the problem of its difficult competitor Elektra Wädenswil by buying up and liquidating the ailing company, five years after the death of Schindler-Jenny, who had founded the company. The young engineer Hans Dietler acted as administrator, having been recommended to Samuel Blumer for this role by Elektra's main shareholder, Von Roll'sche Eisenwerke (Gerlafingen). Impressed by Dietler's energy, Samuel Blumer subsequently found a post for him in Schwanden, where he took up the role of Technical Director in November 1925.[16] In 1928, Blumer was forced to relinquish his responsibilities as Delegate Representative of the Board of Directors for health reasons and proposed Dietler as his successor as Director. The latter held this position until his resignation in April 1954. He oversaw the company's development throughout this lengthy period with its various crises, booms and important building projects, including the construction of the production hall (1928) and the enameling plant (1931) during the phase covered in this chapter. (→2.5)

2.14 Electric fireplace with cast-iron housing, retouched photograph, ca. 1928.
2.15 Electric fireplace with the back open: cast-iron housing, sheet metal cover.
2.16 The heating stove, made of folded sheet metal over an octagonal base, was added to the range ca. 1925 and remained in production with structural-design and stylistic modifications until the 1950s.
2.17 Hans Dietler, an engineer from the canton of Bern, photographed when he joined the company as Technical Director at the age of thirty-seven, fall 1925.

2.18

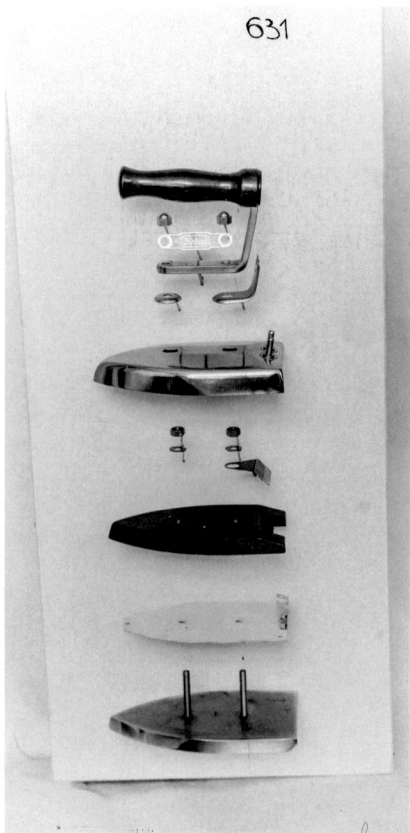

2.19

When the company was commemorating its twentieth anniversary, Samuel Blumer looked back over the two previous decades in the 1927/28 Delegate Representative's report. In the same document, Technical Director Dietler gave the five members of the Board of Directors an insight into activities over the past financial year – information that was probably new to all but Samuel Blumer, at least in this degree of detail. "Growing demand made a corresponding increase in the size of the workforce necessary. Over forty new designs were launched, with special hotplates for England and appliances for commercial kitchens playing a major role. Operating experience and increased sales made it clear over the course of last year that a complete redesign was needed for our tilting caldrons. [...] The accumulator stove, which, as its name suggests, is based on the heat accumulation principle, has been included in the range as an entirely new product. The relevant patents were acquired from engineer [Paul] Seehaus."[17] The accumulator stove, also known as a storage stove, used electricity generated at night to warm up the stove, using this heat for cooking the following day. Electricity companies saw it as a promising option for locations where the high connection load impeded the use of conventional designs.[18]

The photograph of the engineering office around 1931 documents the impressive number of design engineers. As long as Samuel Blumer held the role of Director and Delegate Representative, there was a fairly direct connection between the "workshop" and the Board of Directors. That gradually changed when Blumer was no longer involved in operational management, with the shift becoming even more pronounced with the resignation of the long-standing Chairman of the Board of Directors, Heinrich Jenny-Schuler (1936). The corporate structure later grew more complex and confusing, and the director's role more demanding when the Therma Schwanden company and its sister brands Maxim, Elcalor, Sursee, as well as Volta in Bregenz, formed a group. Quota agreements were concluded between the group's companies to provide leeway to respond to the economic interests of the cantons where they were based; they also agreed to cooperate on component manufacturing on a case-by-case basis. Both arrangements were a repeated source of friction.

Over and above the novel technological concept realized in the accumulator stove, it also displayed a new aesthetic quality in its design. When it was introduced, Dietler mentioned the increased demands concerning the appliance's appearance as an aside in his report to the Board of Directors. "In addition to a number of designs for small appliances, over twenty new designs for professional appliances were drawn up and put into production. In this case, too, the structural designs had to be entirely reworked, as the previous versions no longer met the standard established by new research and perspectives, in terms of both their external form and thermal performance."[19] This comment touches on the connection between technological and aesthetic modernity and thus on "design in industry," a topic discussed intensively in Werkbund circles at the time, although its full significance had not yet filtered through to the Board of Directors nor presumably to Dietler.

After 1930, the altered design language of Therma products becomes unmistakable. The small appliances display pronounced technical ingenuity and originality, especially the travel appliances, such as kettles, irons and a heating device for curling irons. As the mains voltages in different countries had not yet been standardized, the appliance had to be equipped to work at any of the three voltages in use: 110, 145 or 220 volts. The general principle for the solution was already known: three plug contacts, two of which were selected for each of the voltage options. The idea underpinning Therma's specific solution was as strikingly original as it was lucidly implemented: an equilateral triangular plug socket on the appliance and a matching appliance plug with the same cross-section. There were therefore three ways to plug in the cable, with a punched-out window on the

2.20

2.18   A heat storage stove (accumulation
        stove) based on the Paul Seehaus system,
        ca. 1930, probably blue-gray enamel,
        new rotary/slide control.
2.19   Technical construction of an iron,
        demonstration board, ca. 1927, from
        bottom to top: iron soleplate, heating
        element, heat accumulator, nickel-plated
        or chrome-plated cover made using
        chipless forming, handle with attachment.
        All parts were manufactured in Schwan-
        den at this point.
2.20   The structural design office in the anni-
        versary year, 1932: technicians in white
        drawing aprons, with plan rollers, curved
        rulers, protractors as insignia of high
        status. Across the street, the enameling
        plant, recently build to house all this,
        awaits moving day.

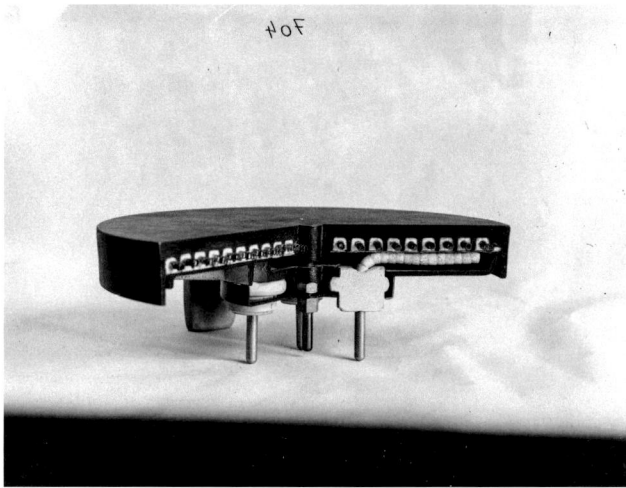

2.21

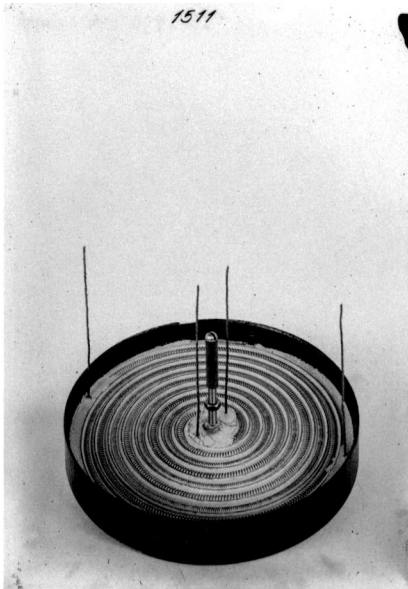

2.22a

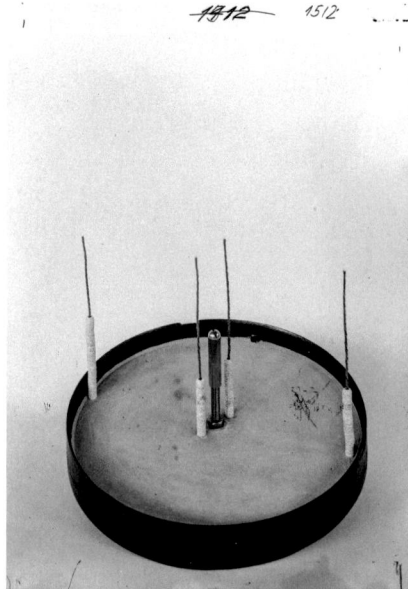

2.22b

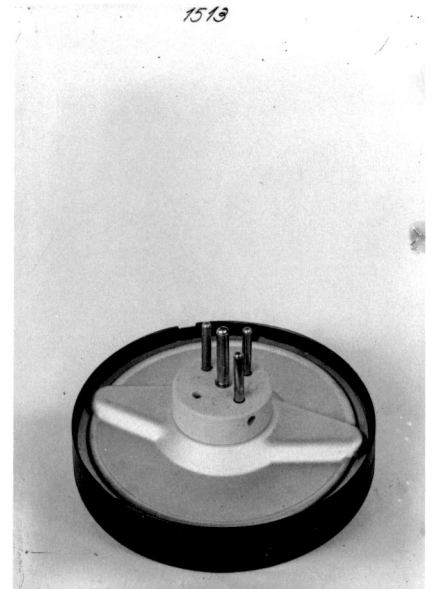

2.22c

2.21   Demonstration model of a grooved hot-
        plate. The grooves run in a spiral from
        the inside to the outside. Numerous
        ceramic rings threaded on as insulators
        enable bending of the conductor wire
        (cf. 1.12).
2.22   Grooved hotplate, three stages of pro-
        duction.
2.23   Travel kettle, probably ca. 1928. The
        three-pin plug socket on the appliance
        (with viewing window for checking)
        is designed for mains voltages of 110,
        145 or 220 volts.
2.24   Demonstration cutaway model of a
        wall-mounted boiler; there is an insulat-
        ing layer of granulated cork between
        the inner tank and the boiler casing.
2.25   Heating device for curling irons with lined
        box and cable with triangular plug for
        mains voltages of 110, 145 or 220 volts,
        ca. 1928.

2.23

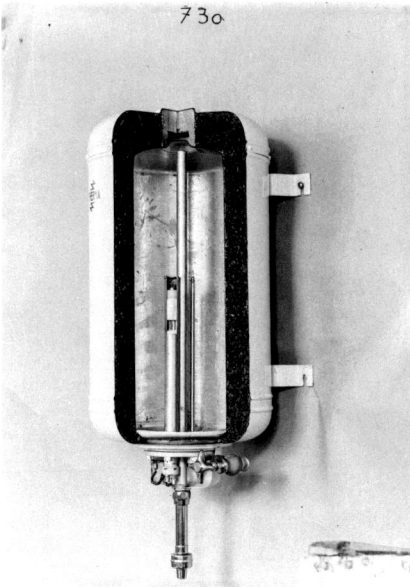

2.24

2.25a

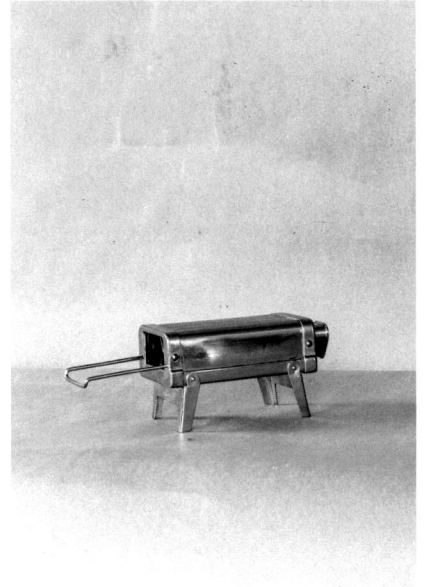

2.25b

2.26

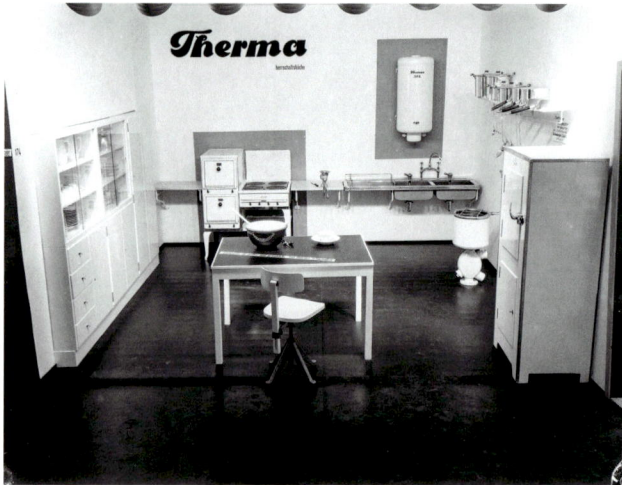

2.27

2.26 Display case with small appliances
at WOBA (Basel Housing Exhibition),
Gewerbemuseum/Mustermesse Basel,
1930.
2.27 Upper-class kitchen at WOBA, the stove
with separate roasting and baking oven,
1930.
2.28 The *Siedlungsherd* in the version
mounted on wall brackets in Neubühl
housing estate in Zurich-Wollishofen,
1931. This variant was created for
the architects involved: Paul Artaria &
Hans Schmidt, Max Ernst Haefeli,
Werner M. Moser & Emil Roth, Flora
and Rudolf Steiger and Hans Neisse.

2.28

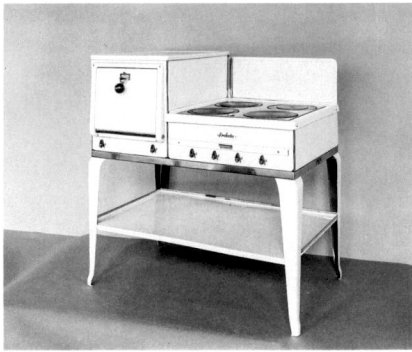

2.29

2.30

2.31

2.29   Domestic cooking stove with high-set
        combined baking/roasting oven, 1930.
2.30   Stove with roasting/baking oven offset
        to the side and a practical shelf above
        it: the model unofficially dubbed the
        Siedlungsherd, 1930. Strangely enough,
        the clearly different stove models
        are not distinguished from each other
        by memorable names, but only by their
        list number.
2.31   Stove with the oven in the base and the
        Siedlungsherd ball handle, ca. 1934.

contact socket indicating the selected setting. Even today, such details reveal the company's ambitious technical and design-oriented standards, aimed at giving its products added value vis-à-vis competitors. The high-quality leather pouch for the kettle and the elaborately crafted strong cardboard box, covered with imitation leather on the outside and fabric-lined inside, that held the travel iron or the curling irons heater are clear indications that these appliances were aimed at a wealthy clientele, particularly customers that could afford to travel at the time. (→ 2.23/2.25)

The 1930 WOBA (Basel Housing Exhibition) was an important event that also in a sense incorporated Therma into a cultural project, thus elevating the firm above its previous status as simply a supplier of particular appliances. Switzerland's first flat-roofed cooperative housing estate, involving various architects from the Neues Bauen (New Building) movement, was built in the Eglisee district, while the second part of the exhibition, under the aegis of the Gewerbemuseum (Museum of Applied Arts Basel) and the Werkbund, was presented for a month in the halls at the Mustermesse Basel (Basel Sample Fair). [20]

A Therma cubicle was set up as an "upscale kitchen," essentially a traditional kitchen equipped with more or less modern appliances. It was spacious, yet brought together a modernized medley of individual appliances; the only Therma products were the new upmarket cooking range with a stacked oven and roaster as well as a boiler, presented alongside a refrigerator, built-in cabinet, kitchen sink and a table. The modern touch was underlined by the work table with swivel chair, not to mention the invitation in lower case: "contact therma schwanden for prices and brochures." Neither the refrigerator – presumably a wooden icebox – nor the double sink were part of the Therma range at the time. (Shortly afterwards, they, too, were manufactured in Schwanden.) The pronounced horizon line formed by the stove, shelves and sink is the most eye-catching feature of this kitchen. Who might have designed the dark, contrasting wall panels behind the stove and boiler that draw the eye to those two appliances?

The simpler version of the new stove model, with only one baking/roasting oven, played a more important role than the double-decker upmarket model. It seems that the company initially favored the model with the oven set higher, comparable to its own model from 1914, but with a more modern structural design and also more advanced technologically. Similar models were also available in the USA. Subsequently, however, the more compact model with the stove in a lower position and to the side won the day and became a household name in the construction universe, where they were nicknamed the *Siedlungsherd* (literally "housing estate kitchen"). Reflecting a new, reduced-rate electricity tariff in Basel, the kitchens in the WOBA Eglisee estate were equipped with this cooking stove. "This is particularly important as it is the first order for one of our new stove models and it has a very special promotional value not only for Basel, but for the whole of Switzerland," Director Dietler informed the Board of Directors. [21] [→ E] He was convinced that the residential buildings of the Eglisee estate, an integral part of the WOBA housing exhibition, "will be one of the main attractions of this exhibition, which is very important for modern housing construction." [22]

One feature in the stove's new design that deserves particular mention is the handle of the oven flap that includes an articulated duroplastic sphere as part of an ingenious venting valve (patented in 1931). [23] [→ F] Therma's use of plastic handles can be traced back to 1930; they rapidly replaced wooden handles on ovens, radiant heaters, kettles, electric tea- or coffeepots, and irons.

2.32

2.33

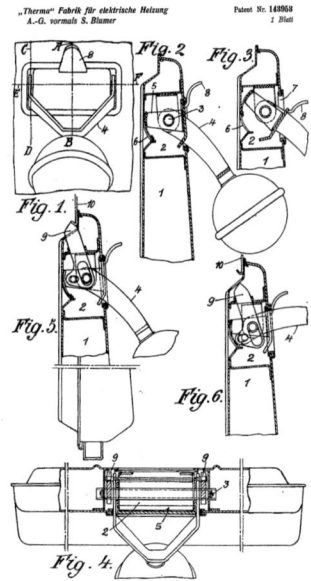

2.34

[← E]

[← F]

[→ G]

"Basel's municipal electricity utility [...] recently issued a new cooking electricity tariff, with which it is now possible to cook economically with electricity in this city. As a result of this tariff, we were the first company to receive an order for 115 family stoves and twenty boilers for a residential estate against fierce competition. This is particularly important as it is the first order for one of our new stove models and has a very particular promotional value not only for Basel but for the whole of Switzerland. All but thirty of the aforementioned stoves will be installed in the residential buildings of the Eglisee housing estate, which will form an integral part of this year's WOBA housing exhibition in Basel and will be a major attraction at this very important exhibition for modern housing construction." (21)

"The disadvantages [of complicated and expensive ventilation openings by means of sliding arrangements in roasting and baking ovens] are avoided if, according to the present invention, the movable door handle and the ventilation slider are arranged in a single aperture in the door for both, the movable door handle and the ventilation slider being rotatably mounted on a common axis" (from the patent specification). (23)

"Our new designs for domestic stoves, and in particular the new types with side ovens, have been well received and won over new friends to the electric kitchen." (25)

2.32   The enameling plant from the west: a clad steel skeleton structure designed by Gustav Thurnherr, Zollikon, start of operation in early 1932.

2.33   The *Siedlungsherd* with three hotplates in the popular gray-blue enamel, 1930.

2.34   CH patent no. 143953: "Door with ventilation opening for roasting and baking ovens," 1930: a technically ingenious combination of handle and valve.

It takes a second glance to realize that the differences between the two stove variants (top-mounted or lower side-mounted oven) are more significant than their egalitarian juxtaposition in the catalog might suggest. The first stove essentially appears to be a pragmatic juxtaposition of an oven and a hob module, conceived as table-style stand-alone hotplates thanks to the legs. The version with the oven offset to the side, on the other hand, was rooted in the decision to use an offset support frame, moving it beyond the kind of additive combination previously deployed and thus optimizing the appliance. The oven was still placed at a suitable height, but there was room for a work surface above it and the cookware handles could move entirely freely. The German critic Hans Eckstein praised this kind of stove designed for modernist housing estates in his book *Die schöne Wohnung.* "The oven is adjacent to the hob, so that its upper side forms a fairly large work surface. The space under the hotplates is very convenient for additional storage." [24] The synthesis of compactness and functionality corresponded to the objectives pursued by the avant-garde, the Schweizer Werkbund (SWB) and the Deutscher Werkbund (DWB). The offset frame also made it possible to rotate the stove by 180 degrees and choose between two configurations for the oven – on the left or right – when ordering. Along with the slightly later variant, which incorporated a unit to keep dishes warm below the hotplates rather than an open compartment, this stove layout indicates the conceptual influence that designs for professional appliances exerted on the evolution of household appliances. This modernist *Siedlungsherd*, with its hint of combinatorial thinking, adopts a more systematic approach than the earlier pre-First World War combinations, although the possible options were limited to the cooking stove per se. Avant-garde architects also incorporated this stove model into the internationally acclaimed Neubühl Werkbund housing estate (Zurich-Wollishofen, 1929–1931), in a further variant: mounted on wall brackets rather than with legs. That version from progressive architectural circles was also included in the catalog. [25] [→ G]

In this context, an almost offhand remark by Director Dietler to the Board of Directors reveals a factor whose true significance probably only gradually became clear to Dietler. He wrote in 1931, "It is becoming increasingly apparent that the new models no longer have the same enduring impact as before, primarily due to the directions adopted by modern housing construction and the somewhat uncertain situation concerning the aesthetics of their appearance. [...] Aggravating this, today almost every renowned architect wishes to receive appliances constructed according to his own ideas and design. This influence on the part of architects can no longer be avoided nowadays and it will be incumbent on us in the future to support young architects in particular, encouraging them to move in a direction favorable to us through suitable visual and written promotional material." [26] Dietler did not yet grasp the full implications of the situation in that period. The issue was not the emergence of individual designs, nor was it fashion, but rather the confrontation between tradition and modernity, with the latter already notching up convincing successes. The avant-garde fundamentally questioned the previous habit of viewing electrical appliances as existing independent of architecture. The "somewhat uncertain situation" concerning design aesthetics that Dietler described was rooted in this cultural debate. The conventional way of thinking about a kitchen as being made up of individual appliances was challenged by emerging modern ideas, which had become much clearer in just a few years, about a meaningful interplay of elements in the contemporary home. Kitchen design moved beyond the conventional arrangement of separate appliances (as still expressed in the WOBA upmarket kitchen), opting instead for a much more coherent functional ensemble in a smaller space.

Therma responded to this with a slim brochure on how the cooking stove had evolved, entitled *Der Herd. Eine Ahnenreihe vom Höhlenbewohner zur*

2.35

2.36

2.37

2.35   Photograph of a toy stove for children:
       scale model (1:2.5) of the *Siedlungsherd*,
       ca. 1933.
2.36   Catalog page for the toy stove; It was
       functional, electrically certified, but only
       better-off families could afford it.
2.37   Enamel advertising sign for the Therma
       cooking stove: The lady of the house and
       the maid are delighted, ca. 1931.
2.38   Hans Tomamichel, *Der Herd. Eine Ahnen-
       reihe vom Höhlenbewohner zur moder-
       nen Hausfrau am elektrischen Kochherd*
       (*The Cooking Stove: A Series of Ances-
       tors from Cave Dwellers to the Modern
       Housewife at her Electric Cooking Stove*),
       a short Swiss history of cooking in eight
       images from the Stone Age to modern
       times: open fire in the Stone Age – under
       the roof with the pile dwellers and still
       with William Tell – confessional peace
       picnic with Kappel milk soup – firing the
       stove with wood – with kerosene – with
       city gas – finally the Therma electric
       stove, ca. 1931.

2.38

2.39

2.39   *Siedlungsherd* production. Left-hand
side: oven production, right-hand side:
oven racks and modules with switches
and hotplates; assembly of the individual
cooking stoves on mobile platforms,
ca. 1930.

2.40   Leaflet for the parabolic radiant heater,
version from 1928.

2.40

modernen Hausfrau am elektrischen Kochherd (*The Cooking Stove: A Series of Ancestors from Cave Dwellers to the Modern Housewife at her Electric Cooking Stove*). Hans Tomamichel's accompanying illustrations depicted steps in this development, starting with the troglodytes' barbecue and spanning kitchens in stilt dwellings, the figure of Gertrud Stauffacher in *William Tell*, Kappel milk soup, and the challenges of cooking with a wood-fired, kerosene or gas stove – devices depicted as prompting the man of the house to fling windows open for ventilation when he returns home – ultimately arriving at the clean Therma stove in a light-filled kitchen with a rectangular window. In which of the eight drawings was the cook still a domestic servant and at which point did the wife take on that role? In the last illustration, the modern housewife and mother was certainly the one doing the cooking, for all her elegant clothing.[27] That was how well-tempered the notion of female emancipation looked back then. Quite apart from that, in other respects, too, this image of a stove in splendid isolation in what was admittedly a bright, light-filled kitchen did not exactly correspond to the ideal of user-friendliness.

However, Therma soon became better attuned to the new insights in residential construction and formulated more comprehensive requirements for functionality. As a result, "the architect" was no longer present only when individual clients stipulated the desired kitchen equipment for a specific home; what was dubbed architectural expertise was instead already incorporated into product development.

This was first noted explicitly in an avant-garde publication when the new design for the Therma parabolic radiant heater was depicted in the magazine *Das Werk*, citing its creator as designer Wilhelm Kienzle (1886–1958), who taught at the Zurich School of Arts and Crafts.[28] There were fundamental differences between this model and previous series of the radiant heater, which first figured in the product lists in 1921. In the previous model, the reflector had been attached to a shaft centrally connected to the circular base. The protective cage that curved outward was included as a precaution if the appliance tipped over, but reinforced the impression of apparent disequilibrium. Wilhelm Kienzle's extensive redesign incorporated a one-piece eccentric base, a handle and power supply from below, with the wiring running through the shaft and the adjustment joint. The cable had previously been suspended and connected directly to the reflector. With its position-locking mechanism, the joint testifies to the technical expertise of the design engineer team, which implemented Kienzle's intentions with impressive sophistication. His previous experience in metal forming techniques (he had completed a traineeship in metal polishing) probably proved helpful. Kienzle's duroplastic handle is shaped to serve as an abutment when the reflector is tilted upwards, with a view to preventing the appliance from tipping backwards. In his design, the protective cage fits snugly around the cylindrical heating element. Creating a convincing synthesis that solves several problems in one fell swoop is emblematic of industrial design and constitutes its function. This was also an important step for Therma.

Wilhelm Kienzle's involvement in designing new Therma appliances is documented in two other cases: in 1934 with the flat radiant heater and its twin, the portable space heater. Another appliance, the 1936 toaster, also appears to reveal signs of Kienzle's structural design thinking and his creative style, as does the universal handle for irons. (→2.81/2.83) In 1937, Kienzle published an article in *Schweizerische Bauzeitung* entitled "An often overlooked relationship between craftsmanship and machinery," in which he emphasized the importance of toolmakers and cited the new Therma household cooking stove, which was much more efficient to manufacture and much easier to keep clean than models that were twenty years older.[29] It is quite possible that he was involved in developing that new stove. There are also at least

2.41

2.42

2.43

2.44

2.41 Worker welding the base of the parabolic radiant heater launched in 1930: the bottom section with the shaft base is deep-drawn; the upper part of the shaft tube is welded on.

2.42 Recently produced parabolic radiant heater designed by Wilhelm Kienzle, 1930: tilt-proof, with ingenious friction joint and adjustment or carrying handle.

2.43 Wilhelm Kienzle, (left) preliminary study for the new parabolic radiation heater from 1930; initially, a cast-iron base was apparently considered. (Right) the finished design, ready to go into production.

2.44 Wilhelm Kienzle, flat radiant heater, 1934. The relationship between form, structural design and the assembly process was factored into development.

2.45a

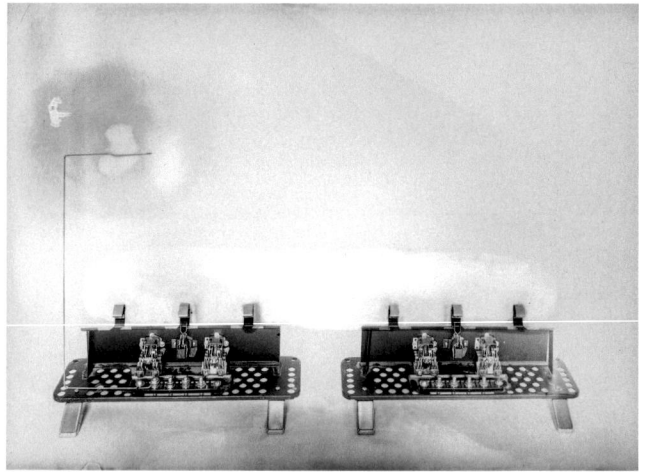

2.45b

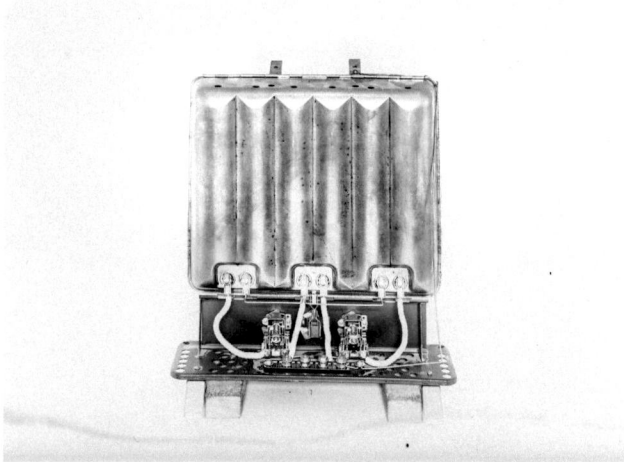

2.45c

2.45d

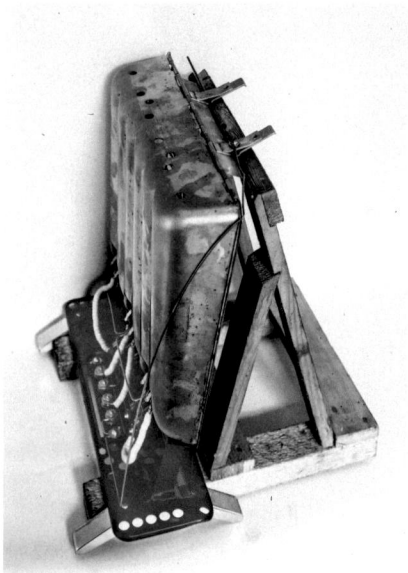

2.45e

2.45f

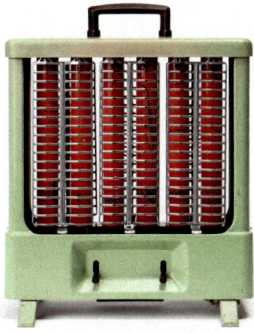

2.46

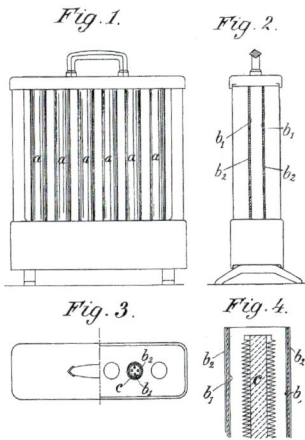

Therma Fabrik für elektrische Heizung A.-G.
vorm. S. Blumer

Patent Nr. 170966
1 Blatt

Fig. 1.

Fig. 2.

Fig. 3.

Fig. 4.

2.47

[→ H]
"I am aware that you sometimes call in an archi-
tect for the design of new constructions.
As we might be interested in such cooperation,
I should like to ask you to provide me with the
address of the architect in question." (30)

2.45   Mounting principle for the flat radiant
        heater. "Therma" was stamped into the
        rear panel – a surprising detail – also
        helping to protect the carrying handle
        from overheating. Price pressure during
        the crisis put an end to production of
        this model after just a few years.
2.46   Portable space heater in the two colors
        available.
2.47   CH patent no. 170966 for the portable
        space heater, a sister model of the
        flat radiant heater. Designed by Wilhelm
        Kienzle in 1934, the heating elements
        were encased in metal tubes sprayed red.

hints that Kienzle contributed to a number of other designs. (→ 2.61/2.62/2.76/2.79) At the aforementioned WOBA exhibition at the Mustermesse, presented under the aegis of Gewerbemuseum Basel, the small Therma appliances were displayed in a showcase; revealingly, the old version of the parabolic radiant heater was still included, tucked away, as development of the new model had apparently not yet been completed. Wilhelm Kienzle's older brother, Hermann Kienzle, was involved in WOBA as director of the Gewer-bemuseum in Basel. Wilhelm Kienzle had already been introduced to Therma by this point, having designed an advertising poster for Therma around 1913 (→ 1.30/1.31) and had selected a toaster and a table-top hotplate from Therma for his highly acclaimed 1926 installation in Zurich for the "one-room bach-elor's apartment" presented in the exhibition *Das neue Heim (The New Home)*. His role was largely in the background, with the exception of the aforementioned cases. In August 1942, Karl Heinrich Gyr, Director of Landis & Gyr in Zug and a member of Therma's Board of Directors, asked Director Dietler for the name of the "architect" that Therma occasionally consulted when developing new designs. [30] [→ H] Dietler immediately gave him the de-tails: "Wilhelm Kienzle, Zürichbergstrasse 10, Zurich."[31] Gyr's enquiry about someone in the role of "architect" indicates that outsiders believed that it was architects who were able to influence designs to reflect the client's wishes. In those years, the job titles "designer" and "industrial designer" were almost entirely unknown, just as the designation "graphic designer" was uncommon.

2.48

2.49

2.50

Nowadays there is a tendency to forget that events turned enthusiastically to the future, such as WOBA or the construction of Neubühl and other residential estates, were overshadowed by the stock market crash in October 1929 and the ensuing global economic crisis. The impact on Therma was delayed, as numerous housing construction projects were still awaiting completion. Business remained extremely good until 1931, as the company had a backlog of orders to work through. However, as of 1932 sales began to decline significantly. There was a strange ambivalence due to what could be called the phase displacement arising from the combination of the stock market crash and the well-filled order books; those in positions of responsibility as well as the workforce must have been aware that this level of orders would not be sustained. Ironically, some of the most cheerful designs date from these years: the *Siedlungsherd*, i.e. the cooker designed for modernist kitchens, the parabolic or flat radiant heater, the portable space heater, the colored enameled irons. The increased use of enameling sheet metal is relevant in that respect, too.

In 1933, Therma launched cooking stoves, irons, parabolic and flat radiant heaters with porcelain enameling in a range of new colors. Until fairly shortly before this, the surfaces of many models had been painted, sprayed (the outside of boilers) or nickel-plated (for small appliances and details such as handles, feet or corner strips). Manufacturers of gas-fired cooking stoves had begun enameling their appliances, prompting other manufacturers to do the same with electric stoves. As late as 1929, only fifteen percent of 7,300 Therma household stoves were enameled; a year and a half later, over ninety percent were enameled. Due to the comprehensive rust protection it provided, the enamel coating applied to all external and internal surfaces of the new stoves became a strong selling point. That was quite an undertaking: In the 1930/31 financial year, 143,000 m² of sheet metal had been enameled by May 1.[32] Therma set up its own test enameling shop in the new production hall in 1928 and achieved good results with it. Until that point, many orders had been placed externally with Metallwarenfabrik Zug, which only produced white enamel. However, Therma had already developed its own formulations for other shades (initially for household cooking stoves), regarding these as a valuable commercial secret. Dietler explained that the company should not disclose these under any circumstances, as he viewed the bright colors as an important way to make Therma products unmistakable.[33] That explains why, just two years after the hall was built, the idea of developing an efficient in-house enameling plant came to the fore. Although Dietler had been cautiously hinting since fall 1930 that this plant would be needed, it was challenging to consider constructing another new building, costing almost half a million francs, in the middle of a severe economic downturn. Although it was not an easy decision, the Board of Directors voted to move ahead with the project (resolution dated June 27, 1931). Once again, construction plans were hastily drawn up – this time by industrial architect and engineer Gustav Thurnherr from Zollikon/Zurich – tenders were obtained, the contracts were awarded and work began immediately on the other side of the road, for a building with a 2,000 m² footprint with a basement throughout. On July 15, the title to the building land was transferred to Therma and construction began the next day! The Sernf-Niederenbach power station had guaranteed to supply the electricity required to operate the four enameling furnaces – and Therma had furnished the corresponding purchase guarante. Amazingly, the new building was completed by Christmas 1931 and the first of four enameling furnaces began work. The decision to go ahead with this project soon proved to be correct and very helpful, as the company was able to carry out lucrative contract work for third parties (traffic signs, road signs, billboards, nameplates) even during the crisis, while retaining the relevant expertise in-house.[34]

2.51

2.52

2.48 Leaflet for irons with the six enameling colors proposed by Ida Störi, 1933.

2.49 Leaflet for irons: color palette reduced to four of Ida Störi's tones, ca. 1937. The newly added universal handle would become the future default option.

2.50 Ida Störi, taken in 1928 in the park in front of Zurich School of Arts and Crafts.

2.51 Lill Tschudi, poster design for Therma iron, gouache, sheet size 65 × 45 cm, undated (ca. 1933).

2.52 Irons in Ida Störi's colors, photographed at Therma Schaulager, Schwanden.

2.53

2.53   The modern housewife does her cooking with electricity with "Therma" appliances. Advertising illustration for the *Siedlungsherd*, first half of the 1930s.

2.54   Therma stand at Mustermesse Basel in 1933. The full force of the economic crisis had not yet been felt. But that all looked different just one year later.

2.55   Therma stand at Mustermesse Basel in 1933. With the refrigerators, Therma entered the new field of cooling and refrigeration.

The photograph from the southeast, taken shortly after the enameling plant was completed, impressively documents the company's structural expansion as a result of construction of the production hall in 1928, with the enameling plant added in 1931 on the other side of the main road. [→ 2.5]

The increased importance of enameling was reflected in 1933 in very special hues for irons and other small Therma appliances, with exclusive color formulations that were a unique selling point. The young Ida Störi (1904–1979) was responsible for selecting the color palette: sandy colors, light brown, reseda green, yellow, red, deep blue for irons – and sometimes also for radiant heaters. The artistically gifted daughter of a Therma employee studied textile design with Sophie Taeuber-Arp and Otto Morach at the Zurich School of Arts and Crafts in the late 1920s. She later worked as a designer for the carpet weaving mill in Ennenda. [35] In 1933, a leaflet presenting irons indicating the various colors available was the first printed material from Therma in four-color printing in which the color range played more than a decorative function and provided substantive information about the products. Another Glarus-born woman, internationally renowned artist Lill Tschudi (1911–2004), created several poster designs for these colored irons. In keeping with her artistic interests, she adopted the Cubist strategy of disassembling solid bodies, echoing for example A. M. Cassandre. Even if they did not achieve the latter's compelling precision, it is regrettable that Tschudi's designs were not printed. [36]

The photographs of Therma's stand at the 1933 Mustermesse Basel clearly reveals how significantly the company's entire appearance had changed in just a few years. Whereas in Milan in 1925 white enameled household cooking stoves had been the exception and black-painted cooking and heating stoves the rule, in Basel white was the predominant color for household cooking stoves, kettles, patisserie ovens, boilers and the refrigerators newly added to the product range, alongside the nickel-plated or chrome-plated surfaces of irons, kettles, coffee machines, electric teapots and toasters. The new color highlights were prominently displayed, in the form of stoves, irons and Kienzle's parabolic and flat radiant heaters as well as the portable space heaters. The options available to customers were demonstrated by color samples hung on the wall next to the kitchen stoves, alongside photographs of the enameling plant from the outside and inside; the functional children's stove, a scaled-down version (on a scale of 1:2.5) of the *Siedlungsherd* aimed at the offspring of upper-class families, was also on display in the various Therma colors. The spectrum of different boiler sizes on offer is striking, as is the choice of different proportions for models with identical capacity: the 75, 100 and 125-liter models were each available in a slimmer and a broader version. Incidentally, the photographic documents include a reproduction of a letter from Bern in which a plumber points out that the room heights in newly constructed residential buildings were lower than had previously been customary. He noted that boiler manufacturers would have to find an answer to this dilemma. Therma immediately took up the suggestion and developed models with a squat shape, which also reduced heat loss. [37] [→ I] A proud announcement was affixed to the wall of the Therma stand at the 1933 Basel Sample Fair: "80,000 Therma boilers in operation, 180,000 Therma cooking stoves in operation."

Therma first presented its own refrigerators at this trade fair in 1933. That marked the company's first move into the completely new field of refrigeration. It offered refrigerators in various sizes. Structurally, the appliances were largely made of wood: a framework of wooden slats covered with planks, with even the cooling chamber made of wood (as in the iceboxes shown in fig. 2.27). As with boilers and ovens, granulated cork was used for insulation, with a textile cord as the door seal. The exterior of the boxes was clad in sheet metal and the cover was also metal. The entire technical construction was still very reminiscent of furniture designs, with the door

2.54

2.55

2.56

Therma
Elektrische Kaffeemaschine

Ausführung:
Verchromt, Griffe und Füsse aus Pressmaterial.

| L.-Nr | Inhalt | | Wattaufnahme | Gewicht | Preis |
	Liter	Tassen à 0,1 Liter	Watt	kg	ohne Zuleitung Fr.
31001	1	10	400	1,7	40.—

Beschreibung:
Moderne kantige Form auf hohen Füssen, mit Kaffee-Einsatz für Kaffeezubereitung nach dem Ueberbrühungs-System. Zubereitungszeit für 1 Liter Kaffee: 17 Minuten bei 15-grädiger Wasserfüllung und 5 Minuten bei 70-grädiger Wasserfüllung.

Anschluss nur an 2-Leiter. Maximale Betriebsspannung 250 Volt.

Preis für 2 m Zuleitung mit Gerätesteckdose und Wandstecker . . . . Fr. 4.40.

Bei Bestellung sind stets Listen-Nummer, Volt, sowie etwaige Wünsche wegen der Zuleitung anzugeben.

S 494 D   1934

2.57

[→ J]
"Locking mechanisms ensure that drawer *a*, which for example is set on runners, cannot be completely pulled out of drawer *b* [...]. The drawer is formed by a rectangular frame and therefore has no base. The container *c*, suspended in it and therefore easy to remove, [...] making it easy to clean and disinfect, is shown as a dotted line in the drawing." (40)

hinged from the outside like a closet. Initially, Therma purchased the units (compressor, evaporator and condenser) from a Detroit-based company, Kelvinator, with which it had concluded an exclusive supply contract. As early as 1933, the firm displayed a commercial refrigerator with several compartments, similar to those used by dairy stores.

How did this come to pass? The Swiss government had announced high import duties on imported refrigerators from March 30, 1932. Director Dietler therefore asked "all existing refrigerator factories" whether they would be prepared "to grant Therma the right to manufacture under license for Switzerland." Dietler proudly reported, "A commitment has been received from the largest and oldest refrigerator factory in the world, Kelvinator in Detroit, USA." He also added that "the Kelvinator refrigerator is considered to be the best existing system." Kelvinator did not demand a license fee; the sole condition was that Therma would purchase the compressors from Detroit and also take on distribution of Kelvinator refrigerators for Switzerland for four to five years.[38]

In 1935, after just three years, Therma was already manufacturing the cooling units. What's more, it even occasionally supplied "made in Schwanden" units to Kelvinator in Detroit! This was the first time that motor components were manufactured in Schwanden for areas other than electrical heat production. In an impressively short time and with great aplomb, the engineers and skilled workers in Schwanden got to grips with the shift from constructing appliances to mechanical engineering with its significantly smaller manufacturing tolerances, in the range of hundredths of a millimeter.[39]

The design engineering department rapidly developed compelling technical solutions. For example, a drawer system with full-extension runners for commercial kitchens was devised, offering scope to lift the drawer box out of the runner with a handle in order to clean it [40][→J] or a hotel coffee machine with a milk container and a suspended pull-out cup rack. The practical arrangement of the components and their interactions are always impressive: the interior's ingenious arrangement and the exterior's calm reliability. Sometimes the solutions were probably a little too imaginative and not really suitable for everyday use, such as the hotel toaster with a sliding rocker arrangement for the bread tongs [→2.65] that was supposed to ensure the toast would slide into the bread basket automatically. Overall, Therma also gained an outstanding reputation as a manufacturer of professional appliances and was contracted to provide the equipment for the kitchen at the international civil airport in Dübendorf near Zurich (1932), as well as the kitchen at Hiltl in Zurich, which was the world's first vegetarian restaurant, Lucerne Cantonal Hospital's kitchen, the Maison des Infirmières in Lyons, not to mention the kitchens of a rapidly growing list of renowned restaurants and hotels, such as the Vitznauerhof, Palace (St. Moritz), Metropol (Bern) or Hotel Brighton (Paris).

The development of ham steaming cabinets should also be mentioned. A whole line of these appliances were delivered to Paris for the Géo meat factory and the Société aux Jambons – in time for the 1937 World Exhibition – in collaboration with the renowned company Gebrüder Grob (Grob frères) in Zurich. The photograph of a reference apparatus in the archive (a reproduction) is tricky to classify. It shows a riveted steaming cabinet with many buckle fasteners. Is this a historical predecessor? A primitive prototype? An illustration of the problem to be solved? What is clear, however, is that the elegance of Therma's technical solution reveals a highly developed grasp of the problem; it includes a single central lever to lock the cabinet steam-tight on all sides by means of several bolts. The other elements in this design (the arrangement of the manometer and thermometer as well as the indicator lights) also demonstrate the depth of technical expertise underpinning Therma's design solutions.

2.58

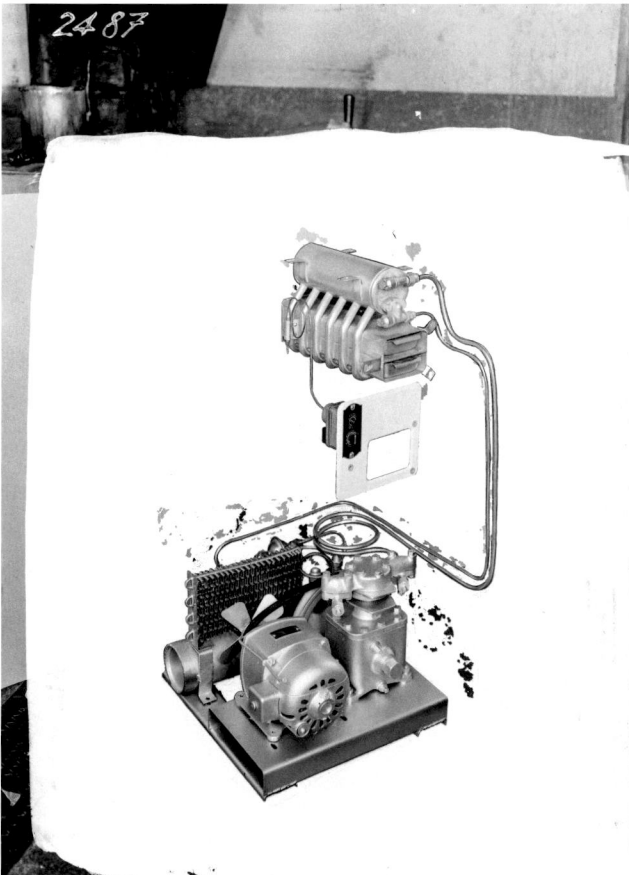

2.59

2.56   New coffee machine based on the
        "pour-over system," with chrome-plated
        housing, 1934.
2.57   Leaflet for the coffee machine with its
        "modern, angular shape," introduced
        in 1934.
2.58   The first refrigerator model from Therma,
        possibly a pre-production series, 1932.
2.59   The refrigerator's cooling module: com-
        pressor and condenser at the bottom,
        cooling coils and evaporator at the top,
        1935.

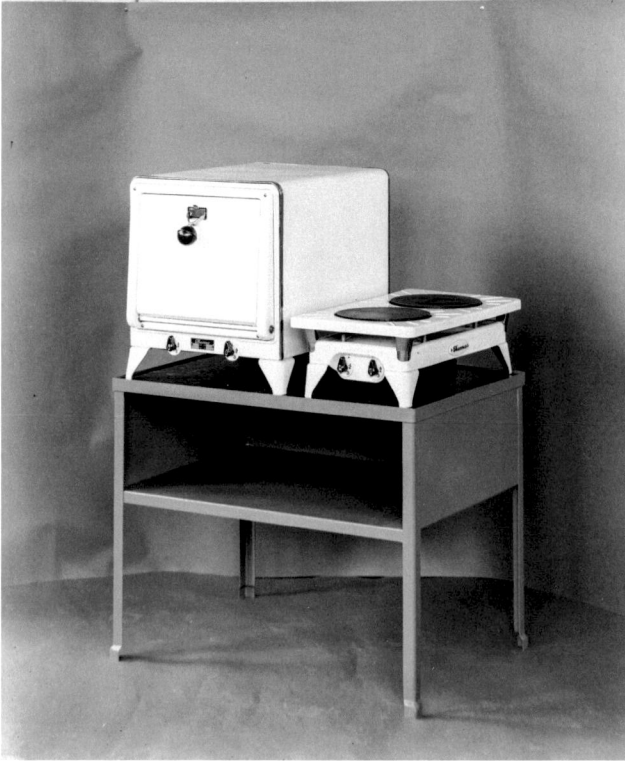

2.60a

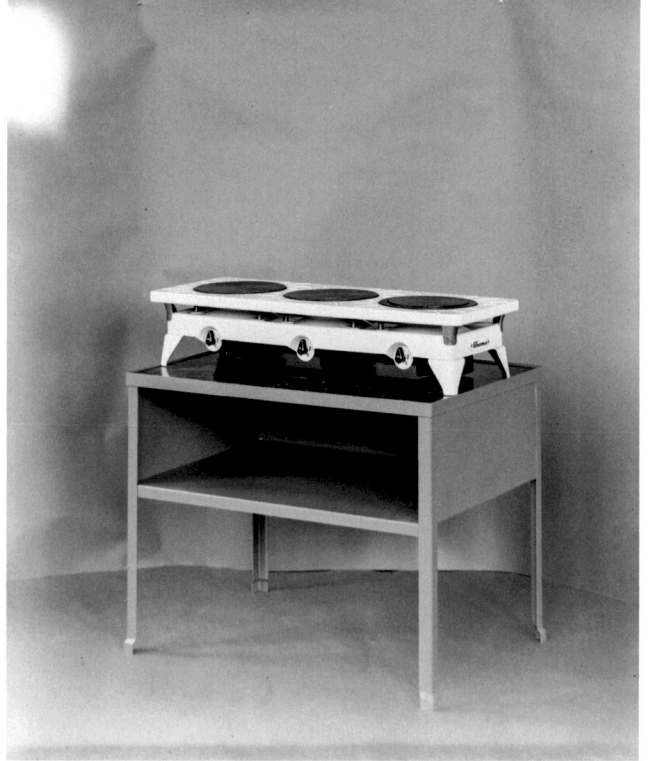

2.60b

2.60c

2.60d

2.61

2.62a

2.62b

2.60 A hint of system design: compact stand-alone hotplate, separate oven and metal underframes, designed as a set of possible combinations to form ensembles, 1933.

2.61 Study for a table-top stove that did not go into production. Wilhelm Kienzle can be assumed to be the designer due to the unusually pared-down elements – the surprising and unconventional fusion of feet and switches. Undated, ca. 1932.

2.62 The table-top stove model that went into production with closed sides, rim beading next to the hotplates and removable, black enameled top plate with feet, probably developed in 1933, documented in the 1934 catalog. Two variants shown. Kienzle may conceivably have collaborated here, too.

2.63

2.64

2.63   Hotel coffee machine, ca. 1931.
2.64   Interior of a hotel coffee machine: on the
        right, the hanging rack with shelves for
        coffee cups on full-extension runners,
        ca. 1931/1932.
2.65   Hotel toaster with pull-out, swiveling
        bread tongs: an experiment that the
        company soon abandoned.
2.66   Structural engineering finesse in com-
        mercial kitchen design: tilting frying pans
        and deep built-in drawers underneath
        on full-extension runners, ca. 1932.
2.67   CH patent no. 160717 for design of easily
        removable drawers on separate full-
        extension runners, 1932.

2.65

2.66

Therma Fabrik für elektrische Heizung A. G.
vormals S. Blumer

Patent Nr. 160717
1 Blatt

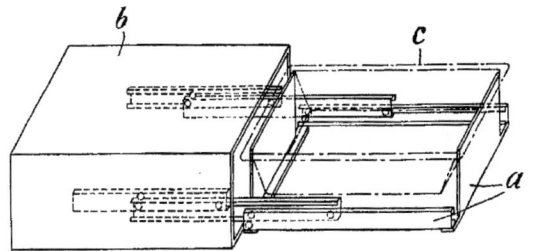

2.67

87

2.68

2.69

88

2.70

2.71

Schweizer Industrie dringt im Ausland immer noch erfolgreich durch. Eine moderne, hygienisch einwandfreie Schinken-Kochanlage, die sich die «Société aux Jambons», Paris, durch die Schweizer Firma Gebrüder Grob, Zürich, einrichten ließ. Auch im Metzgereigewerbe hat die moderne Technik mit ihren maschinellen Anlagen großen Wandel geschaffen.

2.72

2.68   Kitchen at Hiltl, Zurich, reputedly the
       world's first vegetarian restaurant,
       founded in 1898. New fittings by Therma
       ca. 1930, including a full set of bains-
       marie – to keep food warm or cool,
       as required.
2.69   The kitchen in the newly built Dübendorf
       International Airport near Zurich,
       equipped with Therma appliances, 1932.
2.70   Steam cooking cabinet with buckle
       fasteners and riveted housing, probably
       a reproduction of an older third-party
       product.
2.71   Ham steamer cabinets before trans-
       portation, developed with the company
       Grob frères (Zurich) and delivered to
       Paris for the Société aux Jambons for
       the 1937 World's Fair. Door with a central
       lever for all the surrounding bolts.
2.72   The press clipping shows all ten ham
       cooking cabinets installed in Paris,
       presumably in 1937.

2.73

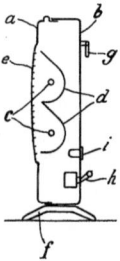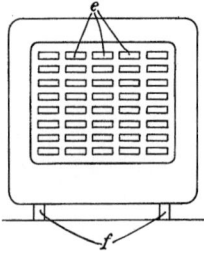

2.74

2.73   Economical to produce: the electric
       heater in two sizes, 1934.
2.74   "Electric heater": CH patent no. 175949
       for rational manufacture of the new elec-
       tric fireplace, 1934. The appliance would
       soon replace the flat heater (cf. 2.45)
       and remained in the range until 1954.
2.75   Type D stove, an economical model,
       priced at 275 CHF, 1934.
2.76   Cooking stove type C (sometimes
       referred to internally as *Sparherd* or *Volks-
       herd* ("low-cost or people's stove")) with
       hinged cover and recessed section
       underneath, presented as most afforda-
       ble model, priced at 260 CHF, at the
       1934 Mustermesse Basel.

As capital goods, the professional appliances offered welcome relief for the company during those difficult economic times, particularly compared to the much more nervous mood in consumer goods. As a result of the multiple crises, the latter division suffered from increasingly dramatic unemployment, exchange rate difficulties, protectionist measures on export markets (sometimes even between cantons!) and political problems in its target countries. On the other hand, it also benefited from protectionist measures in Switzerland.[41] There were growing sources of uncertainty in those years and the confidence that had defined the period after 1925 increasingly gave way to gloom.

In 1931, net sales fell by 9.5 percent, while manufacturing costs rose by 3.5 percent. Although Samuel Blumer was pessimistic about the overall situation, at the same time he expressed "every confidence that our Director would reduce the workforce and adapt to the new circumstances with the same energy and courage with which he had built up the company."[42] The Board of Directors instructed management to "gradually adjust production costs and overheads to reflect the reduced turnover as far as possible."[43] This also involved wage cuts, which the management, as agreed with Blumer, endeavored to make as fair and reasonable as possible. At the same time, it is important to emphasize that looking for ways to make savings in the production process is a constant in industry. Against the backdrop of national and international competition, efforts to boost productivity have formed a persistent undernote throughout Therma's history. Traces of this endeavor can be identified in numerous products, particularly from 1935 to 1945.

One example of this is the new electric fireplace developed in 1934, described in the patent specification as an "electric heating stove," in which the front and back were joined together in a very simple fashion using a form-fit connection (similar to the lid of a tin confectionery box). "Manufacturing such a stove is relatively cheap," the patent specification notes.[44] It certainly had less aesthetic charisma than the aforementioned twin appliances, the flat radiant heaters and the portable space heaters, but its design concept was very pragmatic and it remained in the catalog for many years.

Efforts to make it possible to reduce sales prices were most evident when it came to the household stoves. At the 1934 Mustermesse Basel, Therma promoted the Type C stove with three hotplates at a price of 260 CHF, a quarter less than the comparable *Siedlungsherd*, the stove designed specifically for modern kitchens (356 CHF gray-blue enameled, 401 CHF in white). The price could be lowered as the weight was greatly reduced (63 kg compared to 91 kg for the *Siedlungsherd*) thanks to a structural design consistently geared toward simplification, coupled with economical finishes for the surfaces. The stoves are made of recycled steel – the base layer for a granite enamel finish to conceal small irregularities.[45] Simple angle iron was used for the legs. These low-cost cooking stoves, complete with finishes that reflected the cost-saving spirit of the age, had a different, more spartan appearance than the homogeneously enameled variants; they even deliberately opted to express the lower price point visually to compete as little as possible with previous models. The Type C, the cheapest version, was refreshingly unconventional in its directness, with a hinged cover that revealed the hollowed-out recess underneath to catch spills. Its circumferential edge beading corresponds to that used in the small cooking stoves and table-top hotplates, although it is unclear which category first used that option. The slightly more expensive Type D model (275 CHF) retained the pull-out drip tray.

Dietler repeatedly assured the Board of Directors that the decision to build the enameling plant had been correct, underlining that it was also operating profitably thanks to the extensive third-party orders mentioned above and

2.75

2.76

2.77

2.78

2.79

was keeping the workforce busy. "Our production would no longer be conceivable without our own enameling plant."[46] At the same meeting, Dietler also gave the Board of Directors an insight into his further efforts to limit the damages caused by the economic downturn, explaining that "we are trying to make up for the large drop in orders and profits by incorporating new product lines, such as aluminum cookware, sinks and compressors. [...] Customs measures and quotas have forced us into compressor production, which, however, proves profitable for us."[47] Reading this today, one cannot but admire this determination to stand firm, all the more so as Therma endeavored to protect the workforce from very painful cuts wherever possible. At the same time, however, the company left the VST (Association of Swiss Manufacturers of Electrothermal Appliances) in late 1934 due to the sometimes unfair competition, even among association partners.

Adding metal dishwashing sinks to the Therma range was an important step in difficult times. There were two reasons for that. Firstly, from a manufacturing point of view, they represented a move toward actual three-dimensional forming of metal sheets. The costly drawing presses already in the company were the means used, with a view to reducing the number of individual parts to be assembled by opting instead for larger single-piece forms. This was the generally accepted route to improved productivity. On the other hand, the sinks extended Therma's scope to include an element that had potential to help customers view the kitchen as a room in which heterogeneous elements could be integrated into an overarching whole rather than simply set side by side. The idea of the kitchen as an ensemble was just beginning to take shape and only began to spread like wildfire after the Second World War; however, in the late 1930s there were already examples of Therma kitchens in single-family homes that revealed a desire for improved functionality and visual uniformity (in some cases perhaps kitchens that were remodeled or fitted after moving in). The metal sinks were an important element in this. And they had the sonorous designation of origin "Therminox," which immediately aroused interest.

The deep-drawing process again came into play for household cooking stoves and was introduced in 1935/1936. "The design office is now intensively involved in studying how our appliances can be manufactured even more simply and cheaply," Dietler had previously reported to the Board of Directors, adding that "we have to do our best everywhere to keep our heads above water and keep calm in the face of all difficulties."[48] At first, the stove consisted of metal sheets bolted directly together, i.e. without a housing. The two identical side panels were extended around the corner, attached to the front and back panels by screws, and also formed the feet. Liquids that boiled over were collected in an internal recess set underneath the cover panel and flowed from there through a central aperture into a narrow "milk drawer" in the front of the stove. This model became the new reference type for Therma household cooking stoves for many years to come, also in the upmarket version with a separate baking and roasting oven, with or without a grill rack. Wilhelm Kienzle's appreciation of this stove has already been mentioned, as has the possibility that he was involved in designing it.

The same period saw the development of the universal handle for irons made of black duroplastic material with recessed thumb grips for both left- and right-handed users.[49] The integrated cover protected the user from heat radiation from below and put an end to the previous distinction between closed and open handles. Did the name "universal handle" also suggest a change in the company's self-image? Scope to choose between products with clear distinctions (in this case: handle variants) had been the hallmark of professionalism, whereas now the focus had shifted to a synthesis of functional properties in one and the same object, the common denominator, so to speak – again, traits that I would read as signs of Wilhelm Kienzle's

2.80

2.81

2.82

2.77 In 1934, production was expanded to include stainless steel sinks, by the name of "Therminox," shown here at the 1935 Mustermesse Basel.

2.78 The large drawing press, which was required for the sinks, was installed in ca. 1934.

2.79 New, no-housing stove construction made of deep-drawn side and front panels screwed together, with collecting tray and milk drawer underneath for liquids that boiled over, 1935.

2.80 Toaster with side-mounted bread tongs, in production from ca. 1925 to 1935.

2.81 Toaster with balanced hanging bread tongs, 1936. This design also hints at the logical and creative touch of Wilhelm Kienzle as its creator. In production until the 1960s.

2.82 Therma stand at Comptoir Suisse in Lausanne, 1936.

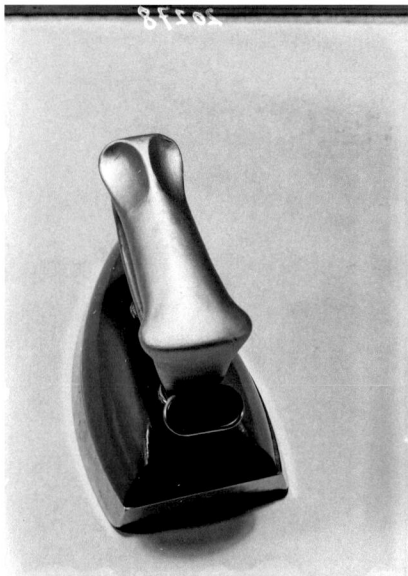

2.83a

2.83b

2.84

design thinking. This heralds something new, an interest in creating integrated designs to benefit customers that would lead after the Second World War, via a circuitous route, to free-standing kitchen furniture sets and subsequently to standardized kitchens.

Created for advertising purposes, the illustration depicting an elegant lady about to step into a warm bath also reflects this theme. A slightly earlier version drew on the same motif, but the bathtub had no cladding and the boiler was visibly attached to the wall. The comparison illustrates points we take for granted today, simply assuming that the bathtub will be built in, with cladding, and that the hot water will arrive in the bathroom via an invisible route from the heating system somewhere in the house. The two advertisements date from the time when Therma was planning to start manufacturing bathtubs, as well as cladding elements, which are the focus in the second, more luxurious-looking illustration. Therma applied for a patent for this variant in 1939, but the outbreak of war thwarted expansion of the product range to include such sophisticated fittings.[50] None of Therma's previous hallmarks appear openly and explicitly here; there is no sign of appliances to heat the room or the water, and the hydraulic system's supply pipes and drains are also not shown. It is all there, yet at the same time concealed, invisible albeit "known" prerequisites in the background. It would be many years before the implicit Americanism of the "good life" manifested in this second advertisement returned full-swing – almost two decades later.

In the first instance, Therma's robust presence at the 1939 national exhibition in Zurich was proof of its technical vigor. It supplied the equipment for various restaurant kitchens at the exhibition, including those in the Turmrestaurant, the Musterhotel and the Fischerstube. With this in mind, the firm had developed the enormous electrode tilting caldron with a capacity of 400 (or more?) liters and set up a mock-up for it in the laboratory on the enameling plant's upper floor, the point being to determine the correct height for the base to allow easy transfer of the food to smaller containers on rollers. The caldron was used in Zurich's recently constructed soup kitchen for the poor, as well as in various locations at the national exhibition, alongside all the other special Therma appliances: restaurant cooking stoves, grills, patisserie ovens, holding cabinets, bains-marie, large metal sinks et cetera. The team of young architects – Max Ernst Haefeli, Werner M. Moser and Rudolf Steiger – who built Zurich's Kongresshaus, which opened at the same time as the national exhibition and was a lasting reminder of it, also chose Therma professional appliances for the kitchen. A major milestone of Swiss modern architecture that emerged after a decade and a half of dedicated efforts to create modern, friendly and humane architecture, the Kongresshaus was a fitting location for Therma to prove to itself and to the general public just how far it had come. The general public, too? Well, they did not really have a chance to see the kitchen. Even the wonderful 2007 book about the Kongresshaus – a belated tribute to the building, then threatened with demolition – only shows the kitchen in the floor plan, like every other commercial kitchen, which publications aimed at a general audience portray as belonging to an architecturally insignificant category: the "service" areas.[51] The photograph here shows its quiet grandeur.

2.83   Bügeleisen mit neuem ergonomischem Universalgriff: Griffmulden für Links- und Rechtshänderinnen und -händer. Gefertigt wurde er in Duroplast, hier das Holzmodell, 1935.

2.84   Frühe Studie zu einem Tischkühlschrank mit seitlichem Kühlaggregat, vermutlich 1933.

1 The plan is attached to the typewritten report by Director and Delegate Representative Samuel Blumer to the Board of Directors on the occasion of Therma's twentieth anniversary. – GWA Elux B 2–3/2, 1926/27, pp. 9 ff.

2 GWA Elux, Neg. P 2_01036

3 Cf. *Therma Schwanden 1907–1932* (Schwanden: Therma, 1932), publication on the twenty-fifth anniversary of the company.

4 Therma – Electric commercial kitchen facilities / "2 Grosse Ehrenpreise an der 'ZIKA,' Zürich 1930," leaflet on professional appliances (with list of references 1913–1929). – GWA Elux H 1–12/5 to H 1–13, folder H 1–13/1

5 CH patent no. 119311: "Antriebseinrichtung bei elektrischen Moment-Drehschaltern," filed on March 30, 1926.

6 Hans Dietler, "Bericht betr. Erstellung eines Fabrik-Neubaues," October 27, 1927, pp. 1–2. – GWA Elux C 1–1/2

7 Ibid., p. 4.

8 20. Jahresbericht [Annual Report], 1926/27. – GWA Elux B 4–1/1

9 CH patent no. 119312: "Walzenschalter zur Serie-, Einzeln-, Parallel- und Ausschaltung zweier elektrischer Widerstände," filed on March 31, 1926.

10 CH patent no. 119184: "Elektrischer Kochherd," filed on April 7, 1926.

11 Hans Dietler, "Bericht des Direktors und des Delegierten an den Verwaltungsrat der Therma über das Geschäftsjahr 1932/33," p. 15. – GWA Elux B 2–3/2

12 GWA Elux, Neg. P 1_20686 and 20687

13 The wage/cost of living differential between Switzerland and other countries, particularly Germany, had a negative impact on Therma's export business; this factor is repeatedly mentioned in the minutes from the Board of Directors' meetings during these years.

14 Hans Dietler, "Bericht des Direktors und Delegierten an den Verwaltungsrat 1929/30," p. 14. – GWA Elux B 2–3/2

15 GWA Elux, Neg. P 2_00892

16 Samuel Blumer, "Lebenserinnerungen," typescript, 1942, p. 37. – GWA Elux B 1–1

17 Hans Dietler, in "Bericht des Direktors und des Delegierten an den Verwaltungsrat der Therma AG über das Geschäftsjahr 1927/28," p. 13. – GWA Elux B 2–3/2

18 Materialprüfanstalt des SEV [Swiss Electrotechnical Association], "Praktische Vergleichsversuche zwischen einem Speicherherd der Therma Schwanden, System Seehaus, und einem normalen elektrischen Herd mit direkt beheizten Platten bei Mitbenutzung eines gewöhnlichen Heisswasserspeichers," *Bulletin de l'Association suisse des électriciens* 23, no. 13 (June 22, 1932): 117–121.

19 Hans Dietler, "Bericht des Direktors und des Delegierten an den Verwaltungsrat der Therma AG über das Geschäftsjahr 1929/30," p. 15. – GWA Elux B 2–3/2

20 Architectural firms involved in Eglisee: Artaria & Schmidt, Hermann Baur, Hans Bernoulli & August Künzel, E. F. Burckhardt, Maurice Braillard, Steger & Egender, Kellermüller & Hofmann. Part of the estate is depicted in the 1932 Therma anniversary book, where it is referred to as a *Wohnkolonie* (a systematically planned settlement with uniform buildings, mostly as workers' housing estates, sometimes used in connection with garden city-inspired developments). The exhibition at Mustermesse Basel (Muba) ran from August 16 to September 14, 1930.

21 Hans Dietler, "Bericht des Direktors und des Delegierten an den Verwaltungsrat der Therma über das Geschäftsjahr 1929/30," p. 10. – GWA Elux B 2–3/2. *Siedlungsherd* is a German term that refers to a specific type of kitchen found in the new housing estates (*Siedlungen*) built in the 1920s and 1930s, particularly in Germany and also Switzerland. These housing estates were often part of social housing or suburban development initiatives and were designed with functional, efficient kitchens that matched the modest, modernist ideals of the time. It could therefore also be called a "modernist kitchen" in English.

22 Ibid.

23 CH patent no. 143953: "Türe mit Ventilationsöffnung für Brat- und Backofen," filed on January 15, 1930.

24 Hans Eckstein, *Die schöne Wohnung* (Munich: F. Bruckmann, 1934), 101.

25 Jahresbericht 24, 1930/31. – GWA Elux B 4–1/1

26 Hans Dietler, "Bericht an den Verwaltungsrat der Therma AG über das Geschäftsjahr 1930/31," pp. 13–14. – GWA Elux B 2–3/2

27 Hans Tomamichel (1899–1984) became famous as the creator of the "Knorrli" figure used to advertise seasoning and stock cubes (1947).

28 *Das Werk* 19, no. 11 (November 1932): 340, Parabolstrahler. Also: Schnellheizer, in *Das Werk* 21, no. 10 (October 1934): 309.

29 Wilhelm Kienzle, "Eine oft übersehene Beziehung zwischen Handwerk und Maschine," in *Schweizerische Bauzeitung*, September 4, 1937, advertisement pp. 38–39.

30 Enquiry from the Therma Board of Directors member Karl Heinrich Gyr (Landis & Gyr) to Hans Dietler, August 12, 1942. – GWA/Elux, B 2–4/6 (correspondence in the Board of Directors and Administrative Committee), K. H. Gyr file

31 Reply from Hans Dietler to Karl Heinrich Gyr, August 15, 1942, ibid.

32 VR-Protokoll [Minutes of Board of Directors meeting] 155, March 1931, p. 2. – GWA Elux, B 2–1/1 (2nd box)

33 "If we wanted to use the metalware factory [in Zug] for other types of enamel [than white enamel], we would have to release our very valuable formulations, which until now have been our manufacturing secret and have not been achieved by any competing company." Hans Dietler, in ibid.

34 "The enamel poster business brought us an increase in orders of almost exactly 100,000 CHF in the 1933/34 reporting year, with a total of 26,615 enamel posters and other enamel articles, and there is still an increase in this business today." Hans Dietler, in "Bericht des Direktors und Delegierten Hans Dietler an den Verwaltungsrat 1933/34," p. 10. – GWA Elux B 2–3/2

35 Message from Ida Störi's son Fredi (Friedrich) Ehrat (Zurich), July 2022; message from Ruth Brechot-Störi (Kilchberg), August 2022.

36 Valuable information on Lill Tschudi was made available thanks to journalist and curator Marcel Just (Zurich), who presented an exhibition on her work at ETH Zürich's Graphische Sammlung (Collection of Prints and Drawings) in 2021/2022.

37 Letter from Zent AG (Bern) to the electrical installation business A. Eichenberger (Bern). – GWA Elux Neg. P 2_01066

38 VR-Protokoll 165, April 1, 1932, p. 1. – GWA Elux B 2–1/1 (2nd box)

39 Note from Thomas Schätti, Schwanden, July 2024.

40 CH patent no. 160717: "Schublade," filed on April 19, 1932.

41 Passim (various minutes from Board of Directors meetings in this period). – GWA Elux B 2–1/1 (2nd box)

42 VR-Protokoll 163, February 15, 1932, p. 2. – GWA Elux B 2–1/1 (2nd box)

43 Ibid., p. 3.

44 CH patent no. 175949: "Elektrischer Heizofen," filed on March 31, 1934.

45 Anniversary publication *Fünfzig Jahre Therma AG Schwanden, 1907–1957* (Glarus: Therma, 1957), p. 37.

46 Hans Dietler, in: VR-Protokoll 183, January 30, 1935, p. 1. – GWA Elux B 2–1/1 (2nd box)

47 Ibid., p. 2.

48 Hans Dietler, in: VR-Protokoll 186, May 28, 1935, p. 2. – GWA Elux B 2–1/1 (2nd box)

49 CH patent no. 185656: "Bügeleisen," filed on August 15, 1936.

50 CH patent no. 207331: "Verkleidung von Badewannen," filed on January 25, 1939.

51 Cf. Arthur Rüegg and Reto Gadola, eds., *Kongresshaus Zürich 1937–1939. Moderne Baukultur* (Zurich: gta Verlag, 2007).

2.85

Therma, Fabrik für elektrische Heizung A.-G.   Patent. Nr. 207331
                                                1 Blatt

Fig. 1.

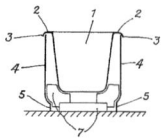

Fig. 2.

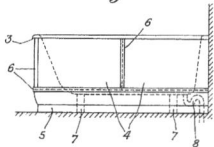

2.86

2.87

2.85   Advertising illustration depicting an elegant bathroom with concealed pipes and bathtub clad with wall elements, ca. 1939.

2.86   CH Patent no. 207 331: "Cladding of bathtubs," filed on January 25, 1939.

2.87   Load testing a deep-drawn bathtub in Schwanden, probably 1939. A decision was taken in 1939 to produce bathtubs but implementation was delayed after the outbreak of war. Production was finally given the green light, but never really took off due to materials shortages.

2.88

2.89

2.90

2.91

2.88 Test installation of a large-capacity electrode tilting caldron, set up in the laboratory on the enameling plant's upper floor (now the Therma Schaulager display space). The base height was probably determined here to ensure liquids could be poured readily into smaller vessels. Large tilting caldrons like these were subsequently used inter alia at the 1939 National Exhibition in Zurich.

2.89 The soup kitchen opened in 1939 in Zurich, in the vicinity of Escher-Wyss and Maag's production premises in the industrial district; Therma electrode tipping caldrons.

2.90 Kongresshaus Zurich kitchen, equipped mainly with Therma appliances, completed for the National Exhibition opening in 1939. Architects Max Ernst Haefeli, Werner Max Moser, Rudolf Steiger.

2.91 Postcard from the Glarus Canton Day at the National Exhibition in Zurich on August 9, 1939.

3

A construction site, viewed from a location opposite it in Therma's former main building on the other side of the road. That part of the complex, which had moved when the enameling plant was established, was now over 200 meters long thanks to extensions added in the meantime. Fall 1941, wartime, another world war. And yet there is a construction site – and construction sites embody faith in the future, not just in any future but a better one. Does this reflect the wartime realities or stand in contradiction to them?

Six months before this photo was taken, Therma's Board of Directors had identified the lack of space in the old office building as the most pressing problem. "Therma AG's building project: The sanitary facilities are inadequate in every respect. It is not possible to make them larger in the existing building, as space is already far too tight in the old offices. As we currently face a shortage of space in all departments throughout the factory, additional production facilities should be created, too."

For the first time since 1908, an established architect was commissioned to design the extension: Hans Leuzinger, then in his mid-fifties, who had offices in Glarus and Zurich, had made a name for himself with various mountain dwellings for SAC, the Swiss Alpine Club, and went on to construct the lovely Kunsthaus in Glarus after the war. An architect with great mastery of the art of building, he had an acute sensitivity for refinement in simplicity. The first plan envisaged creating more space by adding an additional floor to the existing structure but was rapidly rejected. Instead Leuzinger proposed a two-wing building with a rounded front section, to be constructed on the trapezoidal plot southwest of the enameling plant that is visible in this photograph. It would be another building with a flat roof, although the reasons were far from ideological. It was instead to factor in the possibility that additional floors might one day be needed here, too. After all, Therma was only able to develop as it did as flat roofs were incorporated from the outset, pragmatically providing scope to expand upwards. Ideologically fueled cultural debates between advocates and critics of flat roofs that were being waged elsewhere at the time had rapidly run out of steam in the industrialized canton of Glarus.

Once again, everything happened so quickly! A rough overall concept was drawn up for the space needed, a budget defined, an architect commissioned to draw up the plans on this basis, a building permit secured, the volume to be built was determined with a building profile, estimates were obtained, the companies that would

3.0   Construction site for the administration building on December 1, 1941.

101

participate were selected and locked into an ambitious schedule, the underground conduits for utilities were planned – connections to the sewage system, water supply, electricity grid, the telephone and telegraph network – the excavation pit was dug and secured, concrete deployed for the foundations and external basement walls. The construction process is recorded in a photographic journal.

Slender decorticated fir trunks can be seen here, braced together by even slimmer trunks and stretching upwards to support the temporary stairs as scaffolding, making it possible to carry out exterior work, such as plastering, in the coming year. The shell construction for the basement and first floor has been completed and work is underway on the ceiling above the first floor. Large quantities of timber for the ceiling have already been cut to size and installed: upright fixed boards create a substrate for the wooden formwork. It is December 1, 1941; a few days later the onset of winter will interrupt construction work and the whole area will be blanketed in snow. The new building was not inaugurated until November 1942, with a number of complications cited as the reason for the delay. Organizing a construction site during the war after such a short planning phase, particularly with many outside companies providing the internal finishes and technical infrastructure, was quite an achievement and is cited here as emblematic of this period, in which precisely the qualities it embodies were key: a can-do attitude and an ability to work to a particularly tight time frame. And a focus, too, on Therma as an economically significant company during the war – in a country that did not have a professional army, but in which hundreds of thousands of working men took part in exercises and proved their mettle, alternating rapidly between employment and military service. That was an era when having a reserved occupation had nothing to do with a closed shop but signified being (temporarily or permanently) exempt from serving in the army.

1940–1945

Fighting with Kilos, Struggling for Kilocalories

Therma During the Second World War

3.1

Hitler's invasion of Poland on September 1, 1939, marked the outbreak of the long-dreaded war. For industrial companies like Therma, immediate mobilization by the Swiss army (a militia force based on general national conscription) removed more than half of the entire workforce from all its business units in one fell swoop: from workers in the factory to the administration or teams working on product development or strategic planning for the firm's future direction. Although some of those mobilized could later return to work (and others, albeit in smaller numbers, were drafted on a rotating basis), much uncertainty remained in those years. That held true in particular for procurement of crucial raw materials and semi-finished products, which were severely affected by this uncertainty for years. More general issues included the likely future trends in demand for electrical appliances, for both private households and as capital goods. What kind of interventions could be expected from politicians to steer the economy? Would such measures prove supportive or obstructive? As ever during wartime, no one knew how long the conflict would last or what its consequences would be.

The aforementioned general mobilization was implemented at the very beginning of this period. On December 20, 1939, Therma's Board of Directors met in the office building with a notary to certify that the firm was complying with the Federal Council's order to move its headquarters to Bern, "the seat of the Swiss government – in case Switzerland should become involved in military entanglements."[1]

By the end of the period covered here, after six years of war and in the wake of the capitulation by Hitler's Germany and its allies Italy and Japan, Therma had gained an important branch office in Zurich, a subsidiary (Elcalor) and a distinguished new administrative building in Schwanden. This seemed almost unbelievable to people outside Switzerland, who had survived the war in other countries, enduring its immense destruction of human lives and assets. Nonetheless, it had been anything but smooth going for Therma, too, as the firm's development had to be wrested from the difficult circumstances. Although the country did not become "involved in military entanglements," it was surrounded by them and – by no manner of means an island – exposed to the prevailing conditions. In March 1940, the shareholders were informed in the 1939/40 annual report that "in line with increased demand for electric heating appliances as a result of coal rationing, higher sales were achieved over the last few months than during the corresponding period in the previous year. This led to an expansion of the workforce. [...] Thanks to comprehensive preparation by the Board of Directors and operational management as well as the dedication of employees and workers not called up, the company could continue to operate – also thanks to support from temporary female workers who had previously been involved in production in the firm. Export business [...] has suffered a setback since the outbreak of war."[2] A year later, the 1940/41 annual report stated succinctly that "the level of orders for Therma appliances was consistently good throughout this reporting year."[3] Similar statements appeared in subsequent years. However, the seemingly serene situation described increasingly revealed a core of tiresome problems during those years: staff shortages, worries about official allocations of raw materials in the wartime economy – too little or far too little? – problems with delivery times for incoming material and the dispatching of goods. Furthermore, the state felt it had to intervene rigorously in private-sector activity. Last but not least, the company faced coordination problems during these years involving "friendly" companies, initially linked with Therma in a kind of cartel comprising various companies and subsequently consolidated into a corporate group. The setup required agreements to be made on quotas for the number of units produced, material quantities and pricing – fertile ground for jealousy and mutual mistrust. In this part, I shall consider how these circumstances affected Therma's products – in terms of structural engineering, manufacture, formal design and utilization.

3.1   "No more spills, no more drips." The art of refinement: shaping the vessel's rim correctly makes a spout unnecessary.
3.2   Express cooker with automatic switch-off device, introduced ca. 1940. Front and back of a leaflet.

3.2a

3.2b

[→ A]
1942/43: "In addition to developing various new designs, especially for small appliances, which were particularly popular as a means to save energy, and for refrigeration, the main work encompassed fault-free structural designs to convert and adapt standard Therma appliances to today's manufacturing possibilities." (5)

Therma director Hans Dietler drew attention to issues of this kind in January 1941 in his report on the inventory to his superior, Therma President Hans Hefti-Haab. "No changes of any kind are planned in the production program. New designs are out of the question. All available personnel are working on the structural designs to address use of substitute materials and save material. All these issues have been discussed with the design engineering office for the long term."[4]

That sounds clear. However, in spring 1943, two years later, the 1942/43 annual report mentioned "various new designs," "especially for small appliances, which were particularly popular as a means to save energy, and for refrigeration" and noted that the development work addressed "fault-free structural designs to convert and adapt standard Therma appliances to today's manufacturing possibilities."[5] [→A] The meaning of the term "new design" shifted over these two years. Previously, novel versions had been attractive as a way of realizing customers' visions of a better life through civilizational progress; now, under wartime conditions, the expression referred to the need for altered manufacturing parameters to improve productivity. This imperative did not arise solely in response to general moral appeals from the national government and management to save resources, but was also a reaction to official constraints, specifically to the material quotas allocated. These quotas caused constant unrest in the Swiss metalworking industry, which played such a key part in the country's economic performance. Against this historical background, the question arises as to the features that distinguish a new design from a reworked one. A peacetime response might distinguish between a new version that is presented to the public as a promising means to improve their daily lives or one that is merely an operational modification that only affects production, yet does not look like progress to the outside world. During the war, "new design" primarily took on this second meaning. In many cases, design innovations were now primarily an internal matter.

Nevertheless, examples of customer-oriented innovations can also be found during these years. These included a subtle widening of the rim on kettles and caldrons, known as a pouring edge, which ensured that liquids, such as water or milk, no longer ran down the outside of the vessel when pouring, but could be dispensed without spilling a drop. For the last thirty years, this type of Therma appliance had incorporated a straight cut-off rim and a spout. As the new rim was a product of increased expertise in metalworking, it was also an indicator of Therma's technological maturity, which proved attractive to the general public.

The express kettle was a new kettle model with a rim. It had a thermostat in the base that could switch the appliance off or turn it on again to keep the water at the desired temperature. The catalog description highlighted the product's technical sophistication. "A fully automated temperature regulator is built into the kettle and cuts off the power if the kettle is left switched on while containing no water, but automatically switches the power on again when the kettle is filled. The kettle remains safe even if it is left switched on for hours with no water."[6] The description underscores the technical expertise Therma has acquired, evoked by the repetition of "fully automatic/automatic," alluding to its technological skills. Four decades earlier, in its fledgling years, Therma had filed a patent for a device that prevented "dry operation" by burning through a specific contact in the heating element. If that happened, a specialized electrical store was needed to repair this predetermined breaking point and get the appliance working again. Comparing this primitive workaround with the mature solution of the thermostat – based, incidentally, on the design for an iron with a regulator switch that offered excellent operational safety and was lauded in the advertising in analogous terms – conjures up a sense of the long trajectory of technical refinements that progress involves, even for appliances like kettles that are not particularly complex.

Between 1940 and 1945, only one truly new Therma product came onto the market: a radiation heater with a reflective surface, which remained a one-off in Therma's history and disappeared from the range again after a few years. Its heating element was rolled out wafer-thin, applied to the inner surface of a clear glass pane and covered by a second pane with the same dimensions. The two sheets of glass were fixed together by a pair of rods that extended vertically from a base, each with a fold-down handle at the upper end. The base and the handles were made of a duroplast material. In technical terms, this development was spurred by the urgent need to do everything possible to cut consumption of sheet steel, the substrate used in earlier Therma heating stoves.[7] The new variant looked almost sophisticated, a Swiss echo of Art Deco residential interiors. For the first time in Therma advertising, comfort is evoked by means of the modern visual language of a close-up: Alongside the heater, a lady sporting fancy shoes, which echo the patterning of the heating element, stretches out her elegant legs, framed to a point shortly above her knees.[8]

In November 1941, Director Dietler informed the Board of Directors about the heater in a short letter. "As one of the many results of the material shortage and adaptations to it, I am sending you one of our radiation heaters separately. I would be very interested to hear what you think of the apparatus, especially from an aesthetic point of view. The parts in duroplast are manufactured by Landis & Gyr."[9] (Originally referred to as a Spiegelofen (literally "mirror stove"), the name was subsequently changed to Heizspiegel (literally "heating mirror").) This is another example of the considerable operational autonomy to devise new models enjoyed by the director and the design engineering office. In this case, however, it is debatable whether the appliance was developed at Therma. There was already a very similar French counterpart produced by Saint-Gobain, a firm specialized in safety glass. Therma had used ovenproof glass from Saint-Gobain in the 1920s for stoves with an optional viewing window in the roasting oven door, which meant there had already been business relations between the two companies. René Coulon, a French architect and member of the Union des artistes modernes (UAM) with close ties to Art Deco, is named as the designer of Saint-Gobain's French variant, the miroir chauffant. He is also known to have produced studies for exquisite glass furniture and designed Saint-Gobain's pavilion for the 1937 Paris World's Fair.[10] In Coulon's heater, the base was more striking than in the Therma version, for it was made of translucent textured glass with a built-in lamp. The design is dated 1937. Is it also conceivable that Saint-Gobain based the heating element on Therma's tried-and-tested design, as its patent had already expired?[11] Be that as it may, Therma's ultra-thin nichrome heating element, meandering in regular loops, was ideally suited to this elegant, even spectacular display of its reflective impact. The heating element per se had never yet played such an explicit role in defining an appliance's design for Therma. The firm's traditional design mentality is only expressed in the base – with a more sober look than its French counterpart – while the dark contrasting duroplastic of the base and handles frames the dematerialized glass heating surface harmoniously.

3.3 The heater with a glazed reflective surface was the most elegant option for a radiation heater, developed for war economy conditions: The zigzagging heating element is vacuum sprayed onto one of the two glass panes. Minimal metal content – only two vertical rods, 1941/1942.

The photographic records show this heating appliance on the Therma stand at Comptoir Suisse in Lausanne in September 1942 and it appeared for the first time in the 1943 general catalog. Although it remained in the range until 1946, it subsequently disappeared from the catalogs and was succeeded by an appliance known as the rapid heater, a version of which, produced under license, was sold in France. The photographs showing the 1942 Comptoir stand are significant as documentation, for they are the only known photographs of Therma exhibition stands from the war years, when

3.3

3.4a

3.4b

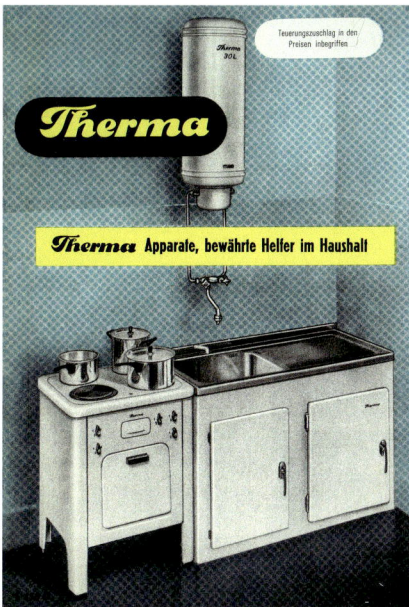

Therma Apparate, bewährte Helfer im Haushalt

3.5a

Ein Therma Kühlschrank der geheime Wunsch jeder Hausfrau

THERMA A.-G. Schwanden Gl. Telephon 7 14 41
Ausstellungsräume in: Bern, Monbijoustrasse 47
Genf, Passage du Terraillet
Lausanne, Rue Pichard 13, (Esc. Lumen)
Zürich, Hofwiesenstrasse 161

Abbildungen, Preise, Maße, Gewichte etc. dieses Prospektes sind unverbindlich   1/1946

3.5b

3.4a The Therma stand at Comptoir Suisse in Lausanne in 1942. Production technology for the cooking stoves was rationalized: Four corner plates bear the body of the stove.
3.4b Comptoir Suisse in 1942, refrigerators and cooling systems section. These appliances were promoted to help prevent food spoilage.
3.5 Cover and back page of the catalog for household cooking stoves, small appliances and dishwashers; in circulation from 1943 to 1946. Dealers would add a handwritten note if a product was no longer being manufactured. Back page: The relationship between the chilled compartment's size and the bulky unit was normal for that period.

only a handful of catalogs and brochures presenting the product range were printed. Catalogs for dealers were no longer updated annually during war; instead, they contained sheets listing the models that were no longer available. The dealers added handwritten notes on the status of particular appliances to those loose-leaf sheets.

Official government instructions impacted Therma's production, as confirmed by the Comptoir photographs and communicated to the dealers in a detailed memo from March 1942. Producing irons with nickel-plated covers was no longer permitted; only beige and green enamel were allowed. When it came to the stand-alone hotplates and table-top hotplates, silver-gray enamel was replaced by a grayish white ("white with a gray undertone and slightly less glossy than white enamel"). Household cooking stoves with a sheet steel base or a side oven were no longer available; to save material they, like the upmarket stoves, were now exclusively produced with feet; electric fireplaces were only sold with a reddish-brown wrinkle finish. Manufacture of the green enameled parabolic radiant heaters had ceased. Flat radiant heaters, portable space heaters and wall-mounted ovens were likewise no longer available, the octagonal oven only in brown and beige. A decision was taken for the refrigeration sector (list 11) to make refrigerators available only in white. The 1944 list also informed dealers that production of parabolic radiant heaters had been discontinued.[12] As it was incumbent on manufacturers to adopt appropriate measures to make the best possible use of the raw materials allocated by the authorities, this was not a planned economy, but instead a market economy that was not really free.

The SSM (Swiss Metal Industry Syndicate) allocated quotas determining the quantities of sheet steel and other materials that could be utilized as a function of the economic significance of each company or corporate group. Every kilogram saved extended production capacity and meant a profit for the company. The household cooking stoves illustrate the impact of efforts in this spirit. Their redesign in 1935 entailed abandoning the concept of a supporting frame or chassis, (cf. 2.79) with the two side panels now supporting the stove and bolted to the front and rear panels. These lateral panels had a rounded cutout at the base, which formed the feet. Although the punched-out part could be melted down for reuse, it generated waste and higher energy costs. In 1942, after being remodeled to save material, the front, sides and back panel of the cooking stove were screwed to four identical rounded corner profiles that extended over the stove's entire height by way of support. The cut-out portions were omitted in this solution, which Therma did not identify as a modernized design, but solely as a manufacturing modification that would have so little visual impact that most customers would not even notice it; during the war, the company still kept the 1936 illustrations in its general catalogs.

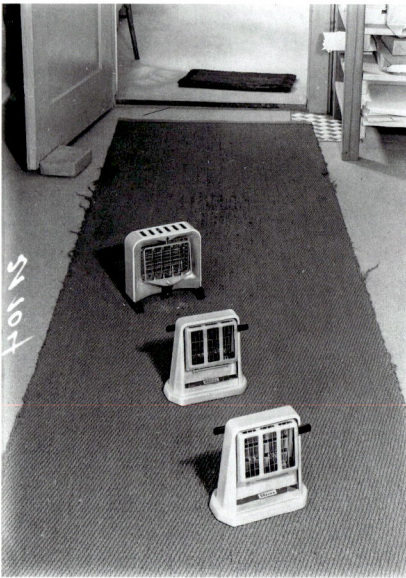

3.6a

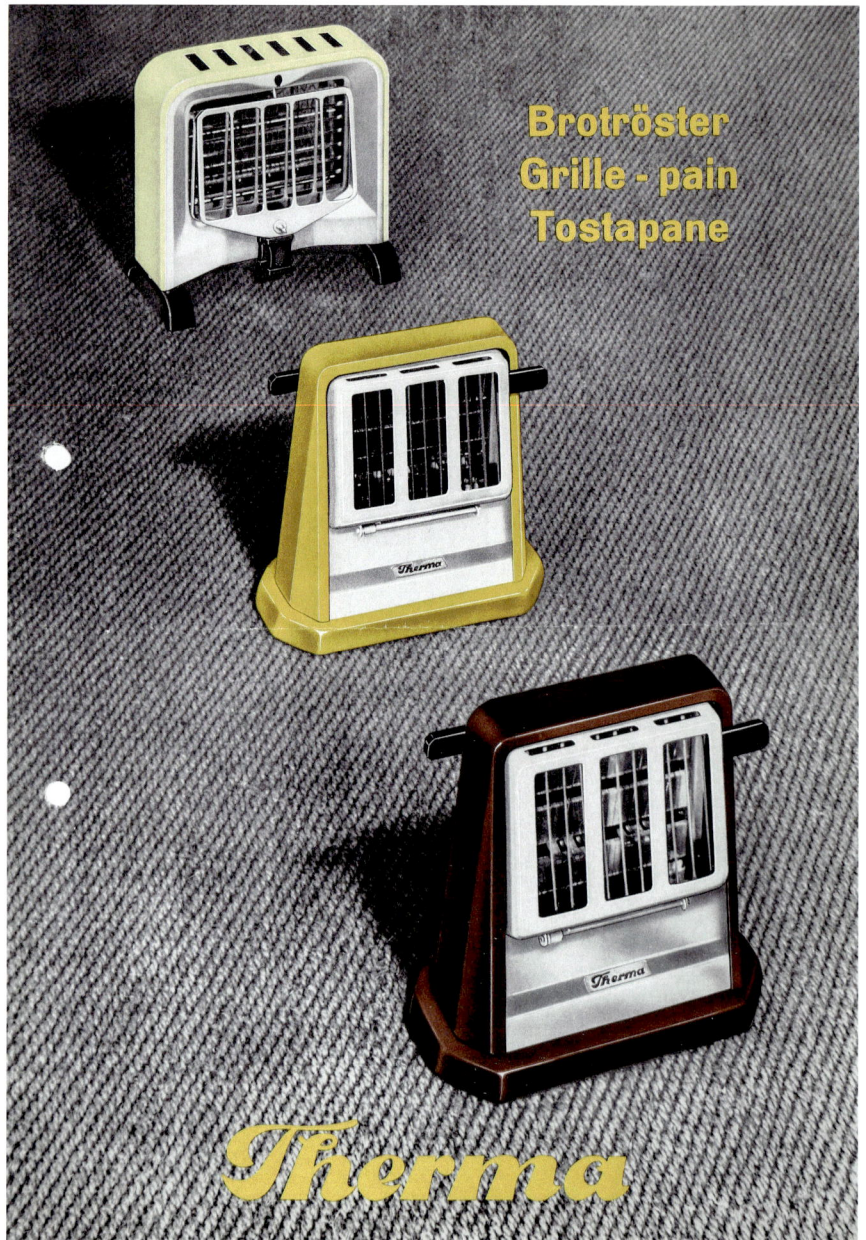

Brotröster
Grille - pain
Tostapane

Therma

3.6b

3.6a   Two toaster models, 1936 and 1942/1943, staging by the photographer.

3.6b   The newer model of the toaster was more compact, 40 percent lighter (700 g compared to 1,150 g), with streamlined production technology and was easier to use thanks to the ingeniously shaped bread holder – the slices of bread are turned over automatically as it is folded down.

3.7   Administrative employees in their old office in the main building, presumably taken in view of the imminent move to the new building, which is visible through the window (cf. 3.12).

3.8   Household cooking stoves, ready for dispatch from Schwanden, in winter. The Therma heating device by the radiator of the truck ensured it did not freeze. Undated, ca. 1940.

3.7

3.8

3.9

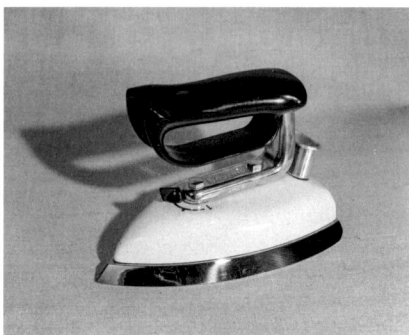

3.10

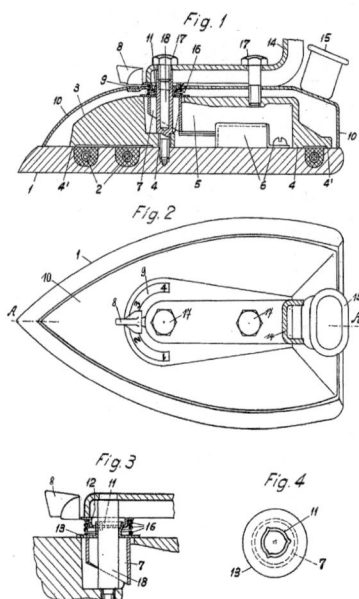

Therma, Fabrik für elektrische Heizung AG.   Patent Nr. **254777**
1 Blatt

Fig. 1

Fig. 2

Fig. 3   *Fig. 4*

3.11

A Side Note: Closing Ranks Against Outsiders

Therma's economic standing within the manufacturing industry was a constant topic of debate for management while the war was raging. In its pioneering days, the company had played a decisive part in paving the way for electrothermal technology and its widespread introduction into daily life. It had become successful in this capacity – as Switzerland's most internationally renowned company in this sector, albeit along with a number of rival companies that had grouped together as the VST (Association of Swiss Manufacturers of Electrothermal Appliances) to set themselves apart from competitors viewed as unprofessional. Those outsiders that attempted to jump on the household electrification bandwagon were regarded by the VST as a reputational risk for modern technology. In addition to Therma, VST members included Maxim (Aarau), Kummler & Matter (Aarau), Zent (Bern) and Sauter (Basel). Therma was the most significant and also best established in export markets. Le Rêve (Geneva), Prometheus (Liestal), Salvis (Lucerne) and a growing number of other non-association members were unwanted competitors. After its pioneering years, competition intensified within the VST, too, during the global economic crisis; some VST companies also moved closer together, adopting a quota regulation that allocated quantities to particular companies and obliged them to agree on pricing. At the time, there was no antitrust law that governed or prohibited such agreements. In the late 1930s, efforts to form a "group" consisting of Therma, Maxim and Kummler & Matter were stepped up, to a large extent to neutralize protectionist measures by individual cantons.[13] It would be too far off-topic to include a detailed account of the group's protracted development, which was by no means devoid of conflict, but a number of aspects related to its development merit a mention. As early as 1930, Therma explored the option of acquiring a majority shareholding in Maxim. Although this attempt was not successful, the two companies sought an "understanding" and harmonized the dimensions of some appliance components, such as the diameter of hotplates. Therma also did enameling work for Maxim. In the challenging 1930s, a kind of proto-group was formed with Therma, Maxim and Kummler & Matter, with Therma clearly the strongest and most prominent partner. Collaboration between the three Boards of Directors was by no means smooth, especially in contacts between Therma and Maxim. A general agreement on joint procurement of semi-finished products and production of components for each other, agreed upon in principle, was at most sporadically implemented; that was mainly due to Maxim, judging by correspondence between Therma's Director and its Presidium, as well as within the Boards of Directors of the individual companies. Therma's President, Hans Hefti, chaired the joint "Administrative Committee" at group level (Therma/Maxim/Kummler & Matter). Therma Director Dietler repeatedly complained to Hefti that Maxim's management seemed to be running the company as if it were Therma's competitor rather than as a business partner. The purported agreement between the individual group companies, which were legally independent but had undertaken to work together as a group, remained largely rhetorical. Their differences of opinion intensified in the face of the war economy and all it entailed. That may in part have been because Therma was considerably more efficient than the other companies and was de facto the senior partner, with individual parts manufactured on behalf of the other group members circulating primarily from Therma to Maxim and only rarely – if at all – in the opposite direction. Demand for sheet steel for production at Therma was several times higher than at the other two companies.[14]

Therma's collaboration with Kummler & Matter, where industrialist Ernst Göhner was an influential partner, functioned better than with Maxim. Shortly after the war began, Therma reached an agreement with Göhner on the acquisition of Kummler & Matter's appliance engineering division or, to be more specific, on the spin-off of this division from the areas at Kummler &

[→ B]
1941: "Throughout the production process as currently implemented in the manufacturing program of the three companies, efforts must be made to attain the greatest possible harmonization of individual components; in the process, the external visual appearance of appliances from each individual company should be preserved as far as possible, but individual components can be substituted between companies without further ado." (18)

[→ C]
1941: "Each of the companies manufactures a certain category of appliances as small series, which cannot possibly be profitable. Nowadays, each company designs their entire manufacturing program independently, as the catalogs proclaim, without any consideration for this or that group company. Each company has its own porcelain, steatite and plastic or duroplast models, for example, and pays for the associated tools, while these models often scarcely differ. It is therefore not possible for one company to help out the other with this or that particular component, as the designs are often just a hair's breadth apart and, as a result, the entire production process is expensive." (21)

3.9   The heating pad: probably the most economical way to create a sense of coziness when you have to save energy.
3.10   The new easy-regulation iron with beige enameled cover and universal handle, 1940. Given the change to the universal handle, the slider is a more elegant solution than the earlier rotary knob from 1931.
3.11   CH patent no. 254777 for the easy-regulation iron, filed on June 5, 1945: The patent claims concerned a design improvement to prevent dust from entering through the semicircular regulator slot.

Matter that remained responsible for overhead line construction and trolleybuses.[15] Therma held one hundred percent of share capital (600,000 CHF) in K & M, the new company, which it entered in the commercial register shortly afterwards under the new designation "Elcalor AG, Fabrik für elektrothermische Apparate, Aarau."

The decision in April 1941 to add a fourth firm to the group, namely Ernst Göhner's other company, Gasotherm (Zurich), is an indication of how challenging business had become in the face of pressure from global politics and economic policy. It also shows that earlier antagonism between electricity and gas as energy sources had now been put into perspective; businesses seized any opportunity to secure market share. Therma cooking stoves equipped with gas burners (or studies for such appliances) also suddenly start appearing among the photo negatives at this time. The articles of incorporation concerning integration of Gasotherm into the group, dated March 13, 1941, stated that "the companies Therma AG, Schwanden, Maxim AG, Aarau, Kummler & Matter AG, Aarau, and Gasotherm AG, Zurich, shall form a joint economic group with the purpose of achieving the best possible competitiveness for their manufacturing products on domestic and foreign markets through group-wide cooperation and market regulation."[16]

The main concern in the metalworking industry in 1941, the third year of the war, was securing supplies of raw materials and semi-finished products. "Material shortages are spreading so rapidly in Switzerland that sooner or later we will be forced to adapt better to the circumstances," Dietler wrote to Hefti, going on to explain that "this would lead to construction of a number of appliances being prohibited [...]. Naturally, all competing companies would have to comply with these regulations."[17] Dietler, however, saw the shortages not only as a temporary obstacle but also within the broader context of an intensified price war and sought to counter the fierce international competition that he anticipated would arise in the post-war period through systematic division of labor within the group and highly standardized designs.[18] [→ B] In Dietler's view, having this kind of understanding between Therma, Maxim, K & M and Gasotherm on the category of structural engineering designs did not exclude the possibility that product differentiation could nonetheless be achieved through technological and visual innovations, although he was concerned with more than stylistic issues when he added, "I understand creative work to mean something other than one company designing an appliance's external appearance to look slightly different from the structural design deployed by the other company."[19] But isn't that a contradiction in terms? Not necessarily: Dietler took as his starting point the concept that a new idea within one company can also be realized with individual parts that are harmonized within the group. The ideas he presented to management in May 1941 are reminiscent of the US automobile industry's brand technology, as developed by General Motors under its CEO Alfred P. Sloan.[20] Dietler gives a clearsighted analysis of the lack of efficiency in the "Structural Designs" section and instead calls for the "greatest possible grouping and harmonization of appliance types and details," explaining the concepts by describing practice at the time.[21] [→ C] He assumes that "substitutes will automatically be utilized as soon as it becomes apparent that increasingly scarce materials are needed to construct the appliances." Referring, like a true engineer, to the satisfaction that may lie in any problem, for it also conceals the solution within it, he adds that "solving this problem is in and of itself a great and to some extent rewarding challenge."[22]

However, the demands he made met with marked resistance, particularly from Maxim AG's management, which feared for its independence and corporate profile. In May 1941 engineer Alfred Oehler, Maxim's President, had welcomed Dietler's proposals for systematic coordination, but now wrote to Chairman Hefti that "implementing the Therma proposal would lead to

[→ D]

1941: "The economic opponents we face are ruthless and exploit everything for their own ends; as a result of the war, they have already learned to think economically, save and do without to a much greater extent than we have. Unless we learn promptly to act like that, too, and change our manufacturing methods, our trade and our structural designs accordingly, Switzerland will not only be defeated as an exporting country, but will also fail to attain self-sufficiency after the war, or even during it, and will lose all justification for its existence." (26)

uniform models. Any creative activity of a technical and commercial nature would suffer as a result."[23] Dietler viewed this stance as an illusory standpoint no longer in tune with reality, as he informed Hefti in a detailed and spirited memorandum during his summer vacation. Responding to Maxim's comments from Aarau, he wrote, "I cannot avoid the impression that the authors of these letters are still not able to work their way out of the old free-market-loving way of thinking of entrepreneurship as it existed around fifteen to twenty years ago and to adapt to the constantly changing circumstances."[24] In conversation with an (unnamed) German industrialist with connections to the Reich Ministry of Economics, Hefti had heard in person of the latter's instructions to pull out all the stops when setting the price of a cheap cooking stove to boost international competitiveness.[25] Hefti seems to have largely shared Dietler's assessment, but had to try to strike a balance in the interest of the whole group. Dietler's objections to Maxim's arguments reveal clearly that he was aware of the fundamental changes unfolding in the industry, which meant that the era of small, family-run, niche firms was coming to an end and that there would be relentless competition – internationally.[26] [→ D] Although Dietler's memorandum does not explicitly mention the German Reich, it can be read as an impassioned call to Switzerland as a political entity, as well as a call for Therma to assert itself economically within the group as primus inter pares.

The decision to build a new administration building in Schwanden was also taken during 1941, which proved to be an extremely nerve-wracking financial year. The expansion was becoming increasingly urgent as the offices of the administration, crammed awkwardly into the old building, also took up valuable floor space that could otherwise be used for production. In spring 1941 a study commissioned from architect Hans Leuzinger was presented, proposing that a floor be added to the existing office building along with an extension to the side. Everyone involved felt, however, that this was not a satisfactory solution and thus at the end of May the Board of Directors decided, as stated in Minutes no. 237, to have Leuzinger draw up a proposal for the site to the west of the enameling plant, on the other side of Sernftalstrasse.[27] His astonishing speed in presenting a new proposal has already been mentioned above. The next set of minutes, no. 238 from July, record the formal award of the contract to Leuzinger, who in the meantime had worked up three variants to ease decision-making.[28] The construction project was classified as being "of national interest." Six weeks later (as recorded in the next set of minutes, no. 239), the specific construction method and material form that the extension would take were already anticipated. "The cost estimate envisages solid, functional construction without any luxurious fittings."[29]

By mid-October, a construction machine was busy with earthworks, a crane had been erected and two months later, the basement and first floor had already been constructed before winter stopped work temporarily. Leuzinger had commissioned the engineering firm A. Wickart, specialized in ambitious reinforced concrete work, to handle the load-bearing structure.[30] It was designed to include five stories, which meant the groundwork was already laid for potential later additions, but only two were built.[31]

That same year, 1941, the repair workshop, located in a building on Guggachstrasse in Zurich that had been acquired in 1937, was expanded into a fully fledged "refrigeration office," which offered individual planning for professional refrigeration systems and presumably also carried out the related carpentry work. Therma manufactured these professional refrigeration systems in Zurich and delivered large numbers of these appliances throughout Switzerland. Combating food spoilage was vital and received financial support as a policy measure during the war, when consumption was regulated by food stamps issued by the authorities. Many refrigeration systems in grocery stores, chilled display cases in butchers' shops or dairies and for

3.12 Exterior of the new administration building on completion in 1942, architect Hans Leuzinger.
3.13 Skeleton construction for the administration building with a remarkable flexible supporting structure (suitable for use as an open-plan office), here the first floor, photographed on June 20, 1942. Ceiling made of reinforced concrete.

3.12

3.13

3.14

3.15

3.16

3.14 Therma's second location: the "Refrigeration Office" in the "Guggach" building
on Hofwiesenstrasse in Zurich, acquired
by the City of Zurich's electricity company in 1937 and in operation for Therma
since 1942.

3.15 Kitchen dresser with built-in refrigerator:
cabinetmaker's craftsmanship for
the upper classes, probably produced
in Zurich (in the "Guggach" building).
1942.

3.16 Kitchen with one of the first sink and
refrigerator combinations, photographed
in one of the new employee houses
in Schwanden, 1945.

3.17

3.18

1943: "Conversion of refrigerator production from iron to wood will soon be complete and the new models have without exception been well received by customers. This work can be described as a success. The changeover has freed up large quantities of sheet metal for the rest of our production, which is of great importance in helping us to keep going. [...] Apart from that, the structural engineering [department] has its hands full with preparatory measures due to the shortages and adjustments." (32)

3.17   A domestic kitchen in the 1940s. Individual appliances: sink-refrigerator combination (possibly as part of a central cooling system), water pipes under plaster, stove, storage cabinet with two drawers and a curtain with metal roller gliders.
3.18   A similar arrangement to that in 3.17: refrigerator on a brick base as part of a central cooling system, low-cost stove type G model with hinged top plate and drip tray, sink unit with built-in cabinet compartments underneath.
3.19   Leaflet for the TK 11 refrigerator, ca. 1940. The door could also be opened with a foot pedal, as in American precursors.

vegetable farmers, as well as in fruit storage rooms are documented in the Therma photo archive from this period. Therma installed these systems all over the country. Customers responded well to the appliances' altered appearance as a result of the switch from metal to wood, used to replace the entire front-facing side of built-in refrigerators and refrigerated compartments – with the timber structure left visible and in many cases no longer painted white – all of which reflected the widespread notion of technical progress in a friendly guise.[32][→ E] A lavish advertising folder documents the important role this division played in consolidating the company's professional reputation. Photographs of stores with these systems throughout the country, ranging from refrigerated sales units in western Switzerland or cheese display cases in dairy outlets to jaunty refrigerated display cases for patisserie in cafés (not yet called tea rooms), convey the unmistakable flair of everyday culture in those years.

For wealthy private households, Therma now also offered a three-part refrigerator-cupboard ensemble with a built-in refrigerator in the middle – from today's perspective, a somewhat curious hybrid of a traditional piece of furniture and a technical appliance, which also conveys a sense that the appliance's likely lifespan could be equated with the unlimited durability of the surrounding woodwork. The ensemble was described in the general catalog as displaying "first-class joinery, sprayed white, cream or silver-gray on the outside, stained dark on the inside, with a built-in refrigerator."[33] The refrigerator in the central axis, which does not yet have standardized dimensions, served as a mark of quality: scope to swap out an interchangeable technical appliance for a newer device was not yet an issue in 1942, and would only gradually appear on the agenda over the next two decades – although the prognosis for technical wear and tear must be viewed realistically, also in terms of the technology and structural design. The first step toward these combination configurations was a small-scale variant of a Therminox metal sink with the refrigerator built in below and the technical portion of the refrigeration unit on the side. The kitchen facilities in the houses that Therma had built in Schwanden for its employees in 1944 document the standards current at the end of the war: a small-scale combined sink and refrigerator, a modest wall-mounted boiler above (thirty-liter capacity, the wiring not yet plastered over) and a stove with a drip tray and "milk drawer" – as had already been the standard configuration for the Therma household cooking stove for a decade.

Shortly before the end of the war, Therma developed a method for freezing fruit and vegetables. The deep-freezing process had been introduced in the USA in 1939 by the Birds Eye brand. Therma's method involved boiling the goods in aluminum trays, rapidly deep-freezing them, removing the frozen blocks, wrapping them in paper and storing them in the dispatch building. The process was primarily introduced to ensure the diet of the company's workforce was somewhat less dependent on the seasons. Therma filed a patent for the process in October 1943 (CH patent no. 245658), but by the time the innovative process gradually became part of everyday life, the war was already far in the past. By then, many refrigerators were sold throughout the country, including models with a large ice cube compartment.

An innovation like the experimental introduction of deep-frozen products highlights that phase changes and overlaps always emerge when attempting to divide a historical continuum into eras for a company like Therma with such a broad product range. That kind of extensive repertoire of very different designs can only be replaced gradually, i.e. modernized step by step. That was certainly the case here: Deep-freeze technology would only be tackled in the post-war period.

Energy-saving suggestions, on the other hand, were directly relevant to the era. Advertising for the iron with a regulator switch was also in this spirit

3.19a

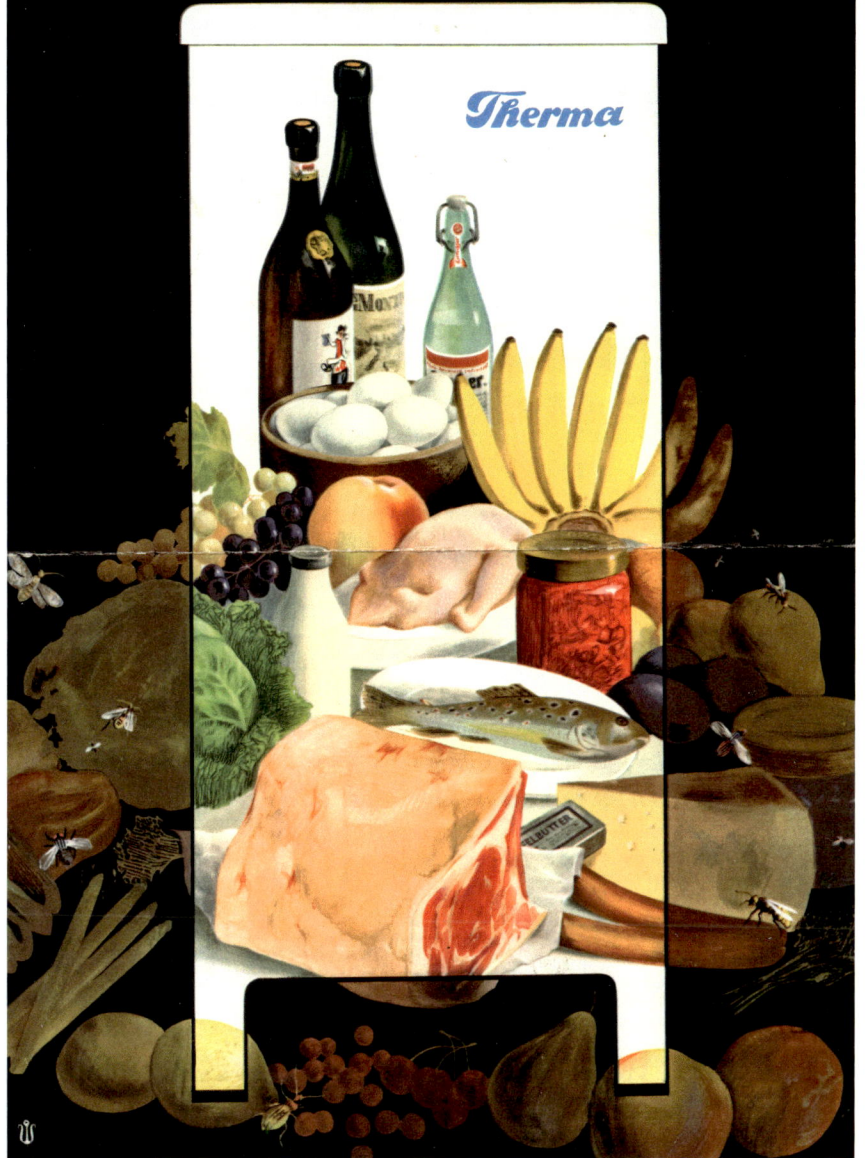

Ein Schweizer Kühlschrank schlägt die andern!

Therma

3.19b

Therma-Tiefkühlanlage

Therma Kühlhaus

Die Produzenten bringen ihre Produkte

Die Annahme & Kontrolle

Die Kühlfächer

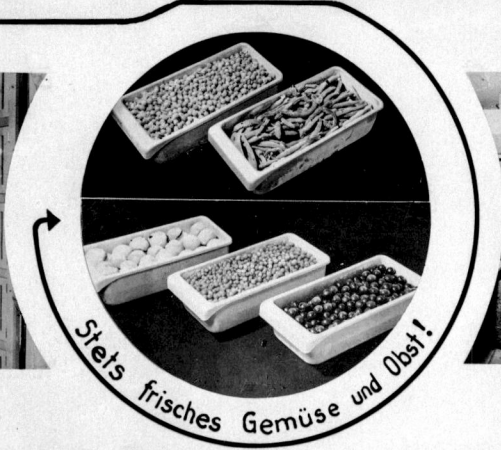

Stets frisches Gemüse und Obst!

Im Vorkühlraum

Verpacken der tiefgekühlten Ware

Die Tiefkühlung

Sortieren, reinigen & blanchieren

3.20

3.21

3.20 "Always have fresh fruit and vegetables!" Sheet with information on production and consumption of frozen food, probably published shortly before the end of the war. Therma's dispatch building was converted or retrofitted for this purpose. Photographs from August 1945.

3.21 View into a refrigerator compartment with manually packed seasonal vegetables. The refrigerator corresponds approximately to the model in 3.19. It could not freeze food.

3.22 Makeshift device for heating liquids or utilizing an iron's residual heat, ca. 1943. It is unclear whether the wooden holder was made by Therma or whether it was meant to encourage the general public to build their own.

3.23 Leaflet for the easy-regulation iron, with a call to save electricity; here still with chrome-plated cover, photograph from March 1940. From 1943 until the end of the war, the model was only available in beige enamel.

3.22a

3.22b

3.22c

Repassage plus économique, plus rapide

Economie de courant!

Therma

Fer à repasser à régulateur à grand rendement

Facilite beaucoup le travail
satisfait les plus exigeants

3.23

3.24

3.25

("Save electricity!") and likewise for cookware that could be stacked on a stove. Suggestions such as positioning an iron upside down in a special wooden construction to warm up water or using the residual warmth to heat water are almost touchingly serious. You might think that experiments often reveal the purest motifs. While that is probably true, this is not just about experimentation or emergency solutions. Some people even used this setup in practice.[34]

In late 1945, after the war had ended, Director Dietler reported to the Board of Directors on work over the previous year and his expectations for the immediate future. "As the new types of rotary compressors performed very well in the endurance tests, we shall soon be able to move to series production. The redesign of the hotel cooking stoves has proved very successful and will further increase demand. All the preparations have been completed for a new type of domestic cooking stove with an entirely new design, and the tests with hand-made prototypes have been completed. These models will be cheaper to manufacture as they will cut both labor and material costs."[35] The post-war economy's fluctuating fortunes are already audible, albeit quietly at this stage. In the last sentence, Dietler announces an innovative easy-clean stove with a groove around each hotplate, which would become a great success with customers in the following years, with a patent application filed on September 1, 1945 (CH patent no. 252708). That was also a wartime development. And it was to play a significant part in Therma's sales figures over the next decade.

3.24   A Therma commercial cooking stove with the proud restaurant owners and their staff, ca. 1941.
3.25   The newly designed easy-clean commercial cooking stove, 1945.

1   VR-Protokoll [Minutes of Board of Directors meeting] 225, December 20, 1939, p. 1. – GWA Elux B 2–1/1 (2nd box)
2   33. Jahresbericht [Annual Report], 1939/40. – GWA Elux B 4–1/2
3   34. Jahresbericht, 1940/41. – GWA Elux B 4–1/2
4   "Bericht des Direktors H. Dietler an den Präsidenten H. Hefti-Haab," January 20, 1941, p. 1. – GWA Elux B 2-4/5 (correspondence in the Board of Directors and Administrative Committee), Dir. H. Dietler bundle
5   36. Jahresbericht, 1942/43. – GWA Elux B 4–1/2
6   Cf. Gesamtkatalog [General Catalog] 1942. – GWA Elux H 1–11/2
7   The heat retention stoves and tiled stoves also built by Therma were an exception and used clinker bricks as thermal storage mass.
8   In the following fifteen years, this motif was adopted one-to-one and subsequently updated with the wood-burning stove and the rapid heater.
9   Letter from Hans Dietler to Board members: President Hans Hefti, Konrad Auer-Brunner, Karl Heinrich Gyr, November 15, 1941. – GWA Elux B 2–4/5, Auer-Brunner bundle
10 After the Second World War, Coulon also occasionally worked with Jean Prouvé.
11 Coulon's Radiaver model was produced by Saint-Gobain from 1937 to 1952. Cf. Institut national d'histoire de l'art INHA, entry on "Coulon, René," https://agorha.inha.fr/ark:/54721/7edfac64-581e-43cd-bb61-8d56b6f6ab6d.
12 1942 and 1944 catalogs. – GWA/Elux H 1–11/2
13 Questionable experiences with the federalist system in Switzerland played a part, as mentioned in Part 2; cantons effectively favored local companies.
14 "Durchschnittlicher Jahresbedarf an Eisen in den Jahren 1938 bis 1940: Therma: 822 Tonnen, Maxim 219 Tonnen, K & M 296 Tonnen." Hans Hefti, memo of the meeting in Zurich on June 24, 1941, July 2, 1941, p. 8. – GWA Elux B 2–4/5
15 Letter from Hans Hefti to the Therma Board, November 8, 1939, and Board minutes of November 10, 1939. – GWA Elux B 2–4/3
16 "Statut Therma/Maxim/Kummler & Matter/Gasotherm," March 13, 1941, p. 1. – GWA Elux B 2–4/5
17 Hans Dietler, "Grundlagen für Anpassung," exposé for Hans Hefti, May 27, 1941, p. 1. – GWA Elux B 2–4/5
18 Hans Dietler, statement on replies of June 23, 1941 to his proposals of May 27, 1941, addressed to Hans Hefti, August 9, 1941, p. 3. – GWA Elux B 2–4/5
19 Ibid.
20 This refers to the precisely planned technical overlaps and equipment-related differences between various brands of the GM Group, from Chevrolet to Cadillac.
21 Hans Dietler, "Grundlagen für Anpassung," exposé for Hans Hefti, May 27, 1941, p. 4. – GWA Elux B
22 Ibid., p. 3.
23 Alfred Oehler to Hans Hefti, July 19, 1941, p. 1. – GWA Elux B 2-4/5
24 Hans Dietler, statement on replies of June 23, 1941 to his proposals of May 27, 1941, addressed to Hans Hefti, August 9, 1941, p. 3. – GWA Elux B 2–4/5
25 Hans Hefti to Alfred Oehler, June 19, 1941, p. 3. – GWA Elux B 2–4/5
26 Hans Dietler, statement on replies of June 23, 1941 to his proposals of May 27, 1941, addressed to Hans Hefti, August 9, 1941, p. 3. – GWA Elux B 2–4/5
27 VR-Protokoll 237, May 25, 1941, pp. 2–3. – GWA Elux B 2–1/2
28 VR-Protokoll 238, July 15, 1941, p. 2. – GWA Elux B 2–1/2
29 VR-Protokoll 239, August 25, 1941, p. 2. – GWA/Elux B 2–1/2
30 Engineering firm A. Wickart was also responsible for the elaborate foundations of architect Otto Rudolf Salvisberg's villa in Zurich (1931).
31 A fourth floor was ultimately added in 2022/2023 when the building was converted into a retirement home.
32 VR-Protokoll 250, September 8, 1943, pp. 7–8. – GWA Elux B 2–1/2
33 Cf. Gesamtkatalog 1944, p. 110. – GWA Elux H 1–11/2
34 Note from visitors to the Therma Schaulager to Thomas Schätti, 2024.
35 VR-Protokoll 261, December 4, 1945, p. 11. – GWA Elux B 2–1/2

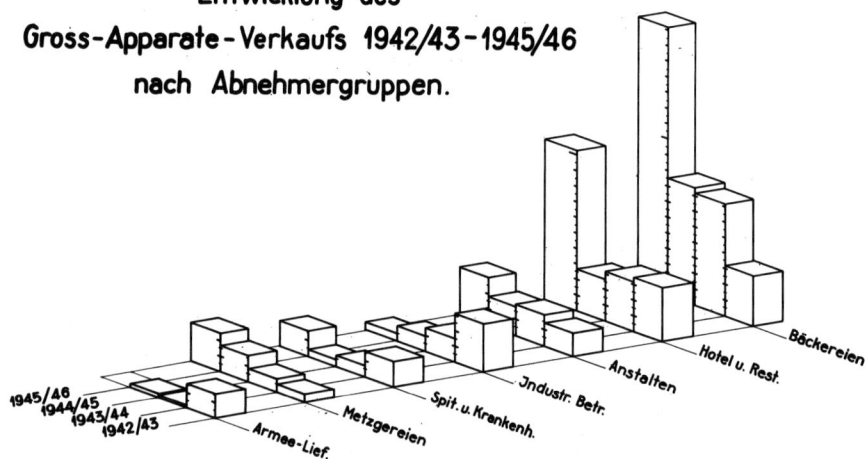

Entwicklung des
Gross-Apparate-Verkaufs 1942/43 - 1945/46
nach Abnehmergruppen.

3.26

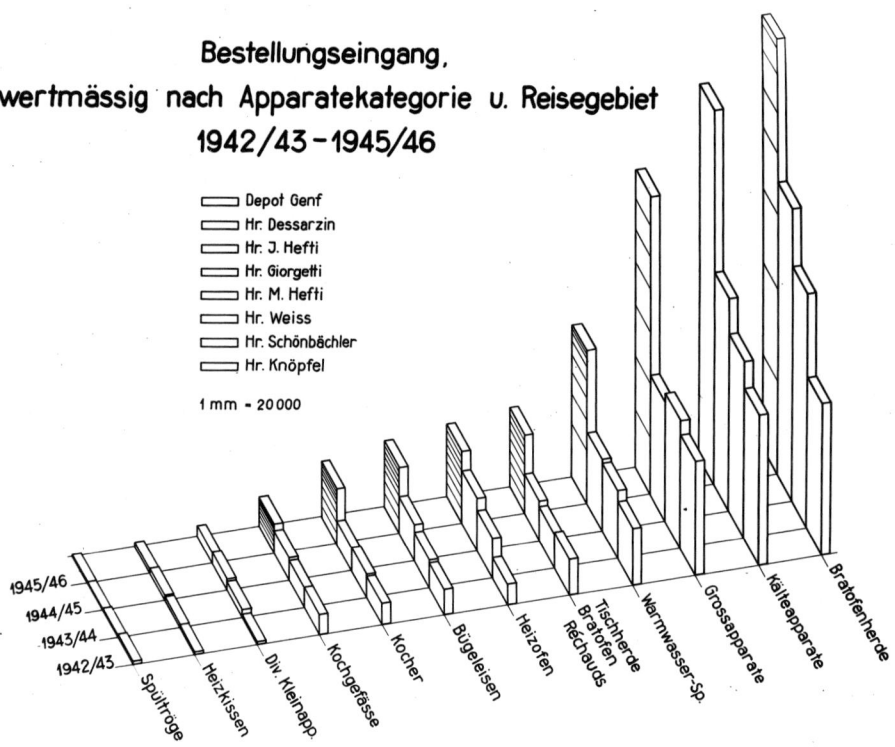

Bestellungseingang,
wertmässig nach Apparatekategorie u. Reisegebiet
1942/43 - 1945/46

Depot Genf
Hr. Dessarzin
Hr. J. Hefti
Hr. Giorgetti
Hr. M. Hefti
Hr. Weiss
Hr. Schönbächler
Hr. Knöpfel

1 mm = 20 000

3.27

3.28

3.26   3D bar chart illustrating statistics on domestic sales of commercial-sector appliances from 1942/43 to 1945/46: Sales of refrigeration systems for butchers' shops (*Metzgereien*) increased steadily, while deliveries to the army and industrial companies (*Armee-Lief./ Industr. Betr.*) decreased. From 1945/46, orders from hotels and restaurants (*Hotel und Rest.*) rose sharply, as did orders from bakeries (*Bäckereien*) for commercial-scale ovens.

3.27   3D bar chart illustrating statistics on domestic orders received by appliance category (catering or household) in the years 1942/43 to 1945/46. From left to right: persistently weak demand for sinks, heating pads and other small appliances (*Spultröge, Heizkissen, div. Kleinapp*), steady demand for cooking pots (*Kochgefässe*). Before the end of the war, demand for cooking appliances, irons and heating stoves (*Kocher, Bügeleisen, Heizöfen)* increased, especially for cooking stoves with roasting ovens (*Bratofenherde*). In the post-war period, stand-alone hotplates, table-top hotplates and roasting ovens (*Tischherde, Réchauds, Bratöfen)* sold particularly well; sales of boilers, commercial-scale appliances and refrigeration devices (*Warmwassersp., Grossgeräte, Kälteapparate*) doubled.

3.28   The administration in the new building, processing orders. Film still from a movie about Therma's production areas, probably 1947.

125

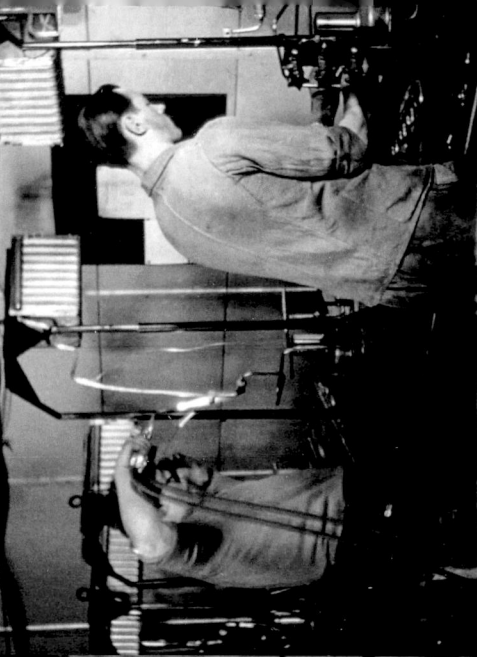

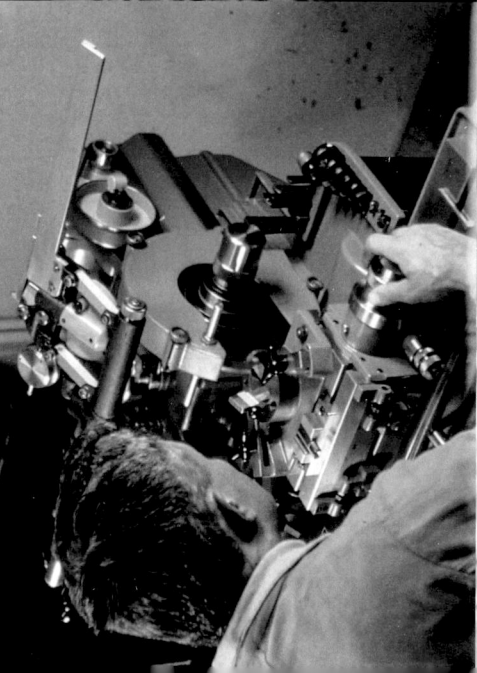

4

4.0 From a film about refrigerator production (around 1947)
From top left to bottom right:
A Housing production
B Roller seam welding for the evaporator
C Soldering of cooling lines
D Production of parts for the rotary compressor
E Precision check for the compressor drive shaft
F Assembly of the cooling module: plate evaporator (top), compressor (bottom), suction line
G The enameled chilled compartment on the assembly line
H Installation of the cooling module: evaporator section at the top, compressor at the bottom, both connected by a suction line
I Finish and checking: Refrigerators of various sizes are completed in rapid succession on the assembly line

A thirty-minute film chronicles the production of domestic refrigerators at Therma. It appears to be a rough version – there are no intertitles, no soundtrack, no commentary. There is no reference to its creator. Whom was this film made for and what was the initial intention? Its striking cinematic quality conveys a sense of what was a highly developed corporate culture for that era. Taking the refrigerator model as a yardstick, it can be dated to 1947. The workers do not look at all as if they are part of an industrial proletariat; instead they convey the kind of pride in the company that was still often expressed by adding the job title "Therma worker" to an entry in the telephone directory.

The film begins by documenting the sheet metal as it is formed for the outer housing and the interior chilled compartment as it is being enameled and ends with the final steps to complete the appliance. Attention is largely focused – for almost two thirds of the film – on production of the cooling unit, including the rotary compressor with the eccentrically rotating rotor and the drive shaft – its functional principle can be deduced from the footage – as well as the evaporator and the circulation lines for the coolant. Therma was particularly proud of its in-house development of a rotary compressor with reduced noise output and vibrations.

The first scenes show the metal sheets for the outer housing being cut and formed. The punching press descends effortlessly and punches out a neat opening in the rear wall and notches in the sheet metal corners for forming. After the housing is formed from the metal, the deep-drawn outer cover is fitted and spot-welded to it – along a line where a horizontal chrome trim will adorn the finished refrigerator.

Things become more mysterious as the film moves on to production of the refrigeration unit. One worker makes the plate evaporator to surround the ice cube compartment from sheet aluminum. Another worker bends the tubes for the coolant and the condenser into the right shapes. We follow his hands for thirty seconds. What else does he do in a nine-hour working day? Does the same person subsequently solder the bent tubes to the cylindrical coolant tank?

The film spends most time observing how the rotary compressor is manufactured. Parts are turned, surfaces are smoothed, screws are tightened and the requisite accuracy – to five thousandths of a millimeter – is checked again and again. Highly qualified precision mechanics subtly adjust measuring instruments to take readings in order to provide the requisite confirmation. For non-experts there is something mysterious about all these processes, clearly intended to impress the public with exclusive insider know-how. In the confirmation phase, each fully assembled cooling unit, consisting of a compressor, tank and plate evaporator, is surrounded by an insulating felt cover and the unit's cooling capacity is recorded by a fountain pen on unspooling graph paper.

A change of location takes us to the enameling plant, where the enamel-coated chilled compartment is removed from the furnace, after which the shot pans round to the assembly line, where this section is fitted into the white enameled outer container and backfilled with cork granulate as insulation. The electrical cooling unit is inserted into the chilled section through the rear wall, the control unit with the thermostat is installed and the ice cube tray is added. Next we see the finishing touches being put to the door; it is constructed as a wooden frame on a wooden base plate, into which a cork panel is sunk with a second cork panel placed above it, wrapped in oiled paper to protect it from condensation. We see its smooth enameled inner cover as the black edges are fitted and the handle is mounted, before the door is hung and adjusted. And during the final inspection, we see hands running over the outer surfaces and wiping away any remaining traces of work, readying the refrigerator to head out into the world.

1946–1957

"Beneficial for the Housewife's Workplace"

The Wish for a United Whole Becomes Visible

4.1

4.2

4.3

As concise descriptions are sometimes needed, the post-war period is often apostrophized as a time of salvation after the war years' long-standing worries. That is probably true from a global political perspective, but is a gross oversimplification of everyday life. Contrary to later attributions, those post-war years were by no means perceived in Switzerland as being on the cusp of a boom. First of all, the global aches and pains of transition to a peacetime economy had to be endured. As far as Therma was concerned, Director Hans Dietler reported to the Board of Directors in December 1945 that the patience that for years had been enforced on customers – installation companies, electrical stores and power stations – had turned into outbursts of discontent. "Customers are so impatient and often aggressive across the board that it is really difficult to respond with the requisite calm and business decorum to all the daily insults and threats received in writing, by telephone or telegraph. With very few exceptions, our customers treat us with a ruthlessness and aggressiveness that we were not accustomed to before the war. It is striking that the smallest defects or material flaws, which are simply unavoidable due to current difficulties in procuring materials, give rise to exaggerated, agitated and unfair complaints from customers. It seems that nowadays the general public and many business people have a completely flawed view of the material supply situation, especially in our area, and of the possibilities for future material procurement due to erroneous newspaper propaganda and because we managed rather well in Switzerland during the war."[1] This is no longer what springs to mind when we think about the post-war period. At the same meeting, Dietler added further information to his personal experience, citing the comparable situation even in the United States, the biggest victor of the war, and the conversion problems it experienced while transitioning to a peacetime economy. "Household items in our sector (refrigeration and heating) are not available. There are no new brochures. Retailers are promised that the first material for peacetime requirements will be delivered at the beginning of next year, but only in very limited quantities. There is therefore a huge shortfall throughout the production sector in the US, which can only be made up very slowly due to a shortage of all raw materials, including aluminum, and of workers, and because peacetime production is constantly disrupted by strikes, transport difficulties and a reduction in labor power of over 30% compared to the pre-war size of the workforce."[2]

It took some time for the economy to settle back into a reliable functional mode. At this stage, however, customers had grown more demanding, which meant the factories and products had to meet more stringent quality demands. In August 1946, Dietler foresaw "that the factories in the reconstruction areas would be equipped with the very latest methods and the very latest machinery" and that "in a few years' time, we will be facing competition that will be considerably more modern and better equipped for production than is the case in our company today." For this reason, as he explained to the group's senior management, Therma was in the process of "revising, reorganizing and rationalizing the entire production process, especially with regard to saving on wages." And he added, "To this end, we are studying new working methods and, above all, the introduction of labor-saving equipment and machine tools."[3] It is not easy to demonstrate what this meant in detail. In one case, it entailed purchasing a new press that weighted 450 metric tons, which required extensive adaptation measures in the workshop, including strengthening the foundations in the basement and raising the roof. Another example was the purchase of a new machine tool in 1954, a tangent bender for manufacturing refrigerator models with the suffix "U," a reference to the one-piece, U-shaped outer housing. The fundamental aim was to use fewer individual parts in production, switching to more interrelated elements and fewer individual operations (e.g., with fewer screwed connections). Dietler described the main task of the engineering design department as "rationalizing and reducing the cost of all old, unconverted designs to save on materials and wages, taking into account

4.4

4.5

4.1 Wet painting of refrigerator housings, 1950.

4.2 Fully assembled boilers on the overhead conveyor, 1953.

4.3 Internal water tanks for boilers, stored temporarily in the yard behind the administration building, 1947.

4.4 Therma stand at Comptoir Suisse in Lausanne in 1949 with the Francophile decorative flair typical of the early postwar years.

4.5 The Mustermesse Basel stand in 1946, "Therma Cooling" section: Presentation of the first refrigerator-sink ensemble. The logo on the refrigerators was only used for a short period.

[→A]
1945/46: "The entire production capacity needed to be available exclusively for handling domestic business, so to speak." – 1946/47: "It was still not possible to allocate an appropriate share to exports." – 1948/49: "The ratio of domestic to export sales shifted to the detriment of the latter in the year under review." – 1949/50: "Exports, which had been rising, fell to a minimum after the currency devaluations in September 1949." (7)

[→B]
"The heightened competition on the market for electrical household appliances is a consequence of greatly increased capacity in our industry. Significant business opportunities arising from meeting domestic demand during the war years, due to the shortage of coal, and in the post-war years, as a result of the marked increase in construction activity, have led to the establishment of new companies and state-sponsored expansions, and consequently supply now exceeds demand. In addition, the volume of cheap imported products, from Germany in the field of heating and from England in the field of refrigeration, continues to rise. It is regrettable that many of these undercut prices are directed against traditional Swiss companies that had to supply what was needed during the years blighted by shortages by keeping prices low and accepting inadequate margins." (10)

4.6   Genealogy of Therma cooking stoves 1924–1947. On the left, two models with a viewing window made of heat-resistant Pyrex glass. In the latest model on the right – here in an export version – the front panel covering makes the two vertical sealing strips from the previous model superfluous, as the joints are moved to the sides.

4./   Cheese shop with refrigerated display in French-speaking Switzerland, 1949.

the anticipated competition from the US."[4] This points to the wartime material shortages experienced in previous years continuing uninterrupted, hand in hand with a new urgent imperative to cut labor and material costs. In addition, after the end of the war, supply chains still faltered for years, which hampered manufacturing activity and affected productivity. In August 1946, for example, it took Therma eight months to deliver an order for a metal sink to an installation company.[5] In the longer term, however, the limiting factor was no longer the absolute shortage of production materials, but rather the struggle to secure the plant's profitability, in other words, to attain low production costs at an attractive sales price, and thus ensure each product's competitiveness on the domestic and international market.

While that sounds so elegant as a formula, it was, however, a major challenge. There was constant concern on this count throughout the entire decade, regardless of the individual products and their success. Therma's production methods still involved a considerable amount of manual labor (also due to the gradual "growth" in the building complex's spatial organization), which was a disadvantage in productivity terms. This was not industrial manufacturing in the true sense of the term. In the first post-war years, the annual reports stated that satisfying foreign demand for Therma products had to take a back seat in order to give precedence to the domestic market. For example, the 1945/46 annual report noted that "the entire production capacity needed to be available exclusively for handling domestic business, so to speak."[6] That, however, was a euphemism; a little later (1949/50) it became apparent that exports in general had virtually dried up. "Exports, which had been on the rise, fell to a minimum after the currency devaluations in September 1949."[7] [→A] However, it should be added that the market share in Switzerland also slowly declined after peaking in 1942.[8]

As a general rule, a groundbreaking company gradually loses its initial pioneering status as the development it initiated becomes the new normal, which means it increasingly has to contend with competitors. A growing number of factors, both positive and negative, came into play in this process for Therma. The lack of a direct rail connection in Schwanden was one disadvantage. When Therma sought to cooperate with the previous "outsider" company Prometheus in Liestal (Baselland Canton) from 1946, it justified this to two of its main shareholders in the draft pool agreement by asserting that "Therma is looking for opportunities to rapidly expand its production in areas with favorable freight conditions."[9] Economic realities became increasingly important during this period. The lack of dynamism afflicting the entire electricity sector in Switzerland shortly after the war was a painful contributory factor, and included in particular the stalled expansion of the grid, while overcapacity had already built up in the kitchen appliance industry.[10] [→B]

After the war, the Swiss metalworking and mechanical engineering industry as a whole had great success in both domestic and export markets and could therefore offer handsome wage increases. However, this mainly held true for the watchmaking, precision instrument and mechanical engineering sectors, while it was less applicable to manufacturing of electrical appliances, as the key players in this field did not enjoy comparable international market leadership. However, Therma could not ignore the rising wages across the industry. In those years, migration of workers to the cities also became a problem; Therma, the most important industrial location (and significant in training apprentices) in the canton of Glarus, attempted to counteract this trend with reasonably good overall conditions. In addition to wage increases, this included improving welfare, as manifested in the next new building the company developed, the Erlenhof.

After the war, the catering facilities at Therma had become increasingly problematic. The previous common room near Schwanden railroad station

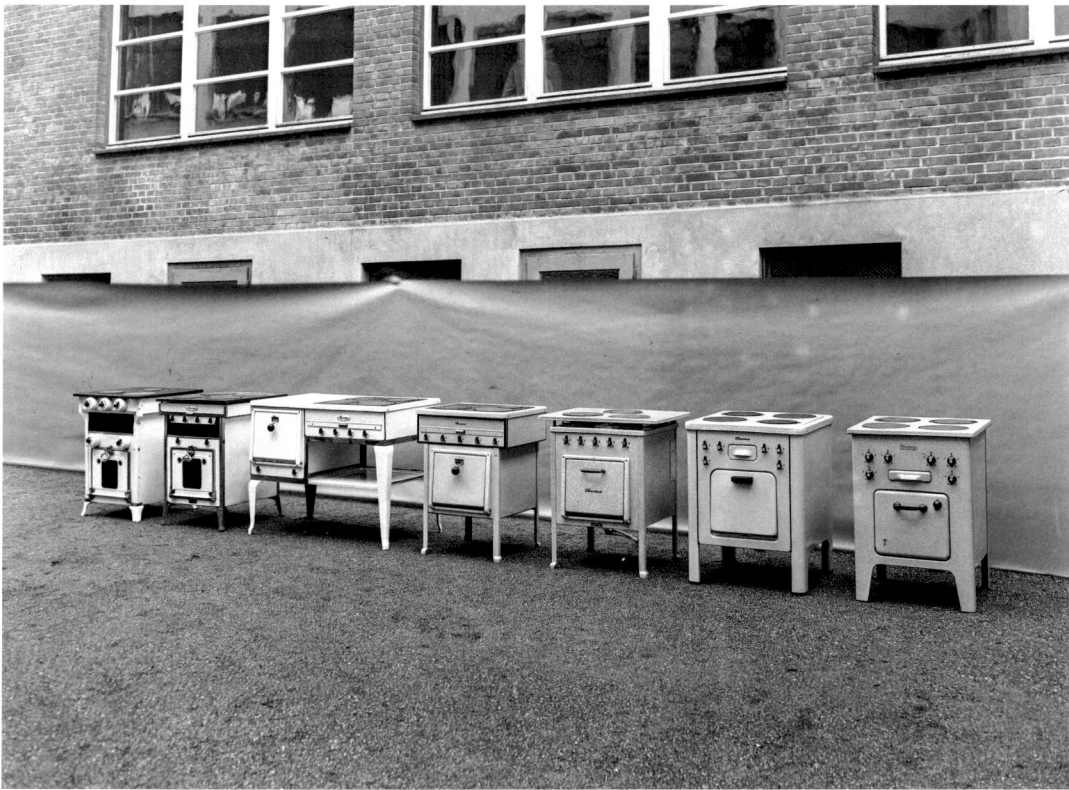

4.6

4.7

4.8

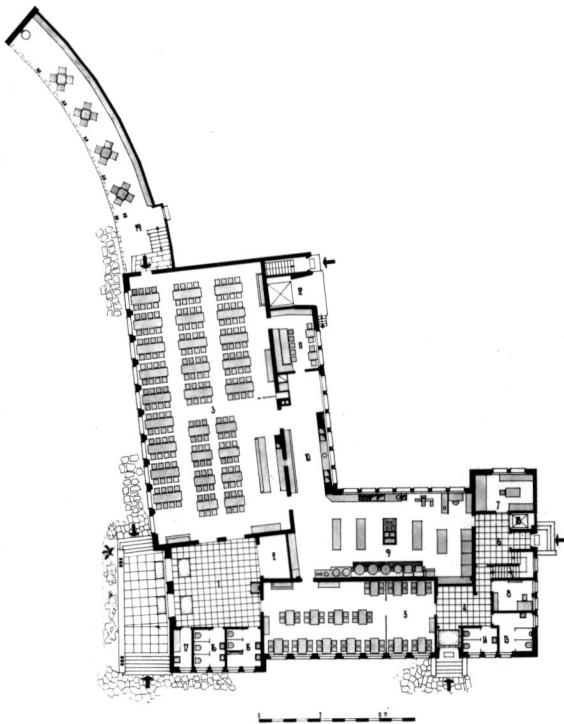

4.9

4.8   Erlenhof welfare center, built in 1947/1948,
        designed by architect Hans Leuzinger
        (Glarus/Zurich).
4.9   Erlenhof, floor plan of first floor: factory
        canteen and assembly hall.
4.10a   Erlenhof, the large dining room for
        workers.
4.10b   Erlenhof, the smaller dining room for
        employees and – behind the partitions –
        the section for management.
4.10c   The kitchen in the inside corner of the
        first floor.
4.10d   Cooks and the tilting caldron group.
4.10e   Building services in the Erlenhof's base-
        ment: heat pumps for river water from
        the Sernf; additional heating with oil
        burners.
4.10f   Erlenhof, switch and fuse boxes.

4.10a

4.10b

4.10c

4.10d

4.10e

4.10f

4.11

4.12

had become far too small for the rapidly growing workforce. That made the company less attractive as an employer. Management therefore once again commissioned architect Hans Leuzinger to design a proper catering facility, a center to boost workers' well-being. Leuzinger, advised by Director Dietler, proposed the angular Erlenhof at the eastern end of the factory site. Construction began in 1947 and the facility was already operational in September 1948. The large dining hall for the workers had three hundred seats; the smaller hall for white-collar employees could seat seventy. Leuzinger's user-friendly architecture with its flat roofs was stylistically confident and, against the backdrop of architectural regionalism, was modern and acceptable to the majority.[11] The building was not just entirely up-to-the-minute, but even ahead of its time thanks to the technical equipment in the kitchen and the building services (including the heat pump used for the underfloor heating). The company expressed its pride in the new building on consecutive information days with factory tours for installation companies, as well as for cooking and home economics schools from all over Switzerland, always concluding with a group photo in front of the Erlenhof.

One new Therma product caused quite a stir even before 1950: the *Rinnenherd*, the new easy-clean household cooking stove with a groove around the hotplates, mentioned briefly at the end of the previous part in the context of Director Dietler's high hopes for its launch. Its design origins lay in the war period, when the intention was to save on sheet steel. Karl Keller, head of design, came up with the idea of draining liquids that boiled over directly into the "milk drawer" without passing through the drip tray under the hotplates, a feature that had been included since 1936.[12] It was possible to scrap the drip tray by introducing a channel-like recess around each hotplate, with an opening punched into it above the drawer. By thus saving roughly a third of a square meter of sheet steel per appliance, the weight and therefore the price were lower. Above all, however, the public was fascinated by the innovative drainage channels around the hotplates, which gave this electric stove its memorable name in German. The top of the stove, which until then had not had any features worth mentioning, suddenly appeared interesting. Instead of the previous flat sheet metal, it now flaunted three-dimensional modeling with circular channels and glossy effects in unexpected spots. The "granite" barrenness of the war era and the memory of years of austerity were suddenly overwritten by a new ambience. The rich, homogeneous enamel finish used for the stove, with rounded forms and fewer visible joints than the previous model, conveyed an impression of greater value, further reinforced by the hotplates' chrome-plated edging along sections partially exposed due to the grooves. Crowds of visitors flocked to the first presentation of this easy-clean stove at the 1949 Mustermesse. It proved to be such a fascinating innovation that in 1951 the Aarau-based Therma subsidiary Elcalor applied for permission to manufacture its own cooking stoves according to the same principle and transferred a license fee of five Swiss francs per unit to Schwanden.[13]

In the 1950s, the easy-clean stove remained one of Therma's most reliable sources of revenue with steady sales, in contrast to the generally dwindling importance of small appliances.[14] [→ C] The table-top model with two hotplates was included in Max Bill's selection for his traveling exhibition *Die gute Form* (*Good Design*) in 1949. In 1954, a new, seven-stage stove switch that allowed for finer temperature regulation was also introduced; the advertising promised that it would obviate the need for housewifely kitchen ballet between cooking ladles, air vents and pan lids.

Since 1930, Therma had carried out impressive development work in its various product ranges. It still went by the name of "Fabrik für elektrische Heizung A.G.," a designation that trumpeted its origins in the heating sector, while also delivering top-notch performance in refrigeration, for example producing laboratory refrigerators and a stratospheric chamber to test

4.11 Delivery of parts, each weighing several tonnes, for the large new forming press, 1952. A new foundation was needed to support it.

4.12 The same sections arriving at the factory.

4.13

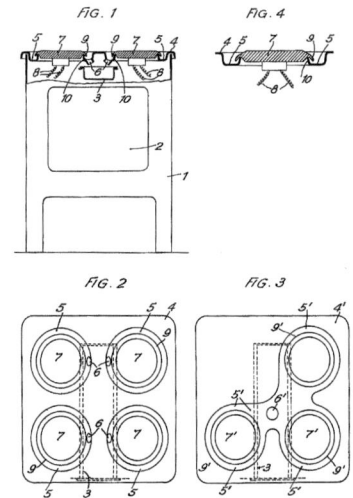

„Therma" Fabrik für elektrische Heizung AG. Patent Nr. 252708
1 Blatt

4.14

„Therma"
Fabrik für elektrische Heizung AG. Zusatzpatent Nr. 261266
1 Blatt

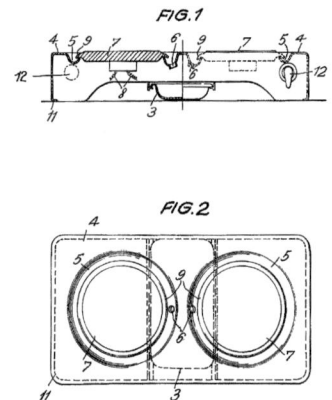

4.15

4.16

4.13   The high-impact innovation for 1949:
the easy-clean stove. Drainage channels
around the hotplates allow boiled-over
liquids to flow directly into the "milk
drawer" without a detour through the
drip tray. Adding a plinth instead of feet,
together with an appliance drawer,
would soon become standard – signify-
ing a move towards kitchen ensembles.

4.14   CH patent no. 252708 on the principle
of the easy-clean stove, filed on September 1, 1945. The drainage openings (6)
are visible, with the drawer to catch spilt
liquids underneath, marked with a dotted
line. The design shown in Fig. 3 remained
a theoretical variant.

4.15   Application of the principle of grooves
for easy cleaning to the stand-alone
hotplates, CH patent no. 261266, "Electric cooking stove," filed on December
23, 1947.

4.16   Underside of the cover plate with recessed areas pressed in for the grooves.

4.17a Flyer for the stand-alone hotplates.
In 1949 Max Bill selected the appliance
for his traveling exhibition *Die gute Form*,
which was shown internationally.

4.17b Back of the flyer for the stand-alone
hotplates.

40 Jahre
Therma

Tischherd
Jubiläumsmodell

4.17a

4.17b

aircraft instruments under extreme temperature conditions. It also cemented its reputation as a technological leader from 1947 with the development of the Megafroster for industrial applications, for example for tempering drill steel at extreme temperatures of minus 85 degrees Celsius. Therma's technological leadership could hardly have failed to impress the shareholders, who probably knew only a little about the sector, especially with statements such as the following assertion in the 1948/49 annual report. "Furthermore, household refrigerators incorporating the rotary compressor developed during the war years, based on the Roots system with an external motor stator, were delivered on an ongoing basis," supplemented by the appliance's classification as part of the broad-sweeping tradition of the natural sciences. "This refrigerator is a new creation in the field of thermodynamics. It will further promote the Therma brand."[15]

Therma continued to manufacture household and catering ovens, industrial baking ovens, large tilting caldrons, boilers, large metal dishwashing sinks, domestic refrigerators in various sizes, refrigeration systems for butchers' shops, slaughterhouses, dairies and grocery stores, refrigerated display cases and refrigeration equipment for cafés and shop windows, as well as a huge number and variety of small appliances: irons, radiant heaters, toasters, kettles and electric tea- or coffeepots. It promoted electrical energy, even though this entailed an ongoing and sometimes problematic dependence on policies pursued by the large electrical utilities, which competed with the gas works that supplied the energy for gas-powered appliances (including household refrigerators).

The appeal of a strong vision of the future was, however, long missing in this decade. At the 1946 Mustermesse Basel, the recent experience of surviving the world war was reflected in the serenely modest headline above the stand: "Therma appliances are faithful helpers in good times and bad." Although this chimed with the general mood, it was far from conjuring up a contagious vision. Over this decade, however, standardization of the household kitchen would become something of a leitmotif, as a slogan in a brochure toward the end of this period pledged: "Therma modernizes the household kitchen!" Therma's understanding of this standardization and modernization will be discussed in greater detail below.

Director Dietler's new home, which was built in 1946, also to a design by architect Leuzinger, boasted a kitchen equipped to a high standard.[16] The photograph shows a continuous work surface with a double sink unit, one of the first wide easy-clean stoves with a warming compartment, a wall-mounted boiler, wooden base units and a worktop with drawers on wall brackets, made by a carpenter working from architect Leuzinger's drawings. (→4.28) An impressive three-piece kitchen cupboard ensemble with a built-in refrigerator stood in the corner (not visible in the photograph). (cf. 3.15) The cooking stove and base units were set on a brick plinth. The room appears tidy and spacious, creating a sense of a neatly planned, fully equipped postwar kitchen. However, there are not yet any wall units, the boiler is placed above the sink and the refrigerator stands alone: this kitchen still follows the concept of distinct individual units. (→4.28) Ten years later, the idea of kitchen furniture ensembles would disrupt this concept of autonomous elements – an epochal change to which Therma made a significant contribution.

The first example of kitchen furniture that combined various units appeared in the 1946 household appliances catalog and brought together a metal sink and a refrigerator mounted below it. It was exhibited for the first time, still rather inconspicuously, at the Mustermesse Basel that same year and marked the modest beginning of an evolution in which the household kitchen ceased to be seen as an "amorphous agglomeration of individual items" (Hans Hilfiker 1967).[17]

4.18

4.19

4.18 Therma stand at the Mustermesse Basel in 1949. The easy-clean stove with feet or a plinth as a major innovation is placed in the left-hand corner at the front, while its predecessor, the upmarket stove, stands head-on; on the right are catering appliances, with a newly designed hotel stove in the foreground; behind it, inter alia, electrode water heater caldrons and tilting caldrons.

4.19 Lively interest at the Therma stand at the Mustermesse Basel in 1949, also for domestic refrigerators.

4.20 The inside of the easy-clean stove: The guide tube for the drip drawer and the wiring of the hotplates and oven are visible. The wires are not yet encased in polyethylene, but are kept from touching each other by ceramic spacers. Along the hinge line between the module and the hotplates, they are pressed flat to function like a joint when opened if necessary.

4.20

4.21a

4.21b

Therma spotted a promising development opportunity and in 1950 began offering combinations of appliances in four basic configurations, with options including the number of appliances and how they were arranged (i.e. the sequence in which they were positioned):
- sink/boiler
- sink/refrigerator
- sink/boiler/refrigerator
- sink/boiler/refrigerator/cooking stove

This new typology of kitchen ensembles tickled the public's imagination, caught on in architectural offices and sparked requests for new kitchen installations or conversions. (→4.29)

As early as 1951, Director Dietler complained to Chairman Hans Hefti-Haab that Maxim, a subsidiary brand within the group, was now also planning to manufacture kitchen ensembles. Therma, Dietler wrote, was "the only company within the group and the first company ever" to build "combined sink-refrigerator ensembles. The introductory work took years, and as this line of business developed into mainstream business, competition emerged within the group."[18] The ambivalence involved in the formation of the Therma Group – the war years' defining theme – that brought together the parent brand Therma and subsidiaries Elcalor, Maxim and Sursee, now became apparent. Originally, the group had been intended as a protective bulwark against competition from outside VST, the industry association. At this stage, however, rivalries between companies in the group were emerging more and more frequently, with Therma claiming leadership on creative issues and quality, while the other group companies – especially Maxim – attempted to undercut prices, repeatedly prompting Dietler to draw these issues to the attention of Hans Hefti, President of Therma and Chairman of the Group.

Before 1957, only a few new designs within Therma's existing product range attracted public attention. During a 1952 stage presentation, probably organized in the canton of Glarus, the Therma product range was primarily showcased with the familiar juxtaposition of individual appliances. The only exception was the compact dishwasher-refrigerator ensemble. As a matter of fact, very few patents were filed by Therma during this period. Was the attractive idea of the kitchen ensemble, as interpreted and materialized by Therma, not patentable? Apparently it was not.

Over the years the significance of the various product ranges shifted. The household iron, which initially crystallized the process of household electrification and was much sought-after, was largely taken for granted later. The Therma iron with a regulator switch faced strong competition on the Swiss market from Schiesser's more modern Rextherm. The latter quickly became the new point of reference, with its plastic handle directly on the cover, the regulator disk below, a horizontal tail fin to stand vertically and its red indicator light that recalled a car's tail light. The Rextherm model received an accolade from "Die gute Form SWB" several times in succession at Basel's Mustermesse and made the Therma model, already familiar for many years, appear outdated. Therma did not come up with the right retort until 1954 when it launched its new regulator-switch iron with an open handle. Therma let the chance to develop a steam iron pass it by due to a lack of conviction about the technology.

The filter coffee machine, however, which came onto the market in 1952, was an immediate hit. (→4.43) It looked novel and formed a uniform whole, devoid of the feet that had been incorporated in pre-war versions. The boiling water rose to the top in a pipe, passed through the coffee powder in the Melitta paper filter and collected again in the container at the bottom. The gently curved volumes of its formal design language depicted the inner workings of the appliance in a manner typical for the era. The advertising

4.22

4.23

emphasized the high quality of the coffee brewed using this method with comic-style drawings in the French style.

The dominant theme of these years was the desire to move away from the mere juxtaposition of individual appliances toward a more meaningful ordering with convincing connections between the sub-units. There was a gradual discovery of the ergonomic dimension of work in kitchens, interpreted more than any other room as framing closely inter-related activities. As mentioned in Part 2, a "horizon line" had already emerged around 1930 as an activity-oriented pattern, extending from the stove to the work surface to the sink. Several alternations between materials had to be bridged: from metal to a wooden surface to the stainless steel sink. [cf. 2.27] There was a genuine desire to make life easier and more elegant for housewives, following the American example; of course, these efforts were primarily aimed at middle-class housewives. Until Therma ceased to be an independent firm in 1978, the unquestioned archetypal figure that the firm envisioned in domestic kitchens was the housewife, provided with a housekeeping allowance and suitable appliances by the male breadwinner so that she could merrily do her unpaid work. Kitchen ensembles offered the key here and Therma was among the first manufacturers to adopt this approach.

4.21 Flyer for the highly efficient Megatherma hotplate: The stainless steel hotplate surround was introduced as a consequence of the easy-clean system implemented for household cooking stoves.
4.22 Therma stand at the Mustermesse Basel in 1950: reference to central cooling systems.
4.23 Example of a kitchen in Zurich with a small refrigerator connected to a central cooling system, 1949.

4.24

4.25

4.24 The administration in the administration building, 1956. Office area with telex machines for communication with customers in Switzerland and abroad.
4.25 The administration (cf. 3.13).
4.26 An exhibition of Therma appliances, probably in the vicinity of Schwanden, 1952.
4.27 Large-format freezer for industrial applications: high-strength steel elements such as drill bits are tempered at extreme subzero temperatures, as low as −85 degrees Celsius. On the left the chilled container with its thick insulation, on the right the cabinet with the refrigeration machinery.

4.26

4.27

145

4.28

4.29

146

4.30

4.31

In 1930, the wall-mounted boiler, which supplies hot water directly to the sink below, was viewed as more progressive than fetching water from a pot kept on the boil on a kitchen range. The next step gave rise to the built-in pressure boiler set lower than the sink, supplying hot water invisibly. Pre-war refrigerators were free-standing appliances to keep perishable food fresh. Fifteen years later, as an alternative to that format, Therma presented a small sink-refrigerator ensemble; the draining board was 85 cm above the floor, with the 110-liter refrigerator positioned underneath it, while the cooling unit alongside it was placed under the sink, next to the water pipes and the siphon. The brochure states, "The Therma dishwasher-refrigerator largely meets the aspirations of modern interior design for space-saving, elegant lines and absolute cleanliness with the most convenient operation and cleaning options."[19] Between around 1945 and 1955, centralized refrigeration systems were not uncommon in apartment buildings, even in Switzerland: as part of the building infrastructure, with the refrigeration equipment in the basement and pipes branching to the evaporator in every built-in refrigerator in the apartments, obviating the need for each unit to have its own separate electrical cooling equipment.[20] At the 1950 Mustermesse, part of the Therma stand presented these central cooling systems. "Several thousand of these cabinets are in operation throughout Switzerland," the exhibition display noted.[21] The Therma photo collection includes examples of such built-in refrigerators without their own cooling equipment, sometimes reflecting detailed, meticulous planning on the part of the architect. However, this technology disappeared as a real option for apartments of the future around the middle of the decade. (→4.22)

Therma aimed to establish a more coherent relationship between the key elements of the domestic kitchen than the previous straightforward juxtaposition of units. The firm was convinced that this could be achieved by extending the sink unit with an angled stainless steel wall panel. This added angled panel, which was firmly attached to the sink unit, covered the tiles or even paint on the walls. Its lack of seams or joints was a symbolic marker of the utmost hygiene. In one particular model, this stainless steel wall surface even extended beyond the length of the sink to cover the front of the hob, giving the cooking stove its own orderly spot alongside the sink or as a continuation of the kitchen ensemble. This was also underpinned by a longing for order and uniformity. Viewed from our perspective today, it looks like a strange solution, for this stove arrangement involved switching colors from chrome-nickel steel to cream-colored stove enamel, introducing a joint between the two conjoined appliances, not to mention the contradiction between the sharp-edged stainless steel sink and the stove's rounded edge. The Therma photo library contains a number of depictions of such built-in units, including advertising photos. As these ensembles were intended as ready-to-transport elements, they also give rise to speculation about the packaging and transportation costs involved. However, around 1950 systematic consideration of an ingenious assembly principle still lay far in the future.

A carefully planned one-off solution was devised for a kitchen extension in a detached house, where the wall panel even extended slightly beyond the front of the stove. (→4.32) In this case, the top of the stove was also made of stainless steel and the remaining space was used for additional storage.[22] Although this attempted uniformity was very costly, the dividing joints were still apparent. There was as yet no realization that the stove surface could merge seamlessly with the sink-top cover thanks to the introduction of the easy-clean principle, which made it possible to clean the channels, punched-out apertures and drawer without a recessed section to catch drips set under the hotplates.[23]

Traces of this remarkably hesitant, tentative process of harmonization and uniformization can be found in numerous photos from these years. At the

4.28   Kitchen in Director Dietler's home, Schwanden (architect Hans Leuzinger), built in 1945/1946, equipped to a high standard, but still as an agglomeration of appliances in keeping with 1940s ideas.

4.29   Sink-refrigerator combination with angled wall panel and attached easy-clean stove, 1949.

4.30   As in 4.29, pragmatic variant with upmarket cooking stove.

4.31   Shipment with orders ready for dispatch; on the left a sink unit with extended wall panel, 1951.

4.32

4.33

4.34

4.35

4.36

4.32   Kitchen installation in a detached house,
        1951. Harmonized materials for the sur-
        faces of the sink unit, stove and counter
        tops, but with separating joints.
4.33   Fittings for a complete kitchen, exhibited
        at Comptoir Suisse in 1955. Unconvincing
        design of the cabinets with downward-
        swinging door flaps on the right-hand
        side.
4.34   Functional design of the wall units with
        sliding doors, in this case probably
        in a detached house. The easy-clean
        stove is fully integrated.
4.35   One-piece cover, hand-made example
        for an individual customer order. Such
        work was good for Therma's reputation,
        but not for profitability.
4.36   Stand at the 1951 Mustermesse Basel:
        The cabinet frontage in the background
        is carefully planned and built, exempli-
        fying a unique custom-made setup.
        The basis for an adaptable measurement
        or organizational system has not yet
        been created.

1951 Mustermesse Basel, a small refrigerator and an easy-clean stove were displayed immediately adjacent to each other as if proudly high-lighting their relationship. [→4.36] Both were indeed the same height, both had a chrome-nickel steel top and a black base – and yet they differed in the radius of their curves, the height of the base and even the height of the edging on the two covers, in other words, only the overall height of each unit was the same. The stove and the refrigerator had evolved to this point at their own pace. There was still no question of systematic uniformization on either a large or small scale. The design and positioning of handles was also a source of constant uncertainty. The downward-facing lever handle in the built-in refrigerators forced users to bend down rather too low. It is only fair to acknowledge that the built-in cupboard ensemble, with the sink unit fitted in precisely on three sides and the two refrigerators – a labora-tory installation? – must have looked impressively well thought out back then. However, the way in which the cupboard space is divided with hinged doors does not follow a modular (additive or multiplicative) logic; instead, it is a sophisticated piece of carpentry work with different divisions for the cupboard sections. [24] The booth wall to the right of it bore the inscription "Therma is the only Swiss company to craft complete cooker/fridge/boiler/sink ensembles." While that was true, the verb "craft" clearly referred in this context to distinctly one-off production.

Therma claimed a special status when it came to creating kitchen ensem-bles. "Therma," the 1956 brochure announced, "is the only factory that man-ufactures all the appliances, stoves, boilers, refrigerators, sinks and metal substructures in-house. This is why Therma ensembles form self-contained units. They are not expensive, but offer advantages in terms of installation and space utilization and above all are beneficial for the housewife's work-place." [25] The 1956/57 annual report commented on the major lines of de-velopment, "Modern construction methods emphasize space- and labor-saving kitchen equipment. This leads to an ever-increasing shift away from mass-produced single cooking stoves and wall-mounted boilers to many variants of combined kitchen units. Here, too, companies of all kinds have become involved." [26] However, these "complete ensembles" and the "self-contained units" did not yet form an entire kitchen. It was only at the 1955 Comptoir Suisse in Lausanne that Therma set up a full kitchen, placing a slogan above it, "Un ensemble Therma pour chaque cuisine" ("A Therma ensemble for every kitchen"). It was a corner kitchen, with an appliance ensemble running along one wall, while the other bore a series of wall units above the worktop, apparently made by carpenters. The design was, how-ever, impractical, as the overhanging flaps were hinged at the bottom. An-other kitchen, built two years later, is also documented, with the same ar-rangement of wall units; here, however, the lower level, again projecting, had sliding doors with elegant handle strips, which was much more func-tional. The "architectural" designer behind this kitchen was obviously also more analytical. It seems fair to conclude that at the time Therma must have lacked the critical expertise to consider the best possible use of the kitchen in a broader systematic sense than through the "complete ensem-bles." In other words, Therma did not – yet! – consider its work as falling within the architectural remit, viewing its role instead as providing the fit-tings. In the 1954/55 annual report, this lack of assurance remains con-cealed; it announced to the public that "building on efforts pursued for years to make the housewife's work ever more convenient, we continue to develop all-around kitchen fittings, referred to by the collective term 'com-bined kitchen units.' As these Therma ensembles are recognized as the ideal solution for workplace design and also simplify and reduce the cost of construction and installation, there has been a clear shift in demand from individual appliances to ensembles." [27] What does an "ideal solution" mean? In the brochure presenting these combined configurations, Therma assured interested parties, "You can adapt your ensemble to your needs by combin-ing the individual elements in a practical manner. The ensemble's total

4.37a

4.37b

4.38

length is the sum of the lengths of the individual units plus 2 mm × 10 mm for the edge of the sink and/or cover." What was meant by "combining in a practical manner"? The list of the individual units with details of their lengths reads as follows: easy-clean stove: 590 mm; 100-liter boiler: 1,150 mm; sink unit with two basins, bucket compartment and cupboard: 1,500 mm and 1,600 mm: 100-liter refrigerator with machine compartment 1,150 mm; cupboard (narrow): 350 mm; cupboard (wide): 450 mm.[28] There was still no modular system, as the cover image from the 1954 ensemble brochure reveals. (→4.37b/4.38) That did not change until 1958 and, as the high degree of customization was not based on fixed measurements for the sub-units, the freedom given to customers to select and sequence the sub-units of an ensemble in their preferred order meant that a great deal of coordination was required, not to mention additional work to produce the individual covers and front sections for the units. Profitability suffered as a result. Although Therma enjoyed customer success with this range and sold large numbers of these combined kitchen sets, this could not be described as economical series production.

This contradiction between public success and the company's performance probably also lay behind the management dispute between the Board of Directors and the Group Directorate, specifically between Group Chairman Hefti and Director Dietler. That conflict had been brewing since 1952 and led to Dietler leaving Therma in April 1954. In formal terms, the dispute was over the question of who held the authority to issue directives or take decisions, along with restrictions on the Group Directorate's autonomy. Dietler had joined Therma as an engineer in 1925 and had unquestionably been an efficient operational manager for decades. After almost thirty years at the helm and despite sales successes, a headwind of low profitability had developed, which the Board of Directors and the group's Administrative Committee sought to counter with a new organizational chart (which entailed introducing a Directors' Conference). Walter Baur, the previous Deputy Commercial Director, and Richard Scherrer, Head of Operations and Deputy Director, were both promoted to full directors, while Dietler was appointed Head of the Group Directorate. He was, however, dissatisfied with this solution and resigned, exhausted if not burned out. A Directors' Conference was held and engineer Oskar Steiger was appointed as the new Technical Director, but the structural problems persisted.

In June 1954, a few weeks after Dietler's awkward departure, the newly constituted team of directors announced their assumption that demand for kitchen ensembles would increase steadily and that four to seven thousand such ensembles could be sold per annum in the following years in the light of construction activity and Therma's market share. They concluded that "as a result, production would largely have to be converted from individual appliances to ensembles, [...] corresponding expansion of the production facilities would have to be clarified and standardized designs would need to be defined as far as possible." This would require extensive purchases of new tools "in order to achieve machine-based production rather than the previous more manual production."[29] That was, however, an ambitious program.

Irrespective of such fundamental structural issues, the problem of the company's diminished creative agility lingered on. Therma's domestic refrigerators testify to this. It took until 1954 for a "fillable door" to be introduced with compartments for eggs, butter and bottles, after the inside of the door had been left smooth for decades. While Therma may not have been lagging behind most refrigerator manufacturers with this significant shift in how refrigerators were used, it was certainly not one of the driving forces for change. Initially, the form that Therma devised for this door with built-in compartments seems to have been determined by stylistic considerations rather than analytically and functionally, as becomes apparent in

Connaissez-vous le jeu du pochon ?

La soupe commence à bouillonner - Glissons vite le pochon sous le couvercle de la marmite. La soupe s'est calmée - Enlevons le pochon! Si les commutateurs de votre cuisinière n'ont encore que 4 positions seulement, vous connaissez bien ce petit jeu, auquel vous renonceriez volontiers si vous pouviez régler pour chaque met la chaleur juste nécessaire pour que la cuisson puisse se faire en ustensile couvert, sans risque de débordement. C'est maintenant le cas avec les cuisinières à gouttières Therma à réglage fin, où chaque plaque de cuisson possède 7 positions: 7-6-5-4-3-2-1, ce qui permet de choisir exactement l'allure de chauffe qui convient. Si vous voulez être plus amplement renseignée sur les grands avantages du réglage fin, sur son application à la cuisson des différents mets, demandez immédiatement la brochure détaillée concernant les 10 modèles de cuisinières à gouttières Therma à réglage fin.

Therma Cuisinière à gouttières à réglage fin*

* Réglage fin de toutes les plaques et non seulement de la plaque rapide Méga!

4.39

4.37   Brochure on the seven-position stove switch, front and back, 1954.
4.38   Front page of the 1955 brochure: The kitchen as a modern workplace gradually takes shape: "Therma modernizes the Swiss kitchen."
4.39   The new seven-position stove switch simplified cooking. "Tired of juggling with a wooden spoon?": A new advertising language is confident the public will be able to decode the photograph's meaning.

151

4.40

4.41

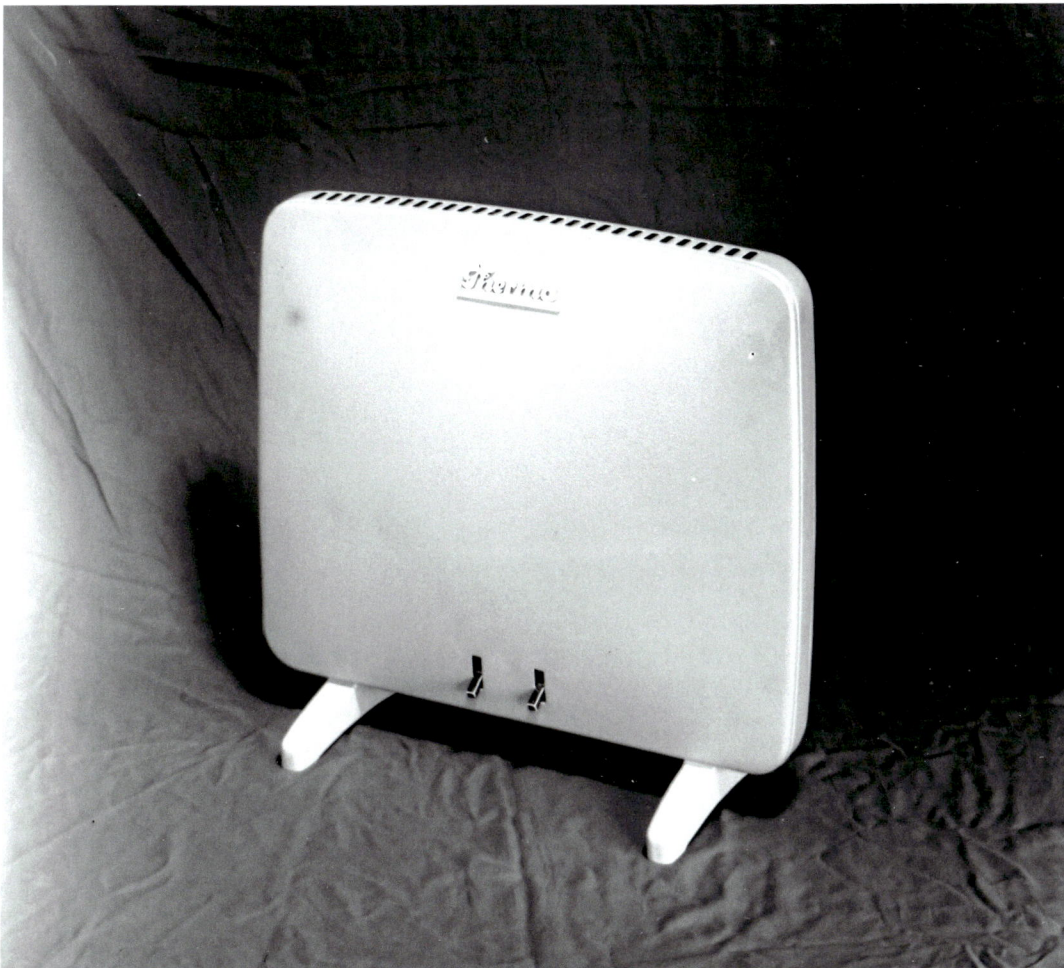

4.42

4.43

NEUHEIT

Therma
FILTRE
la nouvelle cafetière
entièrement automatique

Du café moulu,
de l'eau
dans le réservoir...
Brancher le courant...
et après quelques
minutes déjà
vous obtenez
un délicieux café!

NOUVEAUTÉ

4.44

4.45

[→ D]
Ueli Prager, April, 1958: "I was in our new building in Geneva a few days ago and inspected the kitchen thoroughly, together with the architect. Fortunately, there is ample compensation for the long wait – when building today you really need to have angelic mental calm or nerves of steel like overseas cables [sic] – thanks to the beauty of the highly classical modern building and the magnificent location. [...] I wanted to tell you that I have also or rather above all been generously rewarded by you for the many hundreds of hours and years of planning work. When we visited your factory, I was amazed, as were my employees, by the appliances that you developed for us, by their performance, sophistication and solidity – you could say they were built to last for generations. [...] You know that right from the start I set out the postulate of workplace design. It was not simply about building a large kitchen, but rather workplaces for each individual role. These requirements have been fulfilled in every respect." (30)

two advertising brochures that were published in rapid succession. Only the second tapped into the door compartments' potential. After almost half a century, the innovative flair that had forged Therma's aura over many years seemed to have dwindled. While the fiftieth anniversary in September 1957 was rightly a significant milestone and a fitting time for a celebratory review of half a century of Glarus industrial history, drawing attention to the firm's impressive achievements, concerns about the future were left out of the picture in this context.

In that period, Therma was commissioned to fit out the kitchen for the first Mövenpick restaurant in Geneva on Place de la Fusterie. The project planning must have been challenging, but the firm met the ambitious deadline. A letter of appreciation from Mövenpick founder Ueli Prager in spring 1958 gave Therma an excellent reference. [30] [→ D] It was agreeable to receive this kind of confirmation of the firm's reputation.

A little earlier, on New Year's Day 1958, the now 71-year-old Chairman of the Group Hans Hefti had outlined his thoughts on Therma's situation in a memorandum to the Board of Directors, stating at the outset that "neither the commercial nor the technical managers have precise ideas about the manufacturing program's future structure." He continued, "We are aware that Therma's current manufacturing program is jeopardizing its profitability." Hefti conceded that "a company with smaller output in a densely populated and flourishing area has advantages over a company with large capacity located in Glarus" (probably referring to the subsidiary, Maxim) and added that this factor did play a role, although it was not the main reason why the other companies in the group were more successful. Hefti suggested two approaches as countermeasures: "1. Addressing the price war through more rational and, above all, larger-scale production where necessary; 2. Moving ahead of the competition technically or through particular designs or the use of novel materials." Finally, he mentioned a "new standardized design"; its impact on Therma's success would become apparent in 1958. With a view to developments in the USA, he interpreted the signs of the times, noting that "today, the trend seems to be moving toward overall kitchen design, toward kitchen architecture, in a sense." [31]

This design approach was a new development and a patent application addressing it was filed in spring 1958. Combining standardized interchangeable modules, with the "installation frame" as the underlying design premise, did indeed prove to be trailblazing. These two features formed the technical and conceptual basis for Therma's urgently needed reorientation and renewed upswing over the following decade.

4.45   Until 1953, Therma refrigerators had smooth doors without inner compartments.

1   Hans Dietler, VR-Protokoll [Minutes of Board of Directors meeting] 261, December 4, 1945, pp. 5–6. – GWA Elux B 2–1/2
2   Ibid., p. 10.
3   Hans Dietler, "Bericht über den Geschäftsgang anlässlich der Ausschusssitzung des Verwaltungsrates," August 26, 1946, p. 10. – GWA Elux B 2–2/1
4   Ibid.
5   Ibid., p. 4.
6   39. Jahresbericht [Annual Report], 1945/46. – GWA Elux B 4–1/2
7   Jahresberichte [Annual Reports] 1945/46, 1946/47, 1948/49, 1949/50. – GWA Elux B 4–1/2
8   1929: exports made up 43% of sales; 1935: exports accounted for 11%. The share of exports in total sales was very low during the war and remained low after 1945 due to difficulties in procuring materials. Cf. annual reports in the relevant period without numerical data.
9   Draft of Therma's pool agreement with Prometheus, May 10, 1946, p. 1. – Hefti family fonds, estate of Dr. Hans Hefti-Haab, Schwanden (South Glarus district), "Prometheus" file
10 46. Jahresbericht, 1952/53, pp. 3–4. – GWA Elux B 4–1/2
11 Regionalism is the term used to refer to an architectural and material language that took the basic features of an architectural modernism that aspired to international validity and sought to adapt or further develop it in the spirit of a regional building culture. The term *Heimatstil* (literally "homeland style"), which is also used to refer to this phenomenon, is too imprecise and is usually meant in a derogatory way; it does not apply to Hans Leuzinger.
12 CH patent no. 252708, filed on September 1, 1945.
13 Draft contract Elcalor, 1951 (no precise date). – GWA Elux B 2–4/10
14 46. Jahresbericht, 1952/53, p. 4. – GWA Elux B 4–1/2
15 42. Jahresbericht, 1948/49, p. 4. – GWA Elux B 4–1/2. The rotary compressor was designed by ETH mechanical engineer Henri Soumerai (1923–2023), who emigrated to the US in 1950 and enjoyed professional success there.
16 The Dietler family were tenants of the house financed by Therma.
17 Hans Hilfiker, "Apparateindustrie und Küchenbau," lecture in Montreux, 1967, p. 6. Cf. Part 5.
18 Hans Dietler to Hans Hefti, September 3, 1951, p. 1. – GWA Elux B 2–4/10
19 Brochure, undated (ca. 1950). – GWA Elux H 1–3/1 to H 1–3/4, file H 1–3/2
20 This reminds us that vacuum cleaners were originally designed as centralized systems, too: a vacuum generator in the basement, branched supply lines to each room and a hose connected to the suction nozzle in the rooms being cleaned in the apartments.
21 GWA Elux Neg. P 3_50249
22 GWA Elux Neg. P 2_51416
23 GWA Elux Neg. P 2_53023
24 GWA Elux Neg. P 3_51202
25 Brochure on Therma kitchen ensembles, 1955: "Therma modernisiert die Schweizerküche." – GWA Elux H 1–2/1 to H 1–2/3, file H 1–2/3
26 50. Jahresbericht, 1956/57, p. 4. – GWA Elux B 4–1/2
27 48. Jahresbericht, 1954/55, pp. 3–4. – GWA Elux B 4–1/2
28 Brochure on Therma kitchen ensembles, 1955: "Therma modernisiert die Schweizerküche." – GWA Elux H 1–2/1 to H 1–2/3, file H 1–2/3
29 Protokoll des Verwaltungsausschusses [Minutes from the Administrative Committee], June 2, 1954, p. 4. – GWA Elux B 2–2/1
30 Ueli Prager, letter of appreciation to Therma, April 2, 1958 (reproduction). – GWA Elux Neg. P 2_58172
31 Hans Hefti, untitled (Memorandum to Group Directors/Administrative Committee), January 3, 1958, pp. 1–2. – Hefti family fonds, estate of Dr. Hans Hefti-Haab, Schwanden (Glarus South Local Council), "Organisatorisches" file

Die griffbereite «Fülltüre»

im neuen Therma-Kühlschrank

Die griffbereite Fülltüre macht den Kühlschrank komfortabel. Sie enthält stets streichfertige, nie zu harte Butter im Extrafach.

Sie gibt Ihnen gute 10 Liter Kühlschrankraum: Raum für viele Flaschen, Büchsen, Päckli, die nicht mehr im Schrank verschwinden, sondern übersichtlich dastehen.

Wählen Sie unter den besten Kühlschränken den stromsparenden Kompressor-Kühlschrank, das Schweizerfabrikat mit der großen Kälteleistung ... das neueste Therma-Modell mit der griffbereiten «Fülltüre».

Therma -Kühlschrank R12
Inhalt 120 Liter   Fr. 1100.–

Vorführung und Verkauf durch die Elektro-Fachgeschäfte und Elektrizitätswerke

Therma AG Schwanden / GL
Kältebüro Zürich, Hofwiesenstr. 141   Büro und Ausstellungen
Telephon 051. 26 16 06   Zürich: Beethovenstr. 20 (Claridenhof)
   Bern: Monbijoustr. 47

02178

4.46

4.48

4.47

4.46   Therma only introduced refrigerator doors with storage compartments, known as *Fülltüre* and based on the American model, in 1954 – here an advertising photo from 1956.
4.47   A conventional arrangement with a grateful wife and housewife, 1959. In the 1959 door the arrangement of the storage compartments is more rational than in the previous model.
4.48   New in the range: Beverage cooler on castors for restaurants, 1957.
4.49   And in a new development, the couple as a team; the husband fetches the white wine from the fridge to accompany his partner's chocolate pudding, around 1958.
4.50   The grounds outside the factory, spruced up for the big anniversary. Therma is de facto the gateway to the Sernf valley.
4.51   Speech by Hans Hefti, Chairman of the Group and President of Therma Schwanden, on October 18, 1957, the day of Therma's fiftieth anniversary.

4.49

4.50

4.51

157

4.52

Herd-Boiler-Spültrog-Kombination

Ausführung:
Herd: Rinnenherd mit fest eingebauten Kochplatten, Backofen mit getrennter Temperaturregulierung der Ober- und Unterhitze, Geräteschublade
Boiler: Kessel Eisen feuerverzinkt oder Kupfer 100- und 120-Liter-Boiler mit Thermometer
Kübelabteil: Für 25-Liter-Kübel, mit Kippvorrichtung
Schrank: Mit Tablar, Schublade Holz
Spültrog: Rostfreier Stahl, Becken 340×400×140 mm
Verkleidungen: Stahlblech, Herd crème porzellan-emailliert, übrige Verkleidungen crème email-lackiert
Sockel: Stahlblech schwarz porzellan-emailliert, 100 mm hoch
Mischbatterie: Hochglanz verchromt

L. Nr.	Herd		Boiler		Abmessungen mm			Gewicht kg	Preis Fr.	
	Anzahl Platten	Normalleistung Watt	Inhalt Liter	Normalleistung Watt	Länge	Tiefe	Höhe		Kessel Eisen	Kessel Kupfer
13 50 83	3	6600	50	600	2210	600	850	186		
13 52 83	3	6600	100	1200	2210	600	850	205		
13 53 83	3	6600	120	1500	2270	600	915	220		
13 50 84	4	8400	50	600	2210	600	850	189		
13 52 84	4	8400	100	1200	2210	600	850	210		
13 53 84	4	8400	120	1500	2270	600	915	225		

Auf Wunsch Boiler rechts, Herd links angeordnet
Angaben bei Bestellung: L. Nr., Stromart, Spannung für Herd und Boiler, Anordnung, Randausführung, Sicherheitsarmaturen ½" oder ¾"

4.53a

Herd-Kühlschrank-Spültrog-Kombination

Ausführung:
Herd: Rinnenherd mit fest eingebauten Kochplatten, Backofen mit getrennter Temperaturregulierung der Ober- und Unterhitze, Geräteschublade
Kühlschrank: Mit gekapseltem Rotationskompressor, Innenraum porzellan-emailliert. Nur für Anschluß an 220 Volt Wechselstrom. Anschluß an andere Spannungen (110, 125, 145, 250 Volt) mit Transformator (Mehrpreis). Auf Wunsch mit Gemüseschublade und Innenbeleuchtung (Mehrpreis)
Kühlelenteil: Für 25 Liter-Kübel, mit Kippvorrichtung
Spültrog: Rostfreier Stahl, Becken 340×400×140 mm
Verkleidungen: Stahlblech, Herd crème porzellan-emailliert, übrige Verkleidungen crème email-lackiert
Sockel: Stahlblech schwarz porzellan-emailliert, 100 mm hoch
Mischbatterie: Hochglanz verchromt

L. Nr.	Herd		Kühlschrank		Abmessungen mm			Gewicht kg	Preis Fr.
	Anzahl Platten	Normalleistung Watt	Inhalt Liter	Motorleistung Watt	Länge	Tiefe	Höhe		
13 63 83	3	6600	100	67	2240	600	850	205	
13 63 84	4	8400	100	67	2240	600	850	209	

Auf Wunsch Kühlschrank rechts, Herd links angeordnet
Auch nur mit 1 Becken lieferbar, Minderpreis
Angaben bei Bestellung: L. Nr., Stromart, Spannung Herd und Kühlschrank, Anordnung, Randausführung

4.53b

4.52 Therma stand at the 1957 Mustermesse Basel: The wall units display the traits of a new era, but the ensemble underneath still reflects a gradual, non-systematic evolution over the years.

4.53 Two pages from the catalog on kitchen ensembles, 1957.

4.54 Grocery store, on the left a conventional sales counter; the chilled cabinet by the wall is designed for self-service. Chilled cabinet by Therma, location unknown, 1956.

4.55 Therma stand at the 1958 Mustermesse Basel: The ensemble on the right, with its five drawers and clear joint pattern, has taken a key step closer to full modularity, functioning more as part of a system.

4.56 Stand model for the 1958 Mustermesse Basel with the layout for the appliances.

4.54

4.55

4.56

5

Looking into the newly built assembly hall offers a vista into a light-filled world, unlike the mysteriously introverted locations of the film shots that introduced Part 4. This is where the products that made Therma proud in the 1960s were put together; appliances were assembled and combined into kitchen ensembles, reflecting Therma's growing self-confidence. The photograph by Friedrich Engesser was taken shortly after the hall with a sawtooth roof was commissioned in late 1963 and shows three of the five room axes under the sawtooth sections. The photograph is the coda, in a sense, to the 1965 brochure, *Der Weg zur Küche* (*The Road to the Kitchen*), which Therma couched as a "report to its friends." There were many of these friends. During this decade, engineer Hans Hilfiker was the defining figure for Therma. As Delegate Representative of the Board of Directors, he had directed his full focus to this construction and the production processes it was to house. He planned to transform Therma from an appliance manufacturer into a manufacturer of entire kitchens. He achieved precisely that and it proved to be problematic. (What happened? That will be explained in due course.)

Hilfiker defined his intellectual foundation as rooted in reason. That was the physiognomy of the decade in terms of everyday culture – at least in its first half. In Switzerland, Therma was at the forefront of the consumer goods industry that shaped this physiognomy and played an active part in defining it at all levels: through powerful new developments in its product ranges, at trade fairs, through public appearances, advertising campaigns, catalogs and brochures, with flyers, in manufacturing processes and last but not least with the ambitious service organization. Purpose and means, content and form amalgamated in this decade for Therma to create a new corporate identity that was eager to deal with facts rather than mere assertions. Plausibility was the key issue in this context. Hilfiker sought to enforce it through an approach based on uniformization. Was that a mistake? Which concept of coordinated uniformization did his project involve? In the first instance, it was not about how the kitchens were used, but instead about the construction kit that could be used to model this use in keeping with the customer's individual wishes. The aim was flexibility, not overall uniformity.

The hall with its sawtooth roof housed many more activities than can be described in detail here. It was mainly involved in assembling kitchen ensembles. The formed parts (cut, folded, pressed, deep-drawn, roller-welded and provided with punched openings and bends) were transported from the factory producing components on the other side of the road that has figured in previous sections, moving through tunnels under the thoroughfare into the new building. The parts were, for example, deep-drawn halves of boilers to be built into kitchen sets, front panels with switches for cooking stoves, cover plates, oven housings and refrigerator chilled compart-ments. Downstream, they were degreased, washed and dried in the tunnel at the preparation and phosphating plant. After those cleaning steps, they were primed, wet-painted or enameled (in the sequence: base enam-eling – drying oven – topcoat enameling – drying oven), while suspended on transport chains that sometimes dipped, then rose again, entered a tunnel furnace and emerged on the other side.

It all formed a sophisticated trajectory. Every piece was carefully checked. Small parts were first copper-plated and subsequently nickel-plated, followed by chrome plat-ing, while heated plastic foils for the door linings in chilled compartments were vacuum-formed. The same activities were not repeated every day, but all the measures were organized in daily or weekly schedules that reflected the overall work flow.

The cooking stoves and refrigerators were assembled from these components, either as stand-alone or built-in models, as were the boilers and cabinet elements. These in turn were combined to assemble the kitchen ensem-bles on roller conveyors, moving from back to front toward the camera. Depending on the order selected by the cus-tomer, the stove was on the left, sometimes on the right, sometimes the boiler came next, sometimes the sink, sometimes the ensemble was two and a half sub-units long, sometimes three, four or more. In the foreground here, a kitchen ensemble is visible, probably being pre-pared for transportation by adding a protective cover over the chrome steel worktop. The cooling units for the refrig-erators, which had been Therma's technological pride and joy for fifteen years, were purchased externally at this stage. By this point, Therma's pride was grounded in another strength: the flexible interactions between a sys-tematic approach and modularity.

1958–1968

"Therma – It's All New"

Therma's Rediscovered Creativity During Hans Hilfiker's Decade

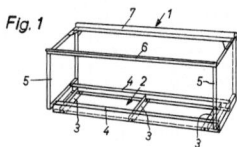

Fig. 1

357526
1 Blatt

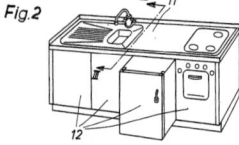

Fig.2

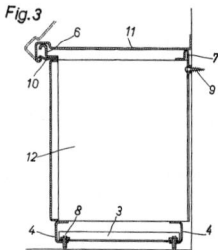

Fig.3

Fig.4

5.1a

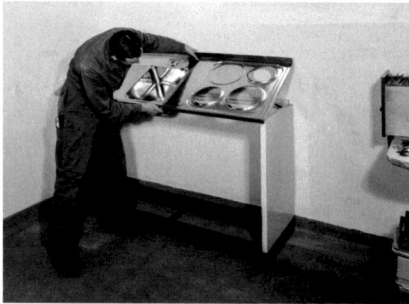

5.1b

From 1958 to 1968, Therma's self-image and public image were redefined, creating an appearance of profound rejuvenation after years of stagnation. In rapid succession, the firm produced numerous innovations – genuine ones, not mere enticing pseudo-innovations – and adopted an unmistakable new corporate image with a determination that makes it thoroughly exceptional in Swiss design history. This fresh look made a substantial contribution to the world of design and expressed a new attitude to life after the tough post-war years. Looking at Therma's achievements, it becomes crystal clear why this is also said to be the era of second-wave modernism – after the first wave during the interwar period. The recently founded research and development office in Schwanden was the nerve center of this development surge. Although the firm was only partially successful in getting to grips with its now confusing corporate structure, that does not diminish the significance of this period.

This renewal process is linked to Hans Hilfiker (1901–1993). A qualified electrical engineer (initially trained as a precision mechanic), his creative interests extended far beyond this discipline and he led the company from 1958 to 1968. Within the corporate group, he took on the newly created role of Delegate Representative to the Board of Directors and the Administrative Committee. Hilfiker's sphere of responsibility encompassed the oversight of the entire group and the management of the Schwanden plant. In his role as Delegate Representative for the entire group, he also handled issues relating to the subsidiaries Elcalor, Sursee and Therma Zurich (formerly Kältebüro). In 1964, he was in addition tasked with developing the Therma Commercial Kitchens division in Schlieren near Zurich, which opened in 1966. Subsidiary Maxim, on the other hand, insisted on its (partial) autonomy during this time and resisted complete integration. As a detailed description of these relationships would go beyond the scope of this book, I shall focus here on Hilfiker's achievements in the household appliances and domestic kitchens sector.

His key success stories arose from the impetus he provided to devise new products based on a clear concept and how he communicated their technical, architectural and social background. The range of developments in these years extended from small appliances to complete household kitchens. The Schwanden site, where Hilfiker was based, played a decisive role in this evolution.

As a young ETH graduate in the mid-1920s, Hilfiker had worked as a telecommunications engineer for Siemens in Argentina, where he was involved in constructing long-distance telephone lines. In 1932, having returned to Switzerland, he began working for Swiss Federal Railways (SBB) and in 1944 became Deputy Head of its District III Construction Department (Zurich/Eastern Switzerland) and Head of Fixed Electrical Installations Services. In 1944, he developed and designed the centrally controlled Swiss railroad station clock and in 1955 added its second hand (which stops briefly every full minute and subsequently makes up for lost time), as well as creating a loading crane that received international accolades for its design and form.[1] His proposal for a new type of station platform roofing also met with much acclaim; initially suggested in 1952, a prototype was erected in Grüze, a suburb of Winterthur, in 1955. Hilfiker's work, such as the spectacular optical timetable reader in Zurich's main station (1957), demonstrated his ability to conduct in-depth analysis and also – by no means a matter of course for an engineer – to oversee its imaginative, convincing design implementation. He combined the rationality of engineering and the eros of creative design work.[2] As the long-time Director of Abendtechnikum Zurich, a specialized engineering evening school, and as a lecturer both there and at ETH, he was experienced in expressing problems verbally and communicating them to others. As a member of SWB, the Swiss Werkbund, he brought to Therma an interest in how function in use, construction, fabrication and formal design interlink.

5.1a   CH patent no. 357526, "Device for installation in kitchens," filed on March 5, 1958, filed under the name of Karl Keller, head of the Structural Design unit.

5.1b   Positioning the chromium nickel steel cover on the upper longitudinal beam. The appliances and cabinet modules below are thus non-load-bearing and interchangeable.

5.2   Probably the study for a new free-standing cooking stove, 1957, design not pursued further.

5.2

[→ A]

"55-60-90: We set ourselves the task of coming up with a benchmark for the Swiss household kitchen. The solution led to the production of ensembles that meet individual requirements and allow rational production. The design is completely new, with an installation frame forming the framework. The stainless steel cover is placed on top. The appliance and box elements are inserted. Every part is completely redesigned and based on standard measurements down to the last detail. The sub-units' dimensions are benchmark-based for width (55 cm or 27.5 cm), depth (60 cm) and height (90 cm). The electrical and hydraulic connections are also based on harmonized measurements. There is a completely novel interchangeability of sub-units. Example: A cooling cabinet may later be replaced by a refrigerator. With the Therma benchmark, you are largely free to combine the various elements. You can expect lower costs and shorter delivery times. And above all: you can plan more easily." (6)

Hermann Budich, Director at the Union Bank of Switzerland and a long-standing friend of Hilfiker, is said to have heard about the difficulties at Therma around 1957 and brought Hilfiker to the attention of top management.[3] As the archival documents reveal, in spring 1958, Hilfiker was recommended to the Therma Board of Directors by its Vice Chairman Wilhelm Bänninger (a management member at the main shareholder Elektrowatt AG, a planning company for power plants in Zurich) for the position of new manager with a remit to oversee Therma's urgently needed reorientation. Oskar Steiger, Technical Director since 1954, was not the right man for this task. The group's executives hoped that appointing a Delegate Representative would lead to more intensive dialog between corporate management level and the operational management of the companies in the group. R. Peter Hefti-Spoerry (1922–2012), Hans Hefti's son and also a doctor of law, had been the group's Chairman since mid-1958. The position of Delegate Representative does not appear to have been advertised. The Board of Directors approved Bänninger's proposal, noting that "although Mr. Hilfiker lacks a certain amount of operational experience, it can be expected that he will rapidly familiarize himself with his area of responsibility."[4] At the age of fifty-six, Hilfiker left SBB (where he had felt constantly hampered in his career development) and took up the position of Delegate Representative to the Board of Directors in mid-1958.

Although Hilfiker made an important contribution to the company's new dynamism, it should be mentioned at this juncture that a decisive technical step toward Therma's reinvention had already been taken shortly before his appointment. That was the development of the aforementioned installation frame, which put the assembly of kitchen ensembles on a new footing. The patent specification was submitted on March 5, 1958 with the title "Device for installation in kitchens" in the name of Karl Keller, head of the structural engineering office. Describing his invention, he noted that "in known devices of this type, the covering portion is supported directly on the elements. The latter must therefore be built as load-bearing components with correspondingly higher manufacturing costs. Logically, the cover portion can only be fitted once the elements have already been installed. This makes it very cumbersome to level the cover and consequently this is therefore not usually done with the requisite care. The cover portion usually accommodates one or more sinks, to which the thick drainpipes can only be connected in the tightest of spaces due to the elements already installed. The need to fit in the sub-units at an earlier stage of construction in view of the installation usually results in damage to them. [...] The invention makes it possible to avoid the disadvantages mentioned above. To that end, the device according to the invention has a fixed frame to which the covering portion and the sub-elements to be built in are affixed."[5]

This invention meant that a kitchen was installed in reverse order (in apartments or detached houses). First, the installation frame was fixed in place, followed by the cover with the sink and the openings for the hotplates. Subsequently, the water pipes were connected and it was only in the final step that the technical modules were inserted (boiler, stove, refrigerator, cupboard elements). Hilfiker now established a causal link between the concept of reversing the order of steps taken and the idea of modularization based on a set of agreed dimensions that offered a systematic spectrum of options. The set of agreed dimensions stipulated that a core kitchen unit should be 900 mm high and 600 mm deep and should take 550 mm as the basic measurement parameter when determining its length. The 900-mm height included a 105-mm-high sheet steel plinth. The two side walls were designed as frame beams and were 40 mm thick (later reduced to 30 mm). In 1960, the catalog text described "the new Therma standard" with its "completely novel interchangeability of sub-units."[6] [→ A]

5.3

5.4

5.3 Advertisement for a modular kitchen ensemble, probably from late 1958 and designed by the Erwin Halpern advertising agency. Typography related to the modular dimensions 90/55/60 (height/width/depth), here still with the old logo.

5.4 Probably the model study for the standard cooking stove introduced in 1961 with the faceted arrangement of the stove front, including its panel of switches, the oven doors and the appliance drawer, photograph taken in late 1958.

5.5 Two pages of the brochure on modular ensembles, design by the Halpern advertising agency. Emphasis on ergonomic aspects. Not dated, probably 1959.

When the patent application was filed in 1958, there was only a study model for a new stove based on the concept of modular appliances. Outgoing Group President Hans Hefti referred to the term "standardized design" in his aforementioned memorandum of January 3, 1958, in which he also talked about a "Muldenherd" or "depressed-section stove" for which Therma had high hopes. This was a new development. Rather than grooves or a milk drawer, the cover had a continuous depression, around 10 mm deep, to collect boiled-over liquids. This was the almost absurdly simple solution to a problem that had been rumbling around for forty years; the technical prerequisite was a liquid-tight enclosure around the hotplates.

The idea of interchangeable modules thus already existed when Hilfiker took up his position as Delegate Representative to the Board. A photograph from 1957 probably documents the aforementioned study model of the free-standing oven. (→5.2) It features a full-width oven door and the hollow-like recess around the hotplates described above, as well as a very slightly slanted front panel with switches and an overhanging front edge.

When Hilfiker visited Therma in Schwanden in March 1958 to glean an impression of the company, Karl Keller must have told him about the ideas circulating and the new design concept. Certain clues suggest that both found this meeting highly encouraging and that it opened up a fruitful collaboration, as the two men were thinking along the same lines.[7] Years later, Hilfiker would arrange Keller's promotion to Vice Director of the Research and Development department – citing his "imagination and talent as a designer."[8]

In contrast to the previous decade, in the ten years or so under Hilfiker's leadership, Therma filed over twenty patents in Switzerland, most of which were highly innovative.

Hilfiker started work officially on July 1, 1958. He had already been attending meetings of the Board of Directors since April and even wrote the minutes on June 25. It proved rather elegant that day for Commercial Director Walter Baur to talk about the company's many problems and in parallel introduce Hilfiker as a problem-solver. In the minutes, Hilfiker gave a striking summary of Baur's assessment of the situation. "Technical development has not kept pace with the times. In the small appliances range, only two items can be marketed viably: the regulator-switch iron and the coffee machine. A new domestic stove cannot be available quickly enough. The previous stove's shape and design are outdated. The Rinnenherd or easy-clean stove is eleven years old. Obsolescence is particularly evident in the new ensembles. Our competitors exploit this to the full. More recently, kitchens have been designed with increasing attention to detail. Kitchen ensembles are therefore becoming more and more popular. As a result, sales of single ovens are also declining. – The new kitchen combinations are convincing because they simplify planning and assembly. However, they also have disadvantages: 1. The hollow base is referred to as a dirt trap; 2. Transportation and storage cause some difficulties. Prefabricated transportation is sought as far as possible; 3. Housewives want this trend to develop further. More elements are needed. They have an endless wish list. The design needs to be completed under high pressure. – Today's rapid heaters are ten years old. Although they are elegant, the shape is a little 'outdated.' A new rapid heater is needed. – Wall-mounted boilers are increasingly being replaced by built-in boilers. – Domestic refrigerators have been improved. The public appreciates them, but they are too expensive. The prices offered by Bosch, Migros, etc. have a very negative impact on our sales. – Commercial appliances have compensated for shortcomings in the household sector: the commercial refrigeration systems department is doing excellent work."[9] Establishing a larger team with an extended skill set for the structural engineering group was described as an important task.

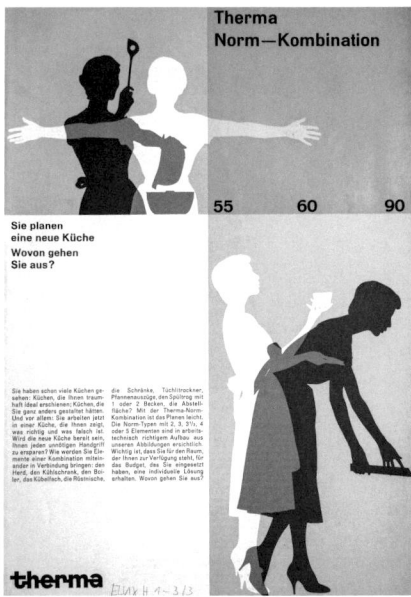

Therma
Norm—Kombination

55 60 90

Sie planen
eine neue Küche
Wovon gehen
Sie aus?

therma

5.5a

therma

55 60 90

Ausgangspunkt Nr. 3

Die Senkrechte

5.5b

[→ B]
"New 'Therma' logo: [The] Administrative Committee requested that the old logo be replaced by the new one, which won the competition. The Delegate Representative provided further explanation. 'Concerns that abandoning the old logo might result in the loss of great conceptual value would only be justified if the name "Therma" were to be abandoned altogether. However, there is no mention of this at all, only of a different graphic representation of the wordmark.' – Unanimous approval of the BoD [Board of Directors]." (15)

It was another four and a half months before the next meeting of the Board of Directors was held, on November 11, 1958. This time Hilfiker gave a presentation on Therma's product range, machinery and manufacturing methods, explaining the urgent need for a comprehensive redefinition. "Too many Therma products have become insufficiently attractive, whether in terms of their usefulness, price, quality or form. For example, in small appliances, once a key business sector, Therma has declined to the level of a small company. Very few of the existing items in this range are still in line with market requirements. In keeping with this, production also bears the hallmarks of small-scale manufacturing. That also holds true for some other product ranges. As a result, and due to the diversity of the manufacturing program, a significant part of Therma is tantamount to a cluster of small businesses."[10] He also noted that a large number of machines were outdated and could no longer hold their own against the competition's powerful means of production; in addition, the operating facilities and how these related to each other would need to be reviewed, which would probably trigger drastic changes. With so many shortcomings, the greatest challenge was "the question of an appropriate starting point to initiate a promising renewal." He added, "It is essential that renewal take place gradually and as organically as possible."[11] "Gradually and organically" – in short, systematically.

Given Therma's overheads, it was clear to him that "the company has no choice but to acknowledge its character as a large company and to achieve corresponding sales again in more product ranges than at present."[12] The minutes record the Representative's intention to "therefore begin a significant expansion of the series appliance ranges, as well as replacing obsolete, no longer marketable products with new designs."[13] This objective corresponds to the goal formulated by former Group President Hefti in January 1958. (cf. p. 154) The minutes concluded by reporting that the Board of Directors had inspected the models for the new range of stoves and approved procurement of new tools to the tune of one million CHF.

Just four months after Hilfiker took up his post, the request from the end of June for a new household cooking stove had already led to a viable design – or, to be more precise, to a template for an entire range of cooking stoves, which were only ready for market launch in their fully developed form two years later and would remain vitally important to the renewed Therma concept throughout the entire Hilfiker era. Hilfiker viewed the congruence between product form and manufacturing method as the prerequisite for the company's renewal; the prototype's new aesthetics can also be read as an expression of this congruence. The stove in the photograph P 1_58318, dated 1958, is probably the manually constructed prototype (→ 5.4) that the Board of Directors inspected in November 1958 – a full two years before its market launch. Its formal conception is markedly different from the model study of the previous year. I shall come back to this.

The new start was rapid. The plan had been to increase the number of staff in the structural engineering office, which was renamed Research and Development in line with its remit and in acknowledgment of its greater independence from day-to-day business. These steps were grounded in an expectation that the department would devise more powerful ideas if its work was not constrained by a need to stick close to reality. In most cases, albeit not always, this proved to be a valid assumption. As early as summer or early fall of 1958, Hilfiker asked graphic designer Carlo L. Vivarelli to draw up proposals for a new wordmark. Hilfiker and Vivarelli had met at the Bel Étage Club at Café Select in Zurich, which offered a meeting place where people with an interest in culture and prominent figures from various professions could share ideas.[14] On December 3, 1958, the management agreed to replace the logo that had been in use for thirty years with a new one.[15][→ B] It was designed in small letters so that it could be punched out of metal as a single piece and attached to the devices.

5.6

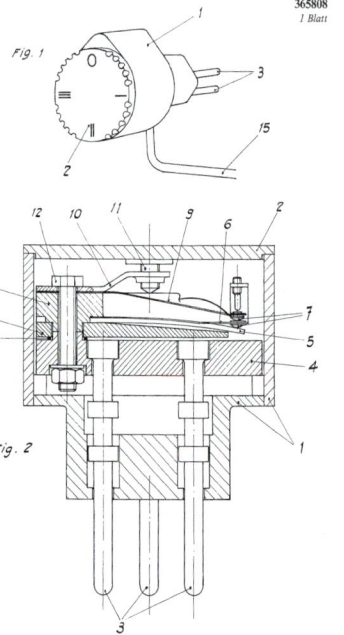

365808
1 Blatt

Fig. 1

Fig. 2

5.7

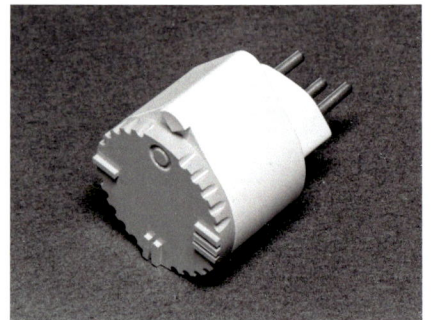

5.8

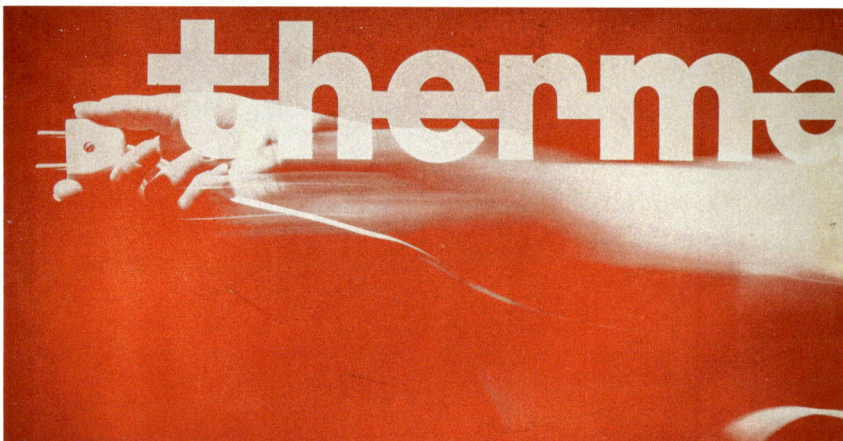

5.9

5.10

5.11a

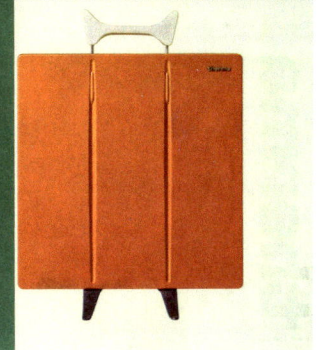

5.11b

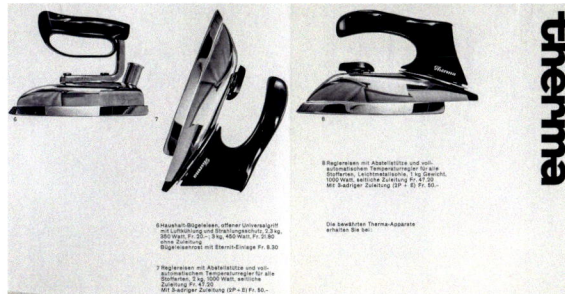

5.12a

5.6 Butterfly heating stove in a photograph from late 1958: already developed to production maturity, but the wordmark is not yet included.

5.7 CH patent no. 365808 on the Butterfly temperature regulation mechanism on the appliance plug: "Regulator device for electric radiator," filed on March 18, 1959.

5.8 The temperature regulation mechanism directly on the plug.

5.9 Symbolizing the new "Therma dynamism" 1959/1960, Photograph probably by Willy S. Eberle.

5.10 Advertisement for the Butterfly heating stove, Halpern agency, photograph by Willy S. Eberle.

5.11 Four-page folded brochure on the Butterfly heating stove, here in French, summer 1959. Sophisticated color combinations: in the pearl gray and yellow model, the handle is black, but it is light gray in the other variants. The square format corresponds to the form of the product.

5.12 Six-page folded brochure on the small appliances, not dated (probably 1959). Attempt to develop a new corporate image, even if the products had in some cases been familiar for many years. Once again the square format forms the basis.

5.12b

[→C]
"Overview by the Delegate Representative concerning new developments. Most urgent task: technical development and new designs. Once this goal has been achieved, planned cooperation between the group companies can become more important again." (16)

The new Therma was presented to the public for the first time at the Mustermesse Basel in April 1959. The Board of Directors heaped lavish praise on Hilfiker for the stand design. At its subsequent meeting, Hilfiker informed the Board of Directors about the latest developments in greater detail. [16] [→C] The new wordmark was presented to considerable effect, while the products also reflected Therma's fresh approach. The public noticed the changes immediately. The flat Butterfly radiant stove was an instant attraction and a sign of a fresh start – just a few years earlier, an English-language product name would hardly have been an option. Butterfly also charmed with its choice of seven colors: pearl gray, slate gray, pastel white, coral red, blue, green, yellow. Its two square metal sheets were held together without screws: at the bottom by spring clips and at the top by a graceful handle in gray plastic, designed by Hans Bellmann. It was an ingenious construction; Hilfiker regarded screw connections as indicating a lack of design maturity. It is not unreasonable to interpret the structural design of Butterfly as implicitly linked to the radiation heater with a reflective surface. (cf. 3.3) Both display a similar flatness and are economical effort-wise in forming the construction with two vertical support bars for the surfaces and handles. [17]

Hilfiker's debut year also saw the creation of the camping cooler, a stele with a circular footprint that contained rotatable and lockable "cages" in two stacked cooling compartments, in which several families could keep their food fresh. The prototype was tested that summer at a campsite in Ticino. Its cantilevered shade-giving roof displayed the new Therma logo prominently. This device's resemblance to the cylindrical advertising pillars still widespread at the time may be a coincidence, but the advertising effect was certainly intentional. It expresses an innovative recklessness that matched the prevalent spirit of optimism. Several such camping coolers were built and installed at Swiss campsites and even in one location in Italy. It is not known how long they remained in operation there.

The main topic, however, was the new standardized ensemble. In fall 1959, Therma presented it at the Olma (Swiss trade fair for agriculture and dairy farming), contrasting it with an ensemble based on the conventional concept. (→5.28) The difference is striking. The conventional version looks heterogeneous, whereas the standardized ensemble conveys clarity and order – despite inaccuracies in the joints due to manual production of the prototype. It adhered to the 55-60-90 formula, which means that a module was 55 cm wide, 60 cm deep, and had a work surface set at a height of 90 cm. These standard measurements were largely defined by Hilfiker and introduced shortly after he joined Therma as a system by the name of SINK (Schweizerische Industriekommission zur Normung der Küche, the Swiss Industry Committee on Standardization of the Kitchen, which in 1996 was renamed SMS: Schweizer Mass-System, the Swiss Dimensions System). SINK was not an exclusive Therma standard; other Swiss manufacturers also participated, such as Franke (Aarburg), Forster (Arbon) and V-Zug (Verzinkerei Zug). Hilfiker, as the driving force behind it, justified the module width of 55 cm with functional considerations. It is not certain whether there was an unspoken strategic calculation behind this, for example an intention to use the 55-cm-wide module to protect Swiss manufacturers from their German competitors, who – not being constrained by a system of standardized dimensions at the time – were building somewhat wider appliances. Therma's problematic experience with price competitiveness, particularly in relation to German manufacturers in the post-war period, may have played a role. The purported greater and more systematic integration of appliances in Switzerland than in Germany may also have been relevant. Other differences between Germany and Switzerland played a role in this context, too: for example, in tenancy law. Definitions in the two countries varied on the issue of which appliances were considered to be part of the home and which were viewed as movable property. In Swiss tenancy law

5.13

5.14

5.13 The camping cooler, photo taken in the plant, 1959.
5.14 Camping cooler installed at a campsite in Tenero, Ticino, 1959. Lockable compartments in rotatable cages.
5.15 A later development under Hilfiker: the rotating frying pan, based on the same rotation principle, for large quantities of grilled meat, 1965.

5.15

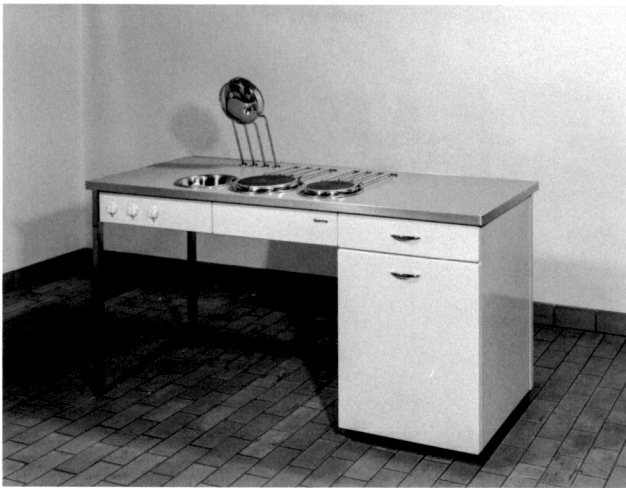

5.16a

5.16b

5.17

5.18

5.16 Compact cooking stove with foldaway hotplates, recessed bowls and circular worktop inserts, first displayed in April 1959 in Basel.

5.17 Modular ensemble with compact cooking stove, 1959. It already includes the vertical six-based unit layout.

5.18 Test setup with a view to the Mustermesse Basel stand in April 1959: presentation of the Therma compact cooking stove and first formulation of the modular system with harmonized measurements and the vertical six-based unit layout.

5.19 CH patent no. 366947, "Fittings with at least one cooking appliance for kitchens," filed on March 10, 1959: description and depiction of wiring and mechanism for moving the hotplates.

5.20 Friedrich Engesser, staging of a kitchen with free-standing compact cooking stove, 1961: a speculative, not fully developed anticipation of the kitchen island.

5.21 Four-page folded brochure on the compact cooking stove, 1959, front page, left-hand inside page, back page. Halpern advertising agency, design by Ernst Hiestand, photographs by Friedrich Engesser.

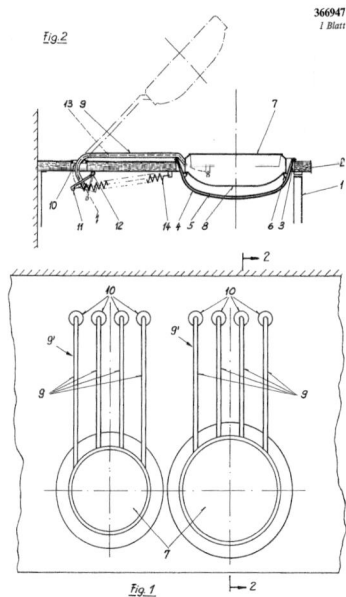

5.19

5.20

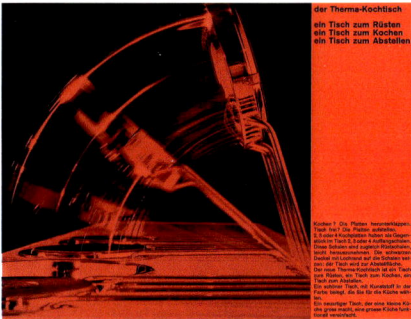

5.21a

5.21b

5.21c

therma

Norm-
Kombinationen
für die
moderne Küche

5.22a

Therma Normkombinationen

5.22b

5.22a Title page of a dealer catalog presenting
Therma's modular kitchen ensembles,
using the same photograph as in 5.3,
designed by Fritz Meyer-Brunner
and J. Wild, 1960. Illustration showing
exchangeability of the sub-units.
5.22b Back cover of the same catalog with
visual reference to the modular proportions 55/60/90.

at the time, the cooking stove was part of the apartment, whereas a free-standing refrigerator fell under the category of movable property. In German tenancy law, only the sink with water pipes was viewed as belonging to the apartment, while appliances tended to be classed as movable property and therefore less permanently fixed in place under a cover unit.[18] This issue reveals the close link between the assembly concept underpinning the installation frame and the idea of interchangeable elements, for which a binding system of dimensions was a prerequisite. Binding means valid in the long term, because any such norm-driven stipulation extends into the future. The SINK concept – relevant to Swiss manufacturers in the group – was also flexible as it allowed SINK products from various manufacturers to be interchanged.

However, in 1959 the SINK standard was still only at project stage behind the scenes. Therma caused quite a stir at the 1959 Mustermesse Basel with a thoroughly unusual and speculative cooking stove concept consisting of individually hinged hotplates, associated preparation bowls and circular cutting boards. The hotplates were attached to four pivoting brackets and could be folded up or down. The power supply for this compact *Kochtisch* (literally "cooking table") or "cooking stove on legs" (also referred to internally by the Board of Directors as a "stove with integrated bowls") was fed into the support tubes, which, according to the patent specification, were balanced with concealed tension springs. When the hotplates were folded down, these tubes also served as a rack to hold the hot pans. "A table for preparing, a table for cooking, a table for storing – that's the new Therma 'cooking table'," the leaflet proclaimed: in other words, several functions in one appliance. Even if questions as to the functionality of this concept persist – concerning, for example, the practical juxtaposition and sequential ordering of preparation and cooking – it was something of a futuristic manifesto. The Board of Directors responded to it with cautious sympathy and wary acceptance. The minutes of the meeting of the Board of Directors note, "Question about the success of the stove with bowls [compact cooking stove on legs]: It was a great attraction at the Muba trade fair. The public realized that Therma was again presenting something new. To date, we have received two orders for these stoves with bowls [compact cooking stove on legs]. We are not yet equipped for production."[19] The plastic surfaces of this cooking stove, which was available in light green or a muted red, also appealed to the general public. It must have been precisely the difference between this version and the erstwhile standard of the chrome-nickel steel cover – long regarded as the epitome of progress! – that determined reception at this point and was the imprimatur of updated modernity.

A few months later, Therma presented a variant of the compact cooking stove on legs as a free-standing unit – a precursor of today's kitchen islands! The firm had great expectations for this product, noting that "further demand for the kitchen ensembles that architects prefer can be expected in the 1960/61 financial year; Therma is recognized as the leading company in this field. Cookers on legs and ensembles with plastic covers are in great demand."[20] The argumentation for the cooking stove on legs in the public brochure (1959) was aimed as much at prospective buyers as at management, which was attempting to reduce manufacturing costs: "The cooking stove on legs with a work surface in rigid plastic can be adapted to the right dimensions for a kitchen much more easily than metal." These two proposals attracted attention and pointed the way forward for the new Therma, even if they did not gain majority support. (→5.20)

Just to recap: the basic features of the new standard household cooking stove had already been defined in 1958, but it was not ready for a market launch until 1961. Its formal character and appearance embodied a seminal new concept. It no longer had a front panel and the oven door extended

across the appliance's entire width (the oven itself was narrower on the inside). Horizontal joints across the front of the stove divided it into the switch panel at the top, the oven underneath and the appliance drawer at the bottom. Two diagonal, overlapping crease lines created trapezoidal surfaces, one on top of the other, extending from the base to the front of the counter as well as in the front of the counter, giving the front-facing side origami-like modeling. The slightly tilted control panel was ergonomically advantageous; it was delimited on both sides by beveled sections that connect the stove front laterally into the flat frontage of the adjoining units in a kitchen ensemble. The effect created by this modeling was iconic. The articulation of this stove front provided Therma with a brilliant and charismatic formulation for the cooking stove of the next decade. With this design language, the stove already carried the genome that would divide the standard ensemble along vertical lines. Photographer Alf Dietrich mentioned in conversation that, to the best of his knowledge, Hilfiker consulted Vivarelli on design issues from time to time – a plausible reference to the design for the trade fair stands, where this connection indubitably existed, as well as to the products, even if there is not any explicit evidence to that effect.[21] Was that also the case with this stove front? Or with other designs, such as the rotary switches and dials? I don't see any reason why not.

5.23 Commercial kitchens remained an important source of orders for Therma. Here the kitchen, with Therma appliances, in the clubhouse of the Swiss Re insurance company in Zurich (Architect Hans Hofmann), 1957/1958.

5.24 Some structural design problems had not yet been solved in the manually constructed prototypes, for example the hinge design. The refrigerator is the existing built-in model.

5.25 Mustermesse Basel stand, 1959: embryonic stage of the complete kitchen with spacious upper cabinet units (→ 5.18).

5.26

5.26 Stand at Comptoir Suisse in Lausanne,
September 1959: prominent presentation
in a tower display case for the small
appliances.
5.27 Public interest in the compact cooking
stove and Butterfly heating stove at the
Therma stand, Lausanne, 1959.

5.27

5.28

5.29

5.28 Therma stand at Olma in St. Gallen, October 1959. The fundamentally different conceptual and design stances of the "old," additive (right) and new, integrated (left) kitchen ensembles are clearly apparent.

5.29 In 1960 a 48-hour repair service was introduced and a series of new service vehicles were purchased for that purpose. Photograph by Friedrich Engesser.

5.30 The new free-standing cooking stove – here the Gamma model, identifiable by the two pilot lights – photographed in spring 1960 immediately before its much-acclaimed premiere in Basel.

5.30

179

There was now an unmistakable correspondence between product form and advertising language at Therma. 1959 was a very dynamic year that saw increasingly close collaboration with the Erwin Halpern advertising agency in Zurich. It is not clear when this began. In early 1958, Therma's outgoing President Hans Hefti had criticized earlier Therma advertising as being too conventional and called for a fresher image.[22] By 1959 a small number of brochures – already bearing the new wordmark – presented a novel concept featuring multicolored overprinted silhouettes of housewives cooking cheerfully.[(→5.5)] This looked more upbeat than the previous advertising campaigns but remained a transitional phenomenon. The Halpern agency was presumably already involved. Hilfiker wrote in an in-house paper at the end of October 1959 that it had proved unnecessary to switch to another agency. "We have to determine the attitude ourselves; the advertising consultant and his graphic designers can only express it. The previous firm of consultants, Halpern, proved to be perfectly capable of giving Therma the required new look in advertising."[23] Shortly afterwards, advertising changed course decisively, turning toward a different visual and verbal language, a completely new rhetoric. Talented young graphic designers and photographers worked for Halpern, for example graphic designers Ernst Hiestand, Fridolin Müller and Hans Heinrich Pidoux, and photographers Barbara Hilfiker, Alf Dietrich, René Beuret, Achille B. Weider and Willy S. Eberle, later Jürg Erni. Hilfiker had already worked with photographer Friedrich Engesser during his time at SBB, and Hilfiker's daughter Barbara had trained in Engesser's studio in Feldmeilen on Lake Zurich since 1957. The collaboration between Hilfiker, Engesser and the Halpern agency, and the pooling of all these creative resources, was to shape the entire decade. Even the early folding brochure for the cooking stove on legs (1959) is a far cry from the earlier pin-up-like advertising photography in its conception and charisma [(→5.21)] – as had been the case for the refrigerator just a year earlier. [(cf. 4.47)] Cooking is evoked here as a pleasurable experience, not through a direct depiction, but rather by means of a close-up with motion blur. This angle of presenting the appliances as if they were the accomplices of key figures was to become part of Therma's advertising language for years to come. However, this is only one side of the story, the "evocative" side. In contrast, objectified information was also required through systematically objectifying factual shots, almost exclusively with a frontal composition, deliberately lacking perspective, sometimes staggered one behind the other, with the camera view parallel to the object (the individual appliance, the kitchen ensemble or the built-in "wall" of the kitchen), often also shown vertically from above. Photo negatives from that era reveal that the cabinet modules, for example, were shot from a distance to minimize perspective foreshortening and parallax deviations, with a view to achieving the desired objectivity. The two-dimensional, abstract-looking photography combines within a composition with the advertisements' typographic elements. The object-based order (the ensemble, the front-facing view of the kitchen units) expressed by multiplying the modular dimensions is intimately linked to the advertising material's typographic structure. Journalist and former advertising expert Markus Kutter paid tribute to Hilfiker's advertising partner Erwin Halpern, whose clients included the then highly innovative Globus department store, remarking, "I've already mentioned the Globus people. Erwin Halpern belonged to this creative group; his specialty was exceptionally refined typography, generally a visualization of sometimes almost Japanese austerity and elegance."[24] Critic and designer Hans Neuburg presented Therma's latest projects in issue 9 (1961) of the trilingual avant-garde trade journal *New Graphic Design*, published in Zurich, under the title "Werbung und Grafik" ("Advertising and Graphics"). Two years later, in issue 15 (1963) of the same magazine, Neuburg addressed the connection between typography and visual language at Therma in some detail. "The tide of evolution that has carried advertising design aloft may also have engulfed designers. At all events, during the same period we recognize in them a growing interest in the formal styling of their products, and to some of them the perfection

5.31

5.31   Erwin Halpern advertising agency, "cook-
        ing stove campaign" (in-house designa-
        tion) in spring 1961. The four full-page
        advertisements, placed in rapid succes-
        sion in the Swiss daily press, became
        renowned internationally as part of
        advertising history.

5.32

5.33

5.34

[→ D]

"Mr. Hilfiker then explained the construction principles of the new Therma kitchen, as represented by two examples in the exhibition. He illustrated the importance of the new hinge sets that were created here in order to enable this simple structure and rationalize the production of components.

In addition to these two kitchens, some of the many possible ensembles combining kitchen units were illustrated and a number of components shown that represent the variety of kitchens under development. One of these is a built-in 115-liter refrigerator, which can be manufactured much more cheaply than the previous R 9 type. With a larger capacity and lower price, it should also offer better refrigeration quality. Mr. Hilfiker intends to design the entire range of refrigerators on the basis of the complete kitchen and only offer models that are not designed for built-in installation if they can be derived from built-in elements. This policy should make it possible for Therma to regain its own 'distinctive look' on the refrigerator market. [...] The Board of Directors applauded the demonstration." (28)

5.32 The striking 1961 stand at Mustermesse Basel (from *New Graphic Design*, no. 15, March 1963).

5.33 The Delta combination stove as a mix of a narrow (420 mm) and standard (550 mm) stove: the modernized successor of the venerable upper-class cooking stove. The cover panel is formed as a single piece, the bases are divided.

5.34 The cover panel of a Delta cooking stove in the photo studio. The camera angle looking straight down at the object – a hallmark of 1960s progressive, abstract object photography – always poses a photographic challenge.

of configuration has become an important object consciously sought." That was doubly true for Hilfiker – also because, as a design-conscious engineer, he accorded advertising a degree of importance it had previously lacked at Therma. Neuburg went on to say, "This endeavour presupposed a method of presentation which, in contrast to the popular conception of propaganda as persuasion, would give reliable information."[25] While we can see what he means, it is nonetheless obvious that even the most factual advertisement is an expression of a wish to catch the eye of the target audience.

In the fifty-fourth annual report to the shareholders in 1960/61, the firm's senior executives recounted Therma's regained leadership in the sector with palpable pride. "At the 1960 Mustermesse, we showed thirty-one of the units Therma has available today, from which the customer can choose to compile a Therma kitchen ensemble; note that subsequent replacements and additions are also possible. This allows scope to take account of individual wishes and varying comfort requirements to a large extent. [...] Introducing plastic outer covers within which stainless steel sinks can be inserted and further development of the cooking stove on legs led to orders from circles with an avant-garde approach to kitchen design. [...] In advertising, the aim was to create a uniform and characteristic line for Therma. The logo introduced two and a half years ago is proving impressive."[26]

In December 1960, Hilfiker was able to present the Board of Directors with a plethora of projects ready for production. These included the new household cooking stove as a differentiated range with various comfort levels in a standard width and a narrow version, the automatic infusion filter coffeemaker and the table-top hotplate set, whose practical features were listed in detail by Ruth Marti, who took the minutes: "1. Operation with only one hand; 2. Effortless simultaneous grasping of two hot plates; 3. Better energy yield; 4. Shorter heating time with a smaller number of plates; 5. No fixed construction size up to the maximum number of plates (plates can be bought in gradually); 6. More suitable for household use (gift items); 7. Significantly lower price; 8. Less space required."[27] Apart from the head of the canteen, management secretary Ruth Marti was the first woman at Therma to be mentioned by name; she appeared repeatedly in the documents. The minutes of the 342nd meeting of the Board of Directors in December 1960 include her detailed summary of Hilfiker's presentation to senior management of the "design principles of the new Therma kitchen." The recently introduced hinge design was explained, as was the concept underlying the new refrigerator range.[28] [→ D] The level of detail and precise eloquence in the minutes was a first; this reflected Hilfiker's efforts to be guided by a clearly outlined program of conditions (to use Hilfiker's terminology; today we would speak of specifications) when developing a new appliance. The advertising material was also characterized by this concern.

The systematic organization of the new cooking stove range included differentiation according to comfort levels, i.e. equipment variants: alpha (normal comfort level), beta (additionally with two rotating spits in the oven), gamma (elevated, the latest special features, light switch). There were also two lines: narrow with an internal oven width of 32 cm and standard width with a 40-cm-wide oven for the 55 cm module. In addition to these six models, a narrow and a normal-width oven could be combined in the two levels, delta B (for example, for "small guesthouses") and delta C (for "top-notch comfort"). These two luxury models had separate plinths but an overlapping top plate and were only available as free-standing models. They were therefore the refined, updated form of the earlier upper-class cooking stoves. The stand design at the 1961 Mustermesse Basel presented a mise-en-scène of this system of variants, which was nothing less than a well thought-out taxonomy, with photographs suspended from the ceiling, turning the planimetric plate images into an effective graphic eye-catcher. (→5.32)

36

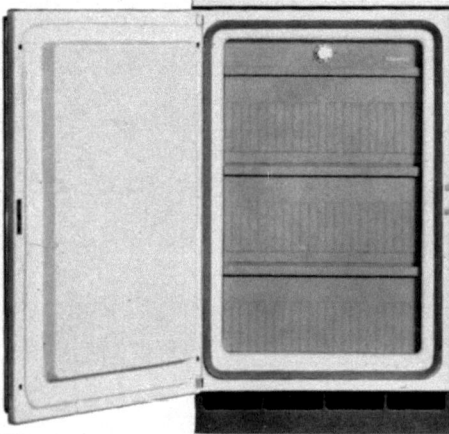

37

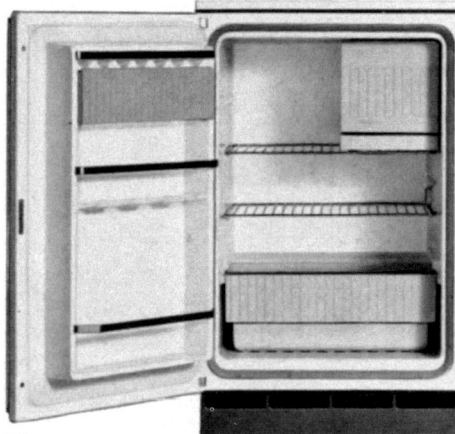

38

5.35

am heissesten
Tag
des heissesten
Sommers

Wäre der kommende Sommer
der heisseste des Jahrhunderts, und Sie
öffnaten am heissesten Tage des
heissesten Sommers Ihren Kühlschrank,
dann müsste alles darin frisch und
verwandfrei gekühlt sein, die Schubladen
voller Eiswürfel und kein Reststück
einer Speise verdorben. Wäre dieser
Kühlschrank ein Therma, dann könnten Sie
ein kühles Glas haben und sich
beglückwünschen, den Kühlschrank mit
so noch bemessener Kompressor-
leistung gewählt zu haben. Sie würden sich
freuen über Ihren guten Schweizer
Kühlschrank, Ihren komfortablen Therma.

Mit diesem Bild, mit diesem Text werben
wir in Tageszeitungen für die drei Therma-
Modelle zu 150, 180 und 265 Liter
Inhalt. Profitieren Sie von dieser Werbung
für den Schweizer Kühlschrank, zeigen
Sie den Therma-Kompressor-Kühlschrank.

Therma AG, Schwanden/GL. Büros
in Zürich, Bern, Basel, Lausanne, Genf

therma

5.36

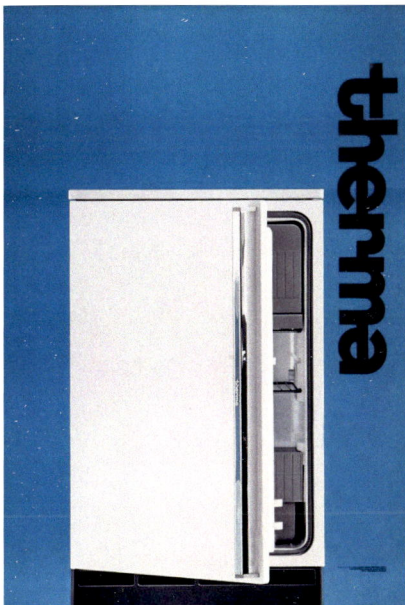

therma

5.37

5.35   1961 Mustermesse Basel: introduction
        of the new refrigerator concept with
        harmonized chilled compartments with
        115-liter capacity for the built-in dimen-
        sions 90/55/60: standard refrigerator
        and freezer compartment side-by-side.
        Or one above the other. The latter can
        be interpreted as a step towards the ver-
        tically arranged fitted kitchen with a flat
        wall-like frontage (from *New Graphic
        Design*, no. 15, March 1963).
5.36   Advertising for refrigerators, probably
        1960. The witty brainwave of the Halpern
        advertising agency for an outdated
        product. From a scrapbook containing
        ads in the Therma archive.
5.37   Hans Heinrich Pidoux / Halpern advertis-
        ing agency, poster in B4 format, for the
        refrigerator with the thinner, supposedly
        higher performance insulation, 1966.

For the stove's market launch in spring 1961, the Erwin Halpern agency came up with a campaign that has gone down in international advertising history. In a rapid succession of advertisements in daily newspapers, the cooking stove was depicted along with its transport packaging – which had its own typographical design, too. Initially shown still completely covered, the appliance gradually became visible as the packaging was torn open. Playing with the audience's attention like this was a novel way to involve the general public. Halpern described this idea for launching a symbolically new product to his international colleagues, entitling his presentation "New Manufacturing Programme and Publicity Campaign." "The change-over to a new manufacturing program involves more than technical adjustments. The new mental concept which goes into these novel articles of daily use is sensed in all the products. The gradual introduction of these novelties will be initiated by publicity for the new Therma Stove. Accordingly this assumes additional significance. It is designed not only to introduce the first item of a new production program, but at the same time, to indicate the direction from which further Therma products may be expected."[29] These considerations were published in 1963 in the aforementioned issue 15 of *New Graphic Design* which addressed Therma, its products and its public presentations in great detail.

In this context, the Halpern agency's advertisement from around 1960 for a free-standing refrigerator is amusing. The ad did not depict the new refrigerator because it was still being developed but showed the previously advertised version, which is unmistakably from the era to be left behind, as a boldly abstracted line drawing; meanwhile, the housewife's enthusiasm was conveyed by means of a photograph.

The motto for the stand at the 1961 Mustermesse was "Therma – It's All New." The cooking stoves were ready for production. Other innovations presented, such as blocks bringing together multiple appliances (ensembles), a full-scale kitchen, the table-top refrigerator as a single and double model, built-in ovens, the electric filter coffeepot and the table-top hotplate set were not yet ready and had to be produced as prototypes, with all the effort that entailed.[30] An entire kitchen with wall cabinets and modular cabinets was even presented in photographs for the 1961 Muba brochure and labeled as "made from prefabricated elements." This concentration of so many trend-setting appliances underlined the company's new dynamism with great vitality.

The structural engineering group faced the major task of developing the standard kitchen ensemble design concept consistently, in terms of its structural design and production, to ensure it reached serial production maturity. The modular dimensions of 550/600/900 mm were established. In addition, the ensembles had standardized vertical divisions; the total height (900 mm) minus the front of the cover (35 mm) minus the plinth height (105 mm) gives a usable height of 760 mm. This measurement divided by 6 gave rise to the vertical unit of measurement of 126.6 mm – the standard height for a drawer, factoring in a narrow gap between the drawers or between the latter and the door leaves. The front panel with the switches on the new cooking stove was also 126.6 mm high. The regularity that emerges from this new set of dimensions becomes apparent on photographs of the new standard ensemble as a reliable ordering system. An interesting point concerning the construction of the metal frontage is that the narrow vertical gap between the doors required a special design for the hinge to align its axis of rotation with the outer edge.[31] The hinge thus remained invisible from the outside. A project version of this kind of complete kitchen was actually built at the 1962 Mustermesse – in other words, before the structural possibilities for manufacturing it had been created.

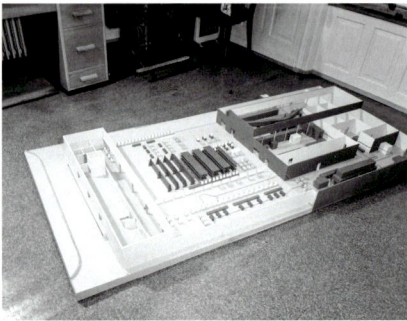

5.38

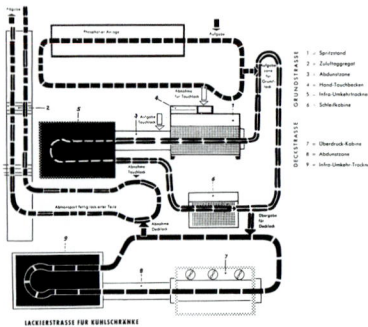

5.39

5.40

5.38 Study model of the factory extension, including the production hall with its sawtooth roof and the multi-story building, 1960. The enameling plant is recognizable, along with the preliminary arrangement of the drying tunnels and machines.
5.39 Diagram with the transport systems for refrigerator manufacture in the extended production facility.
5.40 The steel skeleton of the production hall during construction, probably 1962. The multi-story building behind it has already been constructed.
5.41 New drying tunnel of the painting plant, 1963.
5.42 Switch panels heading to the enameling tunnel furnace.
5.43 New system to transport components heading to the drying tunnel in the remodeled enameling plant. Two drying tunnels are visible in the background.

The aim was to start real-world production of this comprehensive new product concept. In spring 1961, the question of a new factory extension between the enameling plant and the Erlenhof center arose. An extension was needed to enable the requisite increase in output by operating on an industrial manufacturing scale ("from prefabricated elements," as the advertising promised). Hilfiker had already outlined the urgent need for a reorganization in an exposé from late October 1959. The complicated storage conditions in Schwanden were a major source of losses and the standard of transport rationalization at Therma was thus alarmingly low. Anticipating consistently strong demand for kitchen ensembles, it was self-evident to Hilfiker to promote construction of an extensive new building between the enameling plant and Erlenhof; he outlined its main features, noting that "a ground-floor assembly hall (sawtooth roof) would have to accommodate the assembly of all bulky equipment, such as sub-units for kitchen ensembles, ensembles per se, stoves and refrigerators. A basement level of this production hall is intended as temporary storage for the components of these appliances, which would mainly be stored unfinished before undergoing surface treatment in the course of call-off assembly either in the enameling plant or in a new paint shop to be built behind the enameling plant."[32] The following year, young architect Felix Schmid from Rapperswil worked closely with Hilfiker on the building project. The plans envisaged a ground-floor assembly hall with five sawtooth roofing sections and a four-story building, its narrow side facing Sernftalstrasse, and basements beneath the entire construction. Reflecting the remit Hilfiker had previously identified, the design involved comprehensively redefining the production choreography and the way in which production resources were organized. The principal aim was to improve productivity, with particular importance accorded to the mechanical transport equipment, especially conveyor chains with workpieces suspended from them. Total costs of almost six million CHF were envisaged for the construction project, which was a considerable degree of risk. In discussions at the time, Commercial Director Walter Baur argued for more specialization and greater sophistication within the existing product ranges. Wilhelm Bänninger, on the other hand, advocated Hilfiker's approach and called for surprising new developments. "The real art is to have people at the top who can intuit ahead of time what the market needs, create appropriate structural designs and manufacture them cheaply. [...] It is not about specializing within the framework of our [existing] product ranges; instead we will have to constantly identify new needs and pave the way for them."[33] Only one member of the Board of Directors argued against the need for growth and called for turnover to be kept to 15 to 18 million CHF. However, having appraised future prospects as favorable, the Board of Directors managed to consent to the construction project ("We are faced with an either-or choice"), as a "no" would have signified despondency rhetorically and was therefore not an option. The mentality of that era called for the courage to grow.[34] The aesthetically appealing new building was put into operation in September 1963 and signaled that it was a symbol of a company whose program and corporate identity stood for technological innovation, social progress and consistent visual modernity. Compared to the extremely brief planning phase and construction period of all previous factory expansions, this latest round took longer: almost two and a half years from the decision of the Board of Directors to completion. This can be read as a direct correlation with the incomparably greater complexity of the latest planned expansion, which also involved far-reaching restructuring of the manufacturing processes and thus the demanding design of a future-proof production facility. Hilfiker shouldered this task with great dedication. In May 1963, Peter Hefti as Chairman of the Board of Directors thanked Hilfiker "for your commitment to Therma, the success you have helped the company to attain and the marvelous manner in which you supported the planning and implementation of our building project."[35] This was Therma's last major construction project in Schwanden; the building stock there has

5.41

5.42

5.43a

5.43b

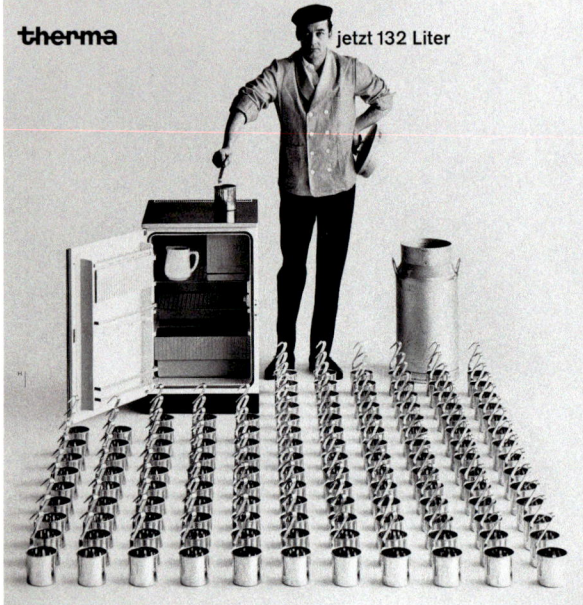

Er ist geräumiger geworden, weil die vorzügliche Isolation weniger Platz braucht. Weil die Isolation gut ist, sind die «Kälteverluste» gering. Weil die Kälteverluste gering sind, läuft der Kompressor nur in grösseren Zeitabständen. Weil der Kompressor stark ist, läuft er jedesmal nur kurze Zeit. Weil die Laufzeiten kurz sind, braucht er wenig Strom. Seine langen Stillstandzeiten sind seine grosse Leistungsreserve. Die setzt er ein, wenn Sie den Schrank korbweise mit marktwarmer Ware füllen, wenn Sie an tropenheissem Tag rasch Eis und Glace wünschen

Das macht diesen Kühlschrank so gebrauchstüchtig.

Wenn Sie zudem die komfortable Innenausstattung beachten: die vielseitig und voll ausnützbare Füllung, das geräumige, abgeschlossene Tiefkühlfach mit besonderem Tablar für Eiserzeugung, den grossen Milchkasselplatz, das verstellbare Tablar, die grosse, glasgedeckte

Gemüseschublade, die richtig plazierte Beleuchtung – dann haben Sie den Schweizer Kühlschrank Therma bereits gewählt.

Dann wollen Sie nur noch sagen, in welcher Farbe Sie das solide, säure- und hitzebeständige Trachtblatt wünschen: schiefergrau, weiss, mit Leinen- oder Teakmuster – und ob die Türe links oder rechts aufschwingen soll.

Der vorteilhafte Preis: Fr. 498.–. 5 Jahre Therma-Garantie. Dieses Modell ist wie jeder Therma-Kühlschrank auch als Einbaukühlschrank lieferbar.

Jetzt im Fachgeschäft erhältlich. Prospekt und Bezugsquellennachweis durch Therma AG, Schwanden GL, Börse und Ausstellungen in Zürich, Bern, Basel, Lausanne, Genf.

der Therma-Kühlschrank
ist (innen)
grösser geworden...

therma

jetzt 132 Liter

5.44

Therma–Kühlschränke
kühlen komfortabel

therma

5.45

[→ E]

"When creating these new devices, we took care from the outset not to design them as individual pieces, but as elements of an organized whole. [...] By using a benchmark measurement for the apparatus and the other components, we created the basis for industrial production, which was our aim from the beginning. It had to be housed in new buildings. Achieving uniformity in terms of the function, construction and design of our products and our information activities is one of the basic concerns of our management. Our products should serve people; however, we want to manufacture them to ensure that they continue to fulfill this role for a long time and design them to ensure that using them is enjoyable. We design our advertising according to these principles, which should primarily inform, yet may also be visually appealing." (38)

since reflected the architectural-historical development of half a century of industrial construction.

Back to 1961. Following on from the cooking stoves, which attracted a great deal of attention and enjoyed rapid sales success, the next issue to address was refrigerators; here the previous model range was considered outdated, too expensive and no longer competitive. Offering scaled models of different sizes, as Therma had been doing for thirty years, was no longer viable, in the light of the notion of a modular construction kit. Hilfiker opted for a radical solution: the refrigerator as a standardized cooling unit with a capacity of 115 liters as the starting point, with one, two or more such units incorporated into the kitchen ensemble. (→ 5.35) The difference lay in their cooling capacity: some configurations had only a ribbed or louver-finned cooling system, with a small refrigerator compartment, others had a wide freezer compartment or were provided as a complete freezer and refrigerator configuration. The full-height handle strip on the otherwise smooth white front was a clear marker. The refrigerators now featured a door with internal compartments as if this were self-evident, incorporating a vacuum-formed plastic inner shell and a magnetic closure device in the surrounding rubber profile – both standard international solutions by this point. [36] Hilfiker was willing to accept that each cooling compartment needed its own electrical cooling unit with this concept. He hoped to be able to offset the additional cost through more consistent industrialized production.

The cooling compartments could be arranged side by side or stacked one on top of the other, which consequently led to the standard ensemble being extended vertically. This meant the refrigerator could be raised to a more convenient height. This extension of the standard ensemble concept was also based on the same set of reference measurement units, with vertical 126.6 millimeter increments. That allowed for a superstructure of one, two or more units to the left or right of the ensemble, as well as a row of wall unit modules, each 55 cm wide and 33 cm deep, at a distance of four vertical modules (51 cm) from the worktop. (→ 5.47) The former stand-alone kitchen dresser was now obsolete. An extractor fan above the stove was available from around 1965. That meant Therma had arrived at the idea of the complete kitchen. If the playing field was already so well thought out, why not separate the oven from the hob and raise it to a convenient height, too? That was also an appealing solution. However, these arrangements amplified one disadvantage that had apparently hardly bothered anyone since the early 1950 ensembles: the frequent proximity of refrigerator and oven, which was thermally very unfavorable. Although avoidable in principle, it is also documented in countless advertising photos. (→ 5.51) Increasing the usable volume of a chilled compartment from 115 to 132 liters in 1964, which was made possible by deliberately reducing the wall thickness (allegedly possible thanks to a higher specific insulation value), did not make the problem any less acute. [37]

5.44 The spatial capacity of domestic refrigerators was increased in 1964 from 115 to 132 liters by reducing the thickness of the walls. Photograph by Jürg Erni from the Halpern advertising agency. The supposed milkman is said to have actually been a barman in the famous Kronenhalle in Zurich. The image was also shown as a cinema advertisement.

5.45 "Therma refrigerators' cooling comfort." Poster made up of 3 Weltformat sheets (F12), in total 128 × 273 cm, for the new refrigerator in 1963, design by Hans Heinrich Pidoux from the Halpern advertising agency. It was recognized as one of the "most beautiful Swiss posters" by the Department of Home Affairs in 1963.

Hilfiker gave a concise summary of the efforts up to that point in the management magazine *Betriebsführung*. "In creating these new appliances, care was taken from the outset to design them not as individual devices, but as elements within an organized whole." [38] [→ E] Stand-alone appliances were now derived from the built-in modules, whereas previously the inverse had applied. He went on to note that "the markedly trade-oriented character of the old business was difficult to reconcile with production that was conceived in purely industrial terms." [39] The new conceptual basis for this "organized whole" – and this is the fundamental difference between previous practice and the firm under Hilfiker's leadership – was the comprehensive matrix that linked a geometric system of dimensions to a set of deliberately selected options for structural design, installation techniques and operation.

5.46

5.47

5.48

5.49

5.46   Model of a complete kitchen, complemented by stand-alone models, not dated (ca. 1964): symbolic representation of the sub-units' modularity and interchangeability. The concept of interchangeable cabinet modules meant they needed to be fitted with double doors. If sliding doors had been used, the sub-units would have needed to be connected as pairs, which would have limited the system's variability (→ 4.52).

5.47   The newly fitted-out Therma exhibition space in Basel in October 1962. The complete kitchen was launched on the market for detached houses and apartments.

5.48   The photographic technique deployed here entails a small degree of parallax, a slight perspectival foreshortening; that means that the camera must be located some distance away from the subject. Draft version for the 1963 complete kitchen catalog.

5.49   Friedrich Engesser, cooking scene in the studio. We believe that there is hot oil in the deep fryer.

5.50   Scale drawing of a fitted kitchen with a length of 7 ½ units, with extractor hood, August 1964. A drawing and list of parts was produced for every kitchen ordered.

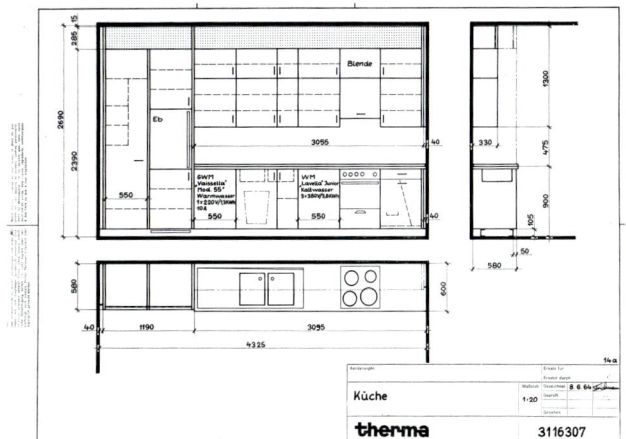

5.50

At Expo 64, the Swiss National Exhibition, held in Lausanne, Therma presented its new holistic standardized kitchen concept and collected data and opinions from the public using a questionnaire. The overarching framework was conveyed in the title "We plan and build for the future" in the exhibition sector "L'art de vivre / Living happily and meaningfully," directed by Tita Carloni, an architect from Ticino. Therma exhibited the prototype of another new show kitchen. Its spectacular eye-catcher was the foldaway cooktop; double, triple or multiple iterations of this appliance were envisaged as replacing a conventional cooking stove when the oven was built into the cabinets. This was a simplified (i.e. more practical) version of the futuristic hob from five years earlier. Therma had the innovation patented immediately before Expo 64 opened. The questionnaire clearly focused on this spectacular innovation in order to ascertain whether it was well accepted, particularly after the less than encouraging overall experience with its more radical predecessor. The MAYA formula coined by Raymond Loewy in the USA (*Most Advanced Yet Acceptable* – the quest to find the point at which fascination tips over into incipient aversion) had also arrived in Schwanden. The hinged cooktop quickly developed into a successful product full of character, even in the somewhat later version as a portable table-top hotplate. The Megastat hotplate with the temperature sensor in the middle oozed technical finesse. Once again, it is striking to note how enthusiastic Therma was at the Expo about using plastic-coated wood panels (brands such as Textolite, Kelco, Resopal) and how pointedly it distanced itself from chrome steel covers; in this context, Hilfiker pronounced a little later that "in fact, women's perception of materials has no affinity with bare steel, in terms of appearance, touch or sound."[40] A somewhat contradictory statement, as all the other surfaces in this complete kitchen set were made of metal.

There was broad recognition of the way in which the concept of the standard ensemble was expanding and moving toward a complete standardized kitchen, also reflected in rapid sales success. Hilfiker informed the Board of Directors that the "breakthrough" nature of the change in demand, which had switched from kitchen ensembles to complete kitchens, had been unexpected. Many architects were now requesting quotes only for complete kitchens when working on large-scale developments.[41] To call a spade a spade, this meant that the most recent new building in Schwanden was already too small for the scale of production. Laying the groundwork to respond to demand for complete kitchens, Therma looked around for suitable options and rented a factory complex in Rupperswil, Aargau. In addition to manufacturing the kitchen ensembles, the appliances were also produced in Schwanden. The 1964/65 annual report noted with satisfaction that Therma's built-in appliances were also chosen by other kitchen manufacturers to incorporate into their carpentry-based designs due to their quality. "Relations with other manufacturers of built-in kitchens could be intensified, as more and more cooking stoves, ovens and refrigerators could be supplied to them for their wooden kitchen cabinetwork."[42] However, the situation rapidly turned on its head – as soon as the other kitchen manufacturers realized that Therma, once an appliance supplier, had now become a direct competitor in their traditional field. This led the Swiss kitchen manufacturers to more or less boycott Therma as a supplier of built-in appliances; they now opted to purchase appliances from other suppliers. That gave rise to a bitter and even enduring setback for Therma.

Even before this resistance had formed, Hilfiker wrote the publication *Der Weg zur Küche (The Road to the Kitchen)*, with the dedication "As a report addressed to their friends from Therma AG, Schwanden GL in spring 1965." The commemorative volume, designed with dignified simplicity by the Halpern agency, featured full-page photographs of Friedrich Engesser and Alf Dietrich, to which Hilfiker added brief comments. Citing company founder Samuel Blumer's bold optimistic faith in progress, the publication

5.51 Fitted kitchen, 5+2 modules long, with drainage tray, cookplates, two extractor hoods and a wall-mounted oven. At Expo 64 a comparable kitchen tested public reactions to the surprising novelty of the built-in cookplates (bottom). Back wall clad with white enameled steel panels, half the width of a module (CH patent no. 424185, filed on June 16, 1965).

5.52 CH patent no. 433624, "Drainage device for sink," filed on November 18, 1965. For Hilfiker, the white enameled sieve base with a pattern of bumps embodied the category of a self-regulating minimal surface.

5.53 Sink with the drainage recess to the right, linked to each other by a drainage pipe, 1966. The inserted enameled sieve, along with the extensible tap fitting, made it easier to wash fruit and vegetables.

5.51

433 624
2 Blätter Nr. 1

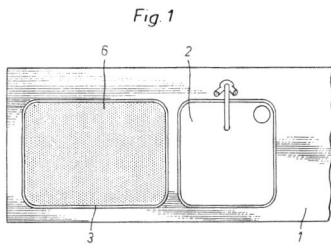

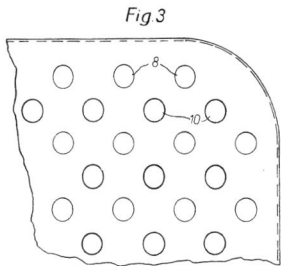

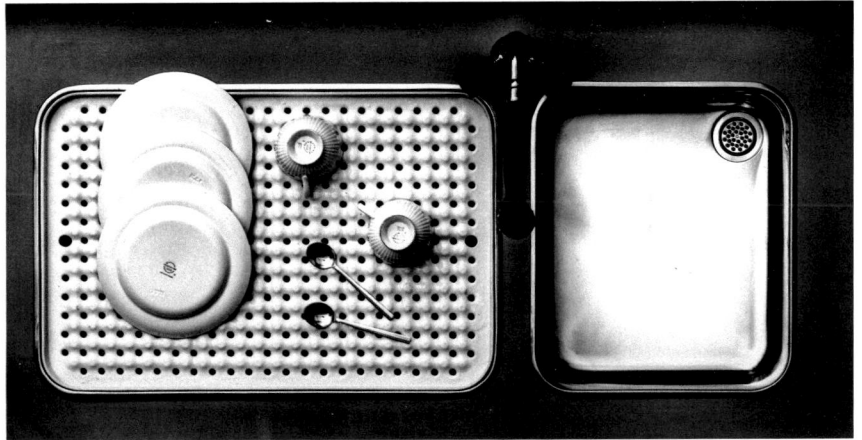

Fig. 1

Fig 3

5.52

5.53

193

5.54

5.55a

5.55b

5.54   An A-class kitchen: low-cost standard for mid-range aspirations, e.g., for large housing estates, photograph taken in early 1964.

5.55   Fire test in the open air during development of the ventilator hood, on the bank of the Sernf River, around 1965. Arnold Gugg is visible and, behind him, in a dark suit, Hans Hilfiker, both with their back to the camera. The identity of the other two men is not known.

5.56a

5.56b

5.57

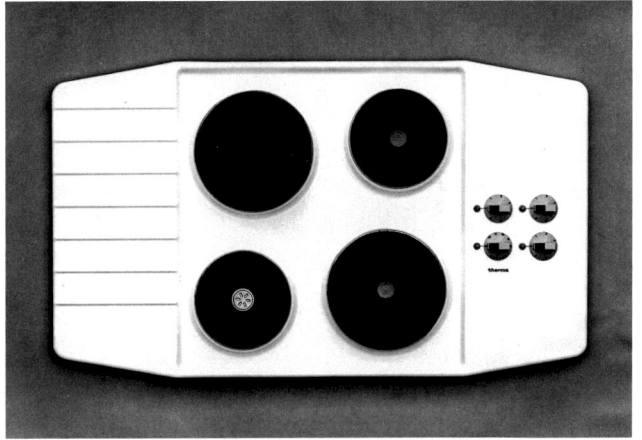

5.58

5.59

5.56a View of the pivotable cooktop, designed by Franz Kaltenbrunner in 1964, which had its market launch in 1966.

5.56b The pivoting mechanism is revealed when the cooktop is folded up.

5.57 A portable table-top hotplate, a variant of the foldaway pivotable hotplate introduced in 1966, here in the chromium steel version with the small (14.5 cm diameter) Megastat heating plate.

5.58 The Oktagon cooking recess, photographed vertically from above. The restrained height of just 4 cm when integrated into a wooden cover panel meant a drawer could be included below. Design by Horst Müller, a designer from Ulm (CH patent no. 423154, "Wooden table panel with built-in cooking recess," filed on July 7, 1965).

5.59 Perhaps a by-product of Hans Hilfiker's technical imagination: ergonomically arranged filing cabinets and filing trays in the administration, 1965.
An experiment?

195

recalled the company's origins and the defining economic role for the local context of a company that was well aware of being at the forefront of development once again. Looking back to the earlier anniversary in 1957, Hilfiker wrote that the company, which had generated so many impetuses, "has since that point probably taken the greatest step forward in its developmental history." He noted that the manufacturing program had been completely overhauled, ensuring that it "did not simply replace previous structural designs with functionally and formally advanced versions, but also coordinated everything conceived to serve the household kitchen, harmonizing its principal dimensions as well as its design concept and tone to ensure that a 'melodious' whole is always created however the various elements are combined. In other words, a stove or a refrigerator, a boiler, a wall-mounted oven, or any of the many cupboard components are not objects in their own right, but are instead consistently conceived with a view to joining them together to form a complete kitchen. They are conceived as interchangeable parts of a whole that aims for good design."[43] The publication, in a compact square format, depicted the work processes involved in the production of individual parts in a not strictly linear sequence through forming, surface treatments (degreasing bath, base and top enameling, drying furnace), intermediate storage and phases of assembly. It is no coincidence that the first image in the series shows the freshly deep-drawn, faceted switch front of a stove, complete with switches, in a worker's hands. One of the last photos depicts a complete mono-front kitchen (eight modules in a row) with two cooking stoves, two extractor hoods, two refrigeration compartments and an oven in three high top-mounted cabinets. There was no dishwasher at the time, but once again the oven and refrigerator were next to each other. Modular enameled metal panels covered the wall between the worktop and the cupboard compartments with the extractor hoods. They were developed to do away with the need for application and grouting of ceramic tiles. Kitchen frontage that is sixteen vertical modules high, including the plinth, therefore ends at a height of 2.14 m above floor level. A pressed-wood panel made of perforated Pavatex adds the finishing touch and extends up to the ceiling. Kitchen cabinet doors and paneling like this were installed and photographed in the basement in Schwanden for advertising purposes. Photographers Alf and Barbara Dietrich report that they must have spent around thirty days a year working in that in-situ photo studio.[44]

The standard-based kitchen, Therma Schwanden's best-selling product, was developed with the construction industry in mind, which had been a flourishing sector for years. The Swiss government responded to the excellent economic situation and the ensuing inflation with measures to cool down the economy. The immediate consequence was a slowdown in orders in 1965/66. Therma's move toward integrated kitchen construction meant that it was now more closely intertwined than other companies with the construction industry and it felt the painful impact of these changes. The prevailing mood also shifted as a result of high cost pressure. Rising wages due to competition and inflation and ever more acute competition led to a deterioration in business results from 1966 onwards. Therma's small appliances were often too expensive for export, even if the public liked them: the table-top portable hotplate, the new cylindrical coffee filter machine (from 1966) with its modern shape and ingenious combination of handle, spout and pressure switch lock at the top of the handle, which was young technician Hans Aebli's brainwave. 1966 also saw the introduction of the Oktagon hob; sunk into a recess in the plastic-coated work surface, this was a thin, thermally well-insulated metal panel in enameled sheet metal with three or four hotplates and work surfaces. At the same time, a horizontally positioned, drained drip tray was proposed for the other end of the worktop, for which Hilfiker had developed a perforated wave structure as the drainage base, corresponding to his preferred concept of minimal surfaces. Both were ingenious ideas, yet did not reach a wide audience. We

5.60 Cross-sectional drawing of a 6/12 filter coffee machine with its key component, the "valve handle," a brainwave of technician Hans Aebli (CH patent no. 483824, filed on February 18, 1969). The product was developed while Hans Hilfiker was at the helm.

5.61 In 1966 the 6/12 cylindrical filter coffee machine replaced the 1952 model. The pouring option was activated via a pushbutton on the upper side of the handle ("valve handle").

5.62 CH patent no. 384807, "Set of food warmer plates with heat accumulation and associated device for heating the plates and keeping them warm," filed on October 20, 1960.

5.63 Set of warming plates, square, the later variant based on the same principle, 1968.

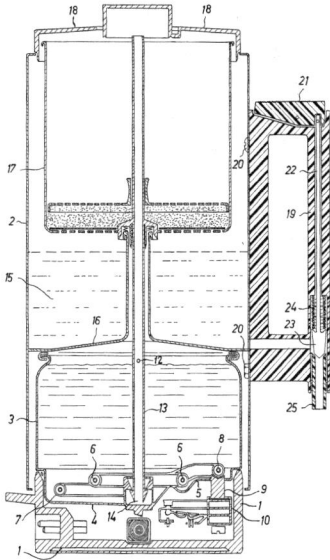

483 824
1 Blatt

5.60

5.61

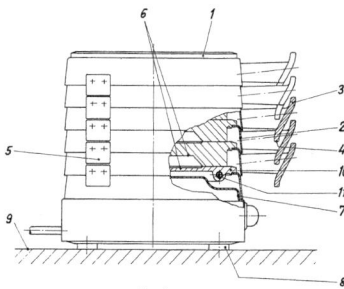

384 807
1 Blatt

Fig. 1

Fig. 2

5.62

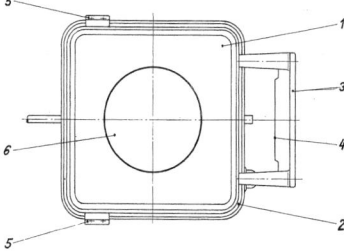

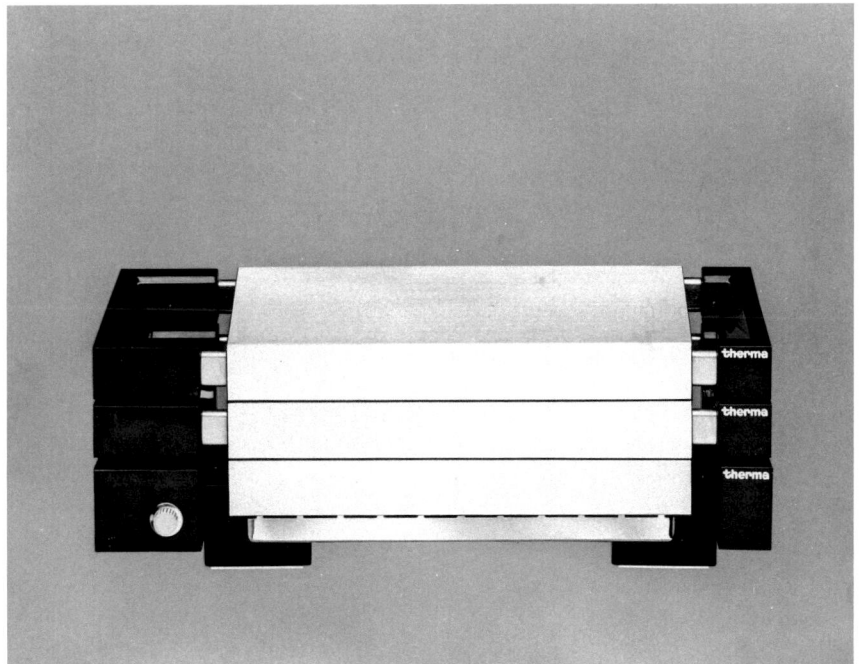

5.63

197

5.64a

5.64b

5.65

5.64 Kitchen with three built-in cookplates and in front of them a table-top hotplate. Below, a kitchen with eight modular units, here, too, with the rear and side walls in chipboard with a wood-look coating. This option was introduced shortly before Hilfiker's departure and essentially against his will.

5.65 Aerial view from the west with Schwanden and the Therma complex at the entrance to the Sernf valley, 1963.

can see how important the plastic-coated wooden worktable had become, in terms of both cost and design ideas. At the same time, it is apparent that the momentum of the early sixties' great awakening had stalled and change was underway. A shift in public taste was also discussed at a meeting of the Chairmen of the companies in the group, held in late September 1967 in Hilfiker's absence in Zurich at the premises of the main shareholder, Elektrowatt. "Demand for wooden cabinet doors and other surfaces seems to be spreading among customers and sales have long drawn attention to this. Mr. Hilfiker is now working on a design that will allow metal or wooden cabinet doors and paneling to be used as required. This should significantly strengthen Therma's position."[45] The latter assertion was not entirely inaccurate. However, it is doubtful that this development was a matter close to Hilfiker's heart. The idealistic space for innovations based on conviction had dwindled, precisely because competition in the industry was so great and because the economy had developed over the years from a supply-side to an increasingly demand-driven business. That meant that there was more room for preferences. Hilfiker's convictions included his rejection of a viewing window for the oven for physical and thermal reasons, unfortunately despite the public's receptiveness to the idea, sparked by market research. Was Hilfiker's rational concept not as irrefutable as it initially seemed? Little by little, doubts began to surface among the group's executives.

In February 1967, the dishwasher, the only missing link for the complete kitchen, was an important development topic. Hilfiker took the view that his production required a product that improved on those on the market. He believed that this approach would prove successful. A set of minutes report in this context that "a patent application has now been filed for a number of new products. The production will probably go to a group company, Mr. Hilfiker is thinking of Elcalor, which urgently needs new products. Hilfiker believes that the dishwasher concept is a contribution to progress, otherwise he would not make it. [...] The aforementioned machine is primarily a sheet metal product; all manufacturers buy in pumps and motors for it."[46] However, the problems that this dishwasher presented for Therma were different problems than for previous appliances and its development took a relatively long time. It was only one year later, in September 1968, with an unfavorable profit and loss account looming, that the Board of Directors was prepared to approve 195,000 CHF for construction of ten prototypes. In the meantime, Hilfiker's age (sixty-seven) had become an issue within the group's Management Board in view of his many responsibilities. He increasingly heard accusations that he had spent large sums of money on misguided projects, such as the 1965 rotating pan, a powerful grill for commercial kitchens. Although the few examples produced worked well, they were too expensive to sell. The whole industry felt the effects of the slowing economy with a decline in construction activity, especially of single-family homes. Therma was only able to pay a small dividend in 1967/68 and none at all in 1968/69. Hans Hilfiker was advised to resign from his position as Representative to the Board in order to save face, and did so, on October 1, 1968.

1 Cf. Max Bill, *Form. Eine Bilanz über die Formentwicklung um die Mitte des XX. Jahrhunderts* (Basel: Werner, 1952), p. 130. Also: *Hans Hilfiker. Ingenieur und Gestalter*, Schweizer Design-Pioniere series 1, exh. cat. (Zurich: Museum für Gestaltung Zürich, 1984).

2 Hilfiker's timetable reader, a mechanical projection device, was installed in Zurich's main station in the foyer adjoining the platforms and is said to have worked well. Cf. *Hans Hilfiker. Ingenieur und Gestalter*, pp. 36–37.

3 Alf Dietrich and Barbara Dietrich-Hilfiker in conversation with the author, July 2023.

4 VR-Protokoll [Minutes of Board of Directors meeting] 328, March 27, 1958, pp. 5–6. – GWA Elux B 2–1/3

5 CH patent no. 357526: "Einrichtung zum Aufstellen in Küchen," filed on March 5, 1958.

6 Brochure "Therma Norm-Kombination – Sie planen eine neue Küche: Wovon gehen Sie aus?" June 1960. – GWA Elux H 1–3/3

7 Message from Karl Keller's daughter Heidi Keller van der Kooij, June 2023.

8 VR-Protokoll 384, February 14, 1967, p. 9. – GWA Elux B 2–1/3

9 VR-Protokoll 330, June 25, 1958, pp. 6–7. – GWA Elux B 2–1/3

10 Hans Hilfiker, "Bericht des Delegierten," in: VR-Protokoll 331, November 11, 1958, pp. 3–5. – GWA Elux B 2–1/3

11 Ibid.

12 Ibid.

13 Ibid.

14 I owe this reference to Jürg Brühlmann, Lenzburg. Vivarelli also designed the brilliant Electrolux logo, the creation and geometric construction of which is documented in the September 1980 issue of Electrolux's in-house magazine ("Das Electrolux-Signet – Made in Switzerland," pp. 6–7). – GWA Elux K 4-1/1

15 VR-Protokoll 332, December 3, 1958, pp. 2–3.– GWA Elux B 21/3

16 VR-Protokoll 333, April 11, 1959, p. 2. – GWA Elux B 2–1/3

17 There is no explicit confirmation that Bellmann designed the handle. However, Hilfiker made a statement to that effect and it seems certain that Bellmann was involved. That probably also related to other Therma products such as the spray for the sink and the soap dish.

18 Cf. Christina Sonderegger, "Zwischen Fortschritt und Leerlauf: die genormte Küche. Anmerkungen zur Entwicklung der Schweizer Küchennorm," in: Klaus Spechtenhauser, ed., *Die Küche. Lebenswelt – Nutzung – Perspektiven* (Basel: Birkhäuser, 2006), pp. 94–111.

19 VR-Protokoll 334, May 27, 1959, p. 3. The photo archive contains several photos of kitchens of this type that were installed in various apartments. – GWA Elux B 2–1/3

20 VR-Protokoll 336, October 29, 1959, p. 5. – GWA Elux B 2–1/3

21 Alf Dietrich and Barbara Dietrich-Hilfiker in conversation with the author, summer 2023.

22 Memorandum from Hans Hefti-Haab, January 3, 1958 – Hefti Family Fonds, Estate of Dr. Hans Hefti-Haab, Schwanden (Glarus South District) [hereinafter: Hefti Family Fonds], "Organisatorisches" file

23 Hans Hilfiker, "Therma und Therma-Konzern. Bericht an den Verwaltungsausschuss der Therma AG" (typescript, 49 pages), October 31, 1959, pp. 10–11. – Hefti Family Fonds, "Organisatorisches" file

24 Markus Kutter, *Abschied von der Werbung. Nachrichten aus einer unbekannten Branche* (Niederteufen: Niggli, 1976), p. 161.

25 Hans Neuburg, "Unity of Function, Construction, Design and Information (Illustrated by the example of Therma AG, Schwanden/ Switzerland)," in *New Graphic Design*, no. 15 (March 1963): 2–38, here p. 6.

26 54. Jahresbericht [Annual Report], 1960/61. – GWA Elux B 4–1/2

27 VR-Protokoll 342, December 6, 1960, p. 2. – GWA Elux B 2–1/3

28 Ibid., p. 3.

29 Erwin Halpern, quoted in: Neuburg 1963, p. 5.

30 VR-Protokoll 347, June 30, 1961, p. 2. – GWA Elux B 2–1/3

31 This was made possible by a small recess in the door leaf, thanks to which the axis of rotation virtually coincided with the exterior. A pivot axis inside the door leaf would have blocked the movement. See CH patent no. 380574: "Verstellbares Türscharnier," filed on December 6, 1960.

32 VR-Protokoll 343, March 21, 1961. – GWA Elux B 2–1/3

33 Hans Hilfiker, "Therma und Therma-Konzern. Bericht an den Verwaltungsausschuss der Therma AG" (typescript, 49 pages), October 31 1959, pp. 46–47. – Hefti Family Fonds, "Organisatorisches" file.

34 VR-Protokoll 343, March 21, 1961. – GWA Elux B 2–1/3

35 Letter from Peter Hefti to Hans Hilfiker, May 30, 1963. – Hefti Family Fonds, "Ing. Hilfiker" file.

36 There were various designs for the doors with compartments depending on the model.

37 In the freezer version, the insulation was more voluminous than in the other versions.

38 "Vom Einzelapparat zur ganzheitlich im Baukastenprinzip geplanten Küche. Ein Gespräch mit Herrn Hilfiker, Delegierter des Verwaltungsrates der Therma AG, Schwanden," in *Betriebsführung. Monatsschrift für Absatztechnik, Betriebsorganisation und Unternehmensführung*, no. 7 (July 1965).

39 Ibid.

40 Hans Hilfiker, "Apparateindustrie und Küchenbau," lecture in Montreux, 1967, p. 31.

41 VR-Protokoll 360, January 16, 1964, p. 5. – GWA Elux B 2–1/3

42 58. Jahresbericht, 1964/65. – GWA Elux B 4–1/2

43 Hans Hilfiker, *Der Weg zur Küche* (Schwanden: Therma, 1965) pp. 4–5.

44 Alf and Barbara Dietrich-Hilfiker in conversation with the author, July 2023.

45 Meeting of the consortium members at Elektrowatt Zurich, September 27, 1967 (W. Bänninger, Bergmaier, P. Hefti, Peyer, Graf, A. Heer). – Hefti Family Fonds, "Analysen F+E"

46 VR-Protokoll 384, February 14, 1967, p. 7 – GWA Elux B 2–1/3

5.66

5.67

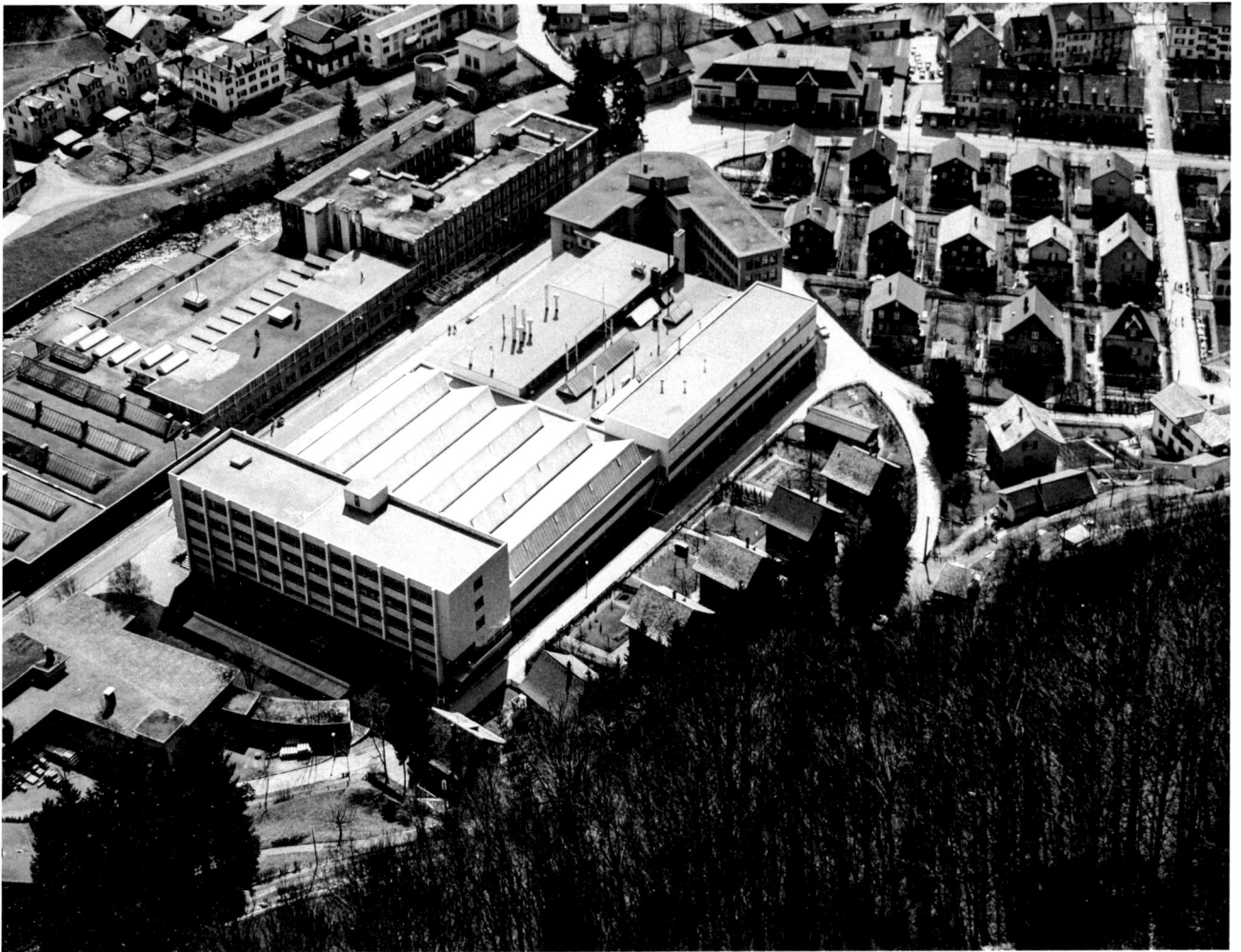
5.68

5.69

5.66 Fully equipped kitchen in an upper-class house: in a sense, an expression of Hans Hilfiker's efforts in a nutshell. On the left-hand side, there is even a built-in dishwasher – it is, however, a Hotpoint appliance, as Therma was still developing its dishwasher at this point, 1965.

5.67 Study of the front panel with switches, etc., for operation of an automatic dishwasher, around 1968. The market launch was four years later.

5.68 The Therma factory complex after the last extension in 1963.

5.69 Transport of Therma appliances. From Hans Hilfiker's 1965 publication *Therma – der Weg zur Küche*. Photograph by Friedrich Engesser.

201

6

The hall with a sawtoothed roof is the same as when it was inaugurated some fifteen years earlier, yet the photograph speaks to us in such a different tone! The activities underway in the hall have changed profoundly. The orderly arrangement of 1963 has given way to a dense juxtaposition of actions whose meaning is not really apparent. This is an image of transition: moving from the 1960s' indubitable confidence in progress to the 1970s' attempt to keep pace with the times. The photograph – a single negative in a transparent case – is not dated and provides no explanation as to why it was taken. It must be from sometime in the late 1970s. That was the period when Therma Schwanden manufactured only a few types of appliances – electric cooking stoves, dishwashers and extractor hoods – before it became a production site for Electrolux in 1979. In later years, after Electrolux's takeover at the turn of the century, reports indicate that the production lines were again very clearly organized and structured. That cannot be said of this earlier photograph. There seem to be only faint recollections at this point of the reasons why this building was originally constructed. Does that also hold true for the bustling figures it depicts? We do not know. Yet we can – must? – assume that the setup at that moment constituted a fitting motif to be recorded.

One particular difference compared to 1963 is the photographic equipment used and thus the specific status of the motif underlying the shot. Whereas the 1963 photograph involved a professional camera on a tripod, here a smaller 35 mm camera was used, most likely for a handheld shot. Was the idea simply to rapidly record the activities going on in the production hall? The photograph is not at all representational, but instead shows a location where something significant happened, yet with no hint of what exactly that might signify. What was happening in this image? We are confronted with an industrial-archaeology picture puzzle.

In the mid-1970s, Therma stopped manufacturing complete kitchens in Rupperswil and ensembles in Schwanden, shifting its focus to producing appliances, either as stand-alone units or for installation by other firms that manufactured and fitted kitchens. The 1963 ensembles are nowhere to be seen. However, no individual appliances are depicted in this image either.

Old office furniture has been repurposed, along with a work surface on trestles, with numerous wooden boxes behind it. Stacks of printed packaging boxes are visible, along with a makeshift structure as a support frame for a power cable in the foreground on the left, to assist

6.0   View into the production hall with its sawtooth roof in Schwanden, a snapshot that does not reveal anything specific as to why this scene was recorded. It is nonetheless a rarity, for there are no comparable photographs that could represent the last chapter (of Therma's history as an independent firm and of this book).

the worker in the white shirt with his activity. But what exactly is he busy with? At first glance, his workpieces might seem to recall the heating elements that the workers were holding in their hands in the photo from 1916, but it is now sixty years later. And what is the worker right behind him doing? That question also remains unanswered. The photograph's appeal stems from its truthfulness, as manifested in its spontaneity and the absence of any stylization; everything we see is related to the activities being pursued. What kind of activities? Is this a standard scenario or a special occasion?

One hypothesis: In summer 1978, the company newspaper mentioned the extensive remodeling project in the production facilities for what was then the beacon of hope, the newly developed Series 77 cooking stove. Much of the existing transport equipment had to be dismantled and reinstalled within a week. A "test carousel" for the stoves was installed as a new piece of equipment, the workstation under a polyhedral structure suspended from the ceiling that can be seen on the right-hand side of the image. This is where each cooking stove's heating performance was checked and certified. However, the image's dense structure makes it impossible to draw reliable conclusions about that kind of process. Does the photo perhaps depict the period in summer 1978 when equipment in the production facility was being dismantled and converted? The moment before the new cooking stove went into production? If so, that would have been a plausible reason for a snapshot like this at a turning point in the company's history. Be that as it may, the image is transitory and calls for a depiction of the changes in those years, because it is per se a reflection of everything that had changed at Therma in the last decade of its independence.

1969–1978

Dream Kitchen and Reality

New Emphases Thanks to Market Observation

In the years when Hans Hilfiker was at the helm, it had become clear that the dual workload involved in being operational manager for the Schwanden plant while also being responsible for the entire group was too demanding. Hilfiker had written to Therma President Peter Hefti-Spoerry in 1959, noting that he had come to a realization that it was only possible to a limited degree for duties in both fields – "the twofold problem of Therma/Therma Group" – to be addressed "in series in terms of the time frame."[1] However, tackling both areas simultaneously proved impractical; there was too much resistance, not to say too many contradictions between the ideal and reality. As already mentioned, Hilfiker, responding to the pressure of circumstances, had a version in wood developed for the kitchen cabinet doors and other paneling. It was not just management that had noticed "that demand for wooden cabinet doors seems to be spreading among customers," for "the sales department has been drawing attention to this for a long time."[2] Despite acknowledging Hilfiker's reaction, the sales team complained in its internal correspondence – unbeknownst to Hilfiker – about his tardy response. "If work on the new design had been started earlier and if it were thus already on sale today, that would probably also already have had an impact on the sales figures. [...] This appears to be just one example of a belated grasp of the market situation."[3] The new, affirmative view of the market set the tone for the coming decade.

After the Administrative Committee opted in 1968 to replace Hilfiker when he turned sixty-seven (referring to his employment contract from 1958), without consulting him at all, the group's senior executives hired a management consultancy firm to shed light on the group's structure as a conglomerate, which had become confusing. The aim was to arrive at a clear analysis of the structural problems and identify ways to overcome them. Half a dozen consulting firms were evaluated and the contract went to ICME (Industrial Consulting & Management Engineering Co.) in Zurich, founded by Henry E. Stettbacher, a graduate of the St. Gallen School of Management with several years of experience in the US. Stettbacher's remit was to "coordinate the activities of the various companies in the Therma Group and create an appropriate management organization structure to manage the group as a whole as well as the individual companies."[4] The main shareholder, Elektrowatt, whose Director Werner Lindecker was Vice Chairman of the Board of Directors (having succeeded Bänninger in 1969), described the assignment as conducting a "study of Therma AG and its subsidiaries" and specified the goal as "a new division of the product range between Therma and its subsidiaries."[5] One important question when ICME was hired was "does the proposed share-out of the product range allow for centralized development and design or would it be more appropriate to divide development work among the companies as a function of their product areas? Today, a central Research and Development department only exists in the organizational chart."[6] A central position for the Research and Development department, and his responsibility for it, played an important role for Hilfiker. In reality, however, Elcalor behaved autonomously to some degree, while Maxim even acted largely independently. In 1969, having analyzed all the companies in the Group and how they related to each other, ICME depicted them with the network planning technique that was just starting to emerge back then. The striking outcome of the 1969 analysis was end-to-end reorganization by structuring the group vertically. That entailed its division into four profit centers: Household Goods, Commercial Kitchens, Cooling and Heating/Industrial Supplies. From this point on, the entire group was called the Therma Group.

Vertical structuring was intended to eliminate overlapping product ranges within the group that had developed gradually over time, sometimes on an ad hoc basis, and that were now no longer welcome, and thus also to alleviate friction caused by divergent views or personal animosities. On the other hand, there was an explicit wish for cooperation between the profit

6.1 The logo introduced in 1970 for the whole group (Therma Group) with the red core for "heat" and the blue ring for "cold."

6.2 "Towards the Future," brochure with information about the newly configured Therma Group, 1970. The graphic demeanor highlights a sense of distancing from the Hilfiker years and gives an early hint of postmodernism. The Erwin Halpern advertising agency was still designing Therma's information material. Their tenure only came to a close in 1973.

6.1

In Richtung Zukunft

6.2

[→A]
"The three companies, Elcalor, Sursee-Werke and Therma, build appliances for kitchens in restaurants, hotels, canteens, hospitals and institutions. Each company can equip entire kitchens with appliances. All three companies have their own areas of specialization, which are constantly being expanded. The Sursee plant, for example, specializes in gas-, coal- and crude oil-fired systems. In addition to appliances, Elcalor also builds chrome steel equipment and sub-units to commercial catering standards. Therma specializes in electrical catering equipment. Each company carries out project planning, construction and installation independently. [...] Sursee-Werke, for example, supplies Pan Am, one of the largest airlines, with tilting frying pan sets heated with natural gas for two canteen kitchens in San Francisco and New York that cater for in-flight meals. [...] Therma and Elcalor can also boast significant installations, including the canteen kitchen system in the renowned Swiss Center in London, which was jointly implemented by the two companies." (9)

centers on substantive matters, for example production of certain units. The new term "profit center" indicated that each of these four pillars was intended to function without making a loss. Group Chairman Peter Hefti communicated this outcome to the staff of all group companies at the end of 1969, although he did not refer to "profit centers," but instead spoke of "four individual companies." That somewhat intimidating reference to profit centers was replaced throughout the group in summer 1970 by the term "division," a neutral and more innocuous expression.[7]

Specific divisions were assigned to each of the production sites:
– Household appliances and kitchens: Therma Haushalt (Household Goods), Schwanden
– Commercial kitchens: Therma with the Sursee plant as Therma Grossküchen (Commercial Kitchens) in Schlieren near Zurich
– and air conditioning equipment and systems: Therma Kälte (Cooling), Zurich
– Heating and industrial supplies: Elcalor Aarau
Together with a subsidiary in Austria (Volta, Bregenz) and in Germany (Therma Hergensweiler, Lindau), the various divisions formed the Therma Group, managed from Schwanden, which continued to be the parent company.

One consequence of this reorganization was the launch of a group newspaper entitled *Therma – Information*, intended for reports from employees of all divisions for their peers, in order to forge a sense of unity within the broader group.[8]

A new logo was also selected for the Therma Group: the letters "th," drawn from Carlo L. Vivarelli's tried-and-tested wordmark and arranged eccentrically in a red dot. As early as December 1970, a blue ring was added around the dot, symbolizing the themes of cold and heat; "th" could also be read as standing for "Therma Holding." Taking the Commercial Kitchens division as an example, the group explained the benefits of the revamped organizational structure, which made it possible for major orders to be handled either independently or cooperatively. Orders from Pan Am for catering equipment for the airline's canteen kitchens in San Francisco and New York, as well as an order for the canteen kitchen in the new Swiss Center London were mentioned with pride.[9] [→A] In citing these examples, the group was clearly keen to recall Therma's international reputation.

In October 1969, the group management addressed questions about Therma's positioning vis-à-vis technical progress, for example, "How does the stove's self-cleaning system make our lives easier?" Or, considering a broader framework, "Are trends moving away from complete kitchens to think in terms of 'wet rooms' [rooms equipped with a water supply] (kitchen plus bathroom)?"[10] The latter question concerned research and projects for large housing estates, specifically linking the kitchen and bathroom as part of building plans, for example in projects developed by Ernst Göhner AG, which had a long-standing, intensive business relationship with Therma. Prior to the 1974 economic crisis, estates built along these lines were often equipped with kitchens from Therma.[11] There were overlaps between fundamental concepts such as the plug-in principle[12] and material developments in the detailing, such as the introduction of catalytic self-cleaning household ovens.

Parallel to ICME's analysis work, a new operational manager had to be found for the group. Hilfiker's position was still vacant more than six months after he had left the role of Representative on October 1, 1968. An ad publicizing the job had been published in May 1969. Almost a year after Hilfiker's departure, forty-two-year-old engineer Robert G. Wimmer was chosen in September 1969, also with input from ICME. From then on, his workplace – and thus also the Therma Group's official headquarters – was in Zurich,

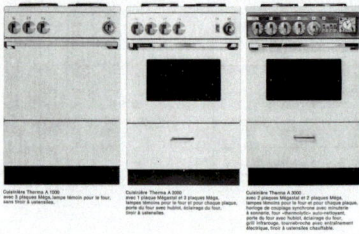

6.3a

6.3b

6.4

6.3 Brochures for the new 1000, 2000 and 3000 oven series, (top) initially still in the down-to-earth, objective style of the Hilfiker years, (bottom) somewhat "spruced up," both 1970. The oven in the basic 1000 model (left) did not have a viewing window.

6.4 "The new large-format family refrigerator," page in the brochure on the two-part fridge-freezer with a 160-liter refrigerator compartment and a 90-liter freezer compartment, 1971.

although it is unclear whether this was at his request or reflected the wishes of the Board of Directors.[13] During Hilfiker's time at Therma, the Schwanden plant, above all the Research and Development unit, had been the living heart of the company and Hilfiker had generally had less attention to spare for the other sites. In coming years under Wimmer, that situation would be turned on its head: Schwanden was not the center of attention for him. Again reflecting this background, only two patents were filed for household appliances in the remaining ten years until Therma lost its independence.[14]

The reorientation of Therma's strategy put market observation on the agenda as a separate topic for the first time, particularly in the Household Goods division. Future developments would no longer be guided by engineers and designers' heartfelt enthusiasm, but instead by attentive analysis of the public's reactions, inclinations or resistance, given that in spring 1969 Group Chairman Hefti had identified Therma Schwanden's "main problem as a production program that no longer conformed to the market."[15] In fall of the same year, the job descriptions for the heads of each profit center or division proved revealing. These included the following requirements for applicants – once again referred to only in the masculine form – "5. Marketing and Sales: He shall supervise the marketing of profit center [XYZ] with the aim of maintaining and increasing its market share in the long term. / 6. Design and development: Taking account of the results of marketing, he shall monitor the programs of profit center [XYZ] with a view to improving existing products and developing new products in order to remain competitive and open up new sales opportunities."[16] "Marketing" was a new term in Therma's toolbox. Positioning it so prominently as an upstream stage before research and development had two implications: It could be read as an implicit criticism of Hilfiker, who had still developed his products autonomously, on his own initiative; at the same time, however, marketing was a typical phenomenon of that era, along with the emergence of management consultancies more generally. The two went hand in hand and were symptomatic of a mode of economic operation that, in the face of ever greater market saturation, was increasingly geared toward stimulating demand – with attention management as a key concept – and no longer based on demonstrating the worth of entirely new inventions, as had been the case in the past. In contrast, the familiar was now offered in a refined form: a spray attachment for the sink, drainage boards with a special water-removal mechanism, soon the self-cleaning oven or the glass-ceramic hob surface – all examples of evolving appliance expertise.

In spring 1970, a new range of cooking stoves was presented for the first time, in a parallel to Hilfiker's early days with Therma. The long-standing characteristically faceted design of the switch front, the oven and the appliance drawer was now replaced by a flat surface, presented as an advantageous modernization from a formal point of view. Designer Klaus Schlensog from the Research and Development unit wrote, "The wide range of installation and equipment variants called for systematization of the appliance's various sub-assemblies, in order to attain rational production despite the extensive overall range. In selecting visual design elements, the focus was on integrating the appliance harmoniously into the kitchen as a whole. The clear display of the operating status and labeling of the control elements is highly beneficial for the purchaser when using the appliance."[17] The latter point refers to the pilot lights and the easily identifiable correlation between switches and hotplates. The ranking in terms of convenience levels was redefined and new designations were selected. The simplest model, A 1000, had three hotplates and an oven, but no appliance drawer; at medium-comfort level, the A 2000 had four hotplates, one of which was a Megastat hotplate with temperature sensor, plus an appliance drawer and, as a major innovation, a viewing window and interior lighting for the oven; the luxury version A 3000 had four hotplates (two of which were Megastat hotplates), individual pilot lights for the hotplates and the oven with

6.5a

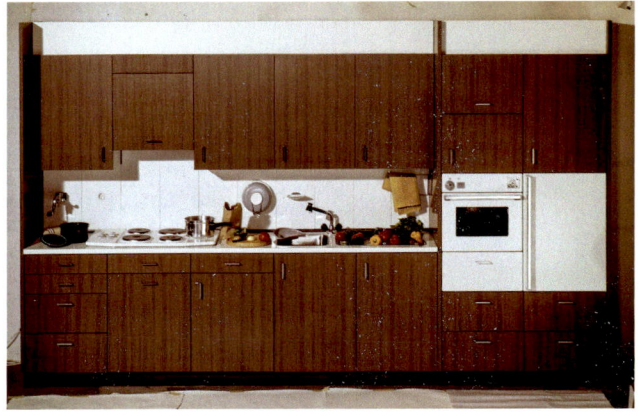

6.5b

6.6a

6.6b

6.5a View of front of kitchen units with wood-look rear wall (coated plywood), new and more angular handles; the built-in cooking stove now has a viewing window, the major achievement after Hans Hilfiker's departure and placed in the limelight in advertising.

6.5b View of front of kitchen units with the rear wall still made up of enameled panels, the frontage, however, in wood-look (coated plywood), appliances in white enamel (Oktagon, oven) or powder-coated (refrigerator).

6.6 Once again, as in 1961, the cooking stove plays the role of signaling a new era. Two studies for built-in models, one with (a) and one without (b) an appliance drawer. The viewing window is lower and somewhat wider than in the version approved for production. Designed by Klaus Schlensog from HfG Ulm.

6.7

6.8

6.7 In 1970 advertisements turned the spotlight on the viewing window in the new
2000 and 3000 cooking stove models.
"Our kitchen window offers you the most
beautiful view." Pop Art style illustration
by Christa Zelinsky for the Halpern advertising agency.
6.8 The French version of the slogan.
6.9 CH patent no. 538249, "Oven with viewing
window," related to a protective grid
on the internal side of the viewing
window as protection against splashes
of fat, filed on October 13, 1972. (The
solution created a new problem: how
do you clean the grid?)
6.10 Page from the in-house magazine
TH Information, 1972: After many years
of development, the dishwasher is finally
available on the market.

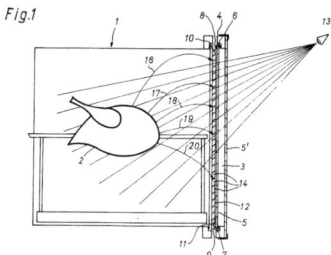

Fig.1

538 249 *
1 Blatt

Fig. 2

6.9

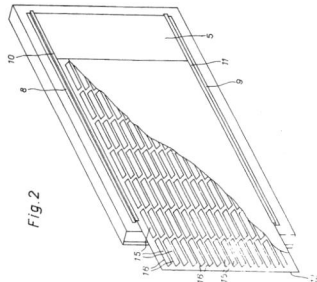

6.10

a viewing window, an infrared grill with a rotating spit, a synchronized timer with a chime and a self-cleaning oven that used the American catalytic process with a special (microporous) coating of the baking chamber (that variant was dubbed "Thermolytic"); in addition, the appliance drawer could also be heated. The technical requirements at the highest comfort level had risen significantly compared to 1961. The range of variants remained somewhat reduced, but was easier to handle from a manufacturing point of view than for the previous generation of appliances.

The most striking distinction between this version and its predecessor was the double-glazed oven viewing window, referred to in the advertising with an ironic twist now inspired by Pop Art and therefore postmodern: "Our kitchen window offers you the most beautiful view." Was that truly irony? Probably it's more accurate to describe it as a calculated tongue-in-cheek joke. The illustration shows a deliberately kitsch stylized sunset in the window, followed by this list: "View of the sizzling roast – view of the browning cake – view of the rising soufflé."[18] The design was once again created by the Halpern advertising agency, yet its idiomatic touch only makes the parallel epochal shift from the pathos of modernity to the whimsical punchline's camaraderie all the clearer – more about that later. Hilfiker had always categorically opposed the viewing window for thermodynamic reasons. Now, however, in year one of the post-Hilfiker era, the viewing window entered the scene playing a leading role. The audience gave it a big hand. The "free market forces" of preferences came into play, and half a century later scarcely anyone would argue that the attitude that won the day in this case was unreasonable. The viewing window does not necessarily have a detrimental effect on heat distribution. The front panel of the A 3000 luxury model in particular, with its horizontal pattern of lines and finely framed additional elements, conveys a further aspect typical of the time by means of the stylistic expression of completeness and prestige (or indeed even excess and opulence) that it creates, in a very similar manner to dashboards in US cars from that time, or more precisely, their Japanese derivatives, which took the market by storm in those years, especially in Switzerland, as well as throughout Europe. (→6.7)

Again analogously to the early 1960s, the round of innovations hit the refrigerator and freezer range after sweeping through the household cooking That assertion certainly holds true. The new approach was less radical, but more practical. What did it involve? The standard chilled compartment with an installation height of 760 mm (6/6) remained unchanged, while a second compartment with a height 4/6 of the first compartment (505 mm) was arranged above it as a freezer. If the lower cell was not set directly on the plinth, but was installed above two drawers, each 253 mm high, the lower door's bottom edge was 61 cm above the floor and the upper door's top edge was 188.5 cm above the floor. This kind of impressive two-part fridge-freezer (1 + 2/3) was a more elegant solution than Hilfiker's concept of integer addition (1 + 1). "The new supersizes from Therma are here!" the leaflet announced. They were also available as free-standing models. (→6.4)

1972 was like an echo of 1961, when "it's all new" was the buzzword. After years of development and hesitation, the dishwasher finally came onto the market, followed by a newly designed ventilation unit called Purair for domestic kitchens, a second option for the self-cleaning oven (the catalytic version was now joined by the pyrolytic process, which worked at higher temperatures of up to 500 degrees Celsius) and a completely new household kitchen – "the most modern domestic kitchen," as the company magazine called it, with cabinet doors and other surfaces available in four color variants.[19]

The dishwasher was designed for ten place settings and had two counter-rotating spray arms with three spray levels and a cross-flow fan with heating for drying. With its "very pleasing appearance," it made a rather different

Der Komfort-Einbauherd von Therma
mit selbstreinigendem «thermolytic»-Backofen

Der tausendfach bewährte «thermolytic»-Backofen von Therma gibt der Hausfrau die Freude am Backen und Grillieren wieder.

Sein katalytischer Spezialbelag erledigt die bisher mühsame Putzerei schon während des Backens und Bratens. «thermolytic» – der Backofen mit dem aktivsten katalytischen Reinigungsverfahren!

«thermolytic»

6.11

Ein Gesamteindruck des Therma-Standes von der «Küchenstrasse» her. Links die Wunschküche, rechts eine Winkelküche aus dem neuen Therma-Küchenprogramm.

6.12a

Kochen Backen Braten Grillieren mit Therma

Unser «Pièce de résistance», das Kochherdsortiment, stiess zu jeder Zeit auf hohes Interesse.

6.12b

Die neue Therma-Haushaltküche ist in den 4 Grundfarben: Weiss, Mooreiche, Walnuss und Grün erhältlich. Bequem zu bedienende Auszugselemente, ein durchdachter Innenausbau und ein vielseitiges Zubehörteile-Programm machen sie zur modernsten Haushaltküche

6.12c

6.11   Brochure for the self-cleaning Thermo-lytic oven, probably 1972.
6.12   "Muba-Report": Photographs of the Therma stand at the 1972 Mustermesse in Basel from the in-house journal *TH Information* (no. 6, 1972):
a   The "Therma Household Goods" stand;
b   wall with the new cooking stoves;
c   cabinet doors and panels in the new subdued tones (bog oak, walnut, dark green) as a proactively promoted alternative to a white kitchen.
6.13a   The prospective "dream kitchen," likewise presented at Muba 1972. It now has a dishwasher and a glass ceramic cooktop with extractor hood included integrated light above it – a remake of the former chimney cap?
6.13b   Detailed view of the 1972 "dream kitchen" with glass ceramic cooktop, here still divided into four sections.
6.13c   Important component of the envisaged "dream kitchen": cupboard with full use of the space thanks to storage sections on the inside of the door and movable or stackable shelves set on joints – a striking idea.

So leer wie auf diesem Bild war die Wunschküche — mit welcher Therma-
Haushalt Trends und Entwicklungen, Wünsche und Träume der Hausfrauen zeigen
wollte — während der Messe nie. Den ganzen Tag über wurde sie von Hausfrauen,
Architekten, Küchenbauern und Hobbyköchen belagert. Sie hat damit einen
wesentlichen Beitrag zur Image-Korrektur von Therma-Haushalt beigetragen.

6.13a

Nicht nur einen konzentrierten, sondern auch einen
eleganten Arbeitsplatz zeigt dieser Ausschnitt aus der Wunschküche mit der neuen Glaskeramik-Kochfläche im Vordergrund
und dem Spülsatz mit Rüst- und Schneidbrett im Hintergrund
sowie dem darunter eingebauten Geschirrspülautomaten.

7

6.13b

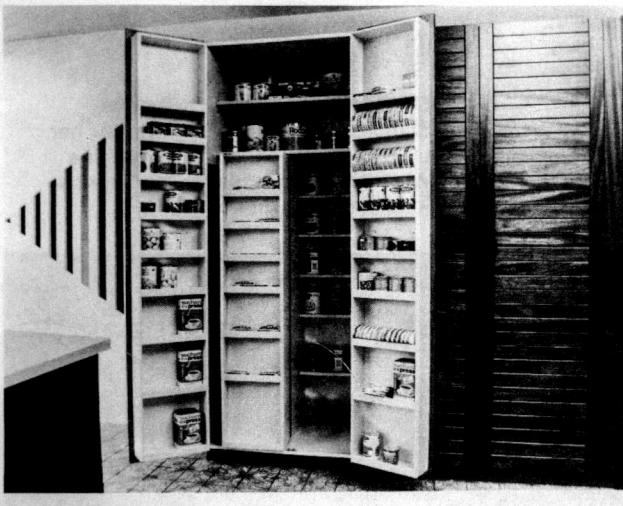

Die immensen Staumöglichkeiten und die Übersichtlichkeit
des Vorratschranks überzeugten jeden Betrachter.

6.13c

213

6.14

6.15

6.14 Interior set up in the photo studio in 1971: typical red-shift of the spectrum as often seen in those years. Fitted kitchen with wood-look imitation cabinet doors and other surfaces. The white appliances ensure an unavoidable (intentional or tolerated?) contrast. The kitchen equipment on the wall (coffee grinder, cake tins) as decorative accessories pay semi-ironic tribute to bygone coziness. The dishwasher is still from another brand (Merker). The most important aspect, however: the open "corner kitchen" had been discovered as a way to establish a closer link between the kitchen and dining area.

6.15 Completion of the tub for the Therma dishwasher, undated photograph from the 1970s.

6.16 CH patent no. 423120, "Dishwasher," filed on April 21, 1965, while Hans Hilfiker was still in charge. The patent application relates to the configuration and mode of functioning of the three spraying arms.

Fig. 1

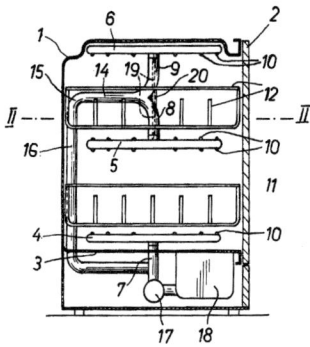

Fig. 2

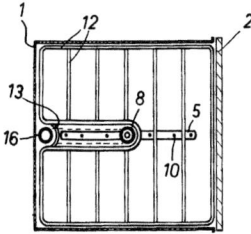

6.16

[→ B]
"Finding a synthesis for a new household kitchen that would also incorporate the most rational production, simple storage of parts, faster assembly, a more varied selection of elements, easy installation of appliances, kitchen technology, color scheme and interior fittings more in line with market demands, as well as scope to assemble the kitchen ready to install on site thanks to back panels and finally making it 'ready to use' with practical appliance components, was not exactly easy. However, that was roughly what the 'new kitchen' specification for the development department demanded. If the new Therma kitchen can lay claim to being called a 'complete' kitchen, it is because a kitchen manufacturer in Switzerland has never before perceived the household kitchen in its entirety and implemented it as a product as comprehensively as Therma Household Goods has done." (26)

visual impression than these appliances generally did.[20] A patent for the arrangement of the spray arms was filed in 1965, while Hilfiker was still with Therma.[21] It took seven years for this appliance to be launched, a much longer time frame than with earlier new developments. Group CEO Robert G. Wimmer told the Administrative Committee in January 1971, "We are late to market [with this], but not too late."[22] An entire folder of international patent documents on dishwashers in the Glarner Wirtschaftsarchiv Archives (GWA), the archives of Glarus' economic history, demonstrates the changing times and how things had even been turned on their head. For decades, Therma had almost always been among the pioneers and could easily file a patent for an invention. Now it had to jostle for position within an already crowded field.

The striking aspect of this new tone was the emerging focus on what was by this point called public relations. Hilfiker had always addressed the "friends of Therma" in his publications. His 1967 lecture at an international trade congress in Montreux had a "sensational" effect, as Walter Baur, Schwanden's Commercial Director, noted at the time.[23] Hilfiker was talking to experts, rather than to the general public; in addressing the latter, he generally relied on the persuasive power of reason. There was no in-house magazine in the Hilfiker years. It was first published in 1955, essentially as something akin to a club magazine with rather anecdotal articles, and was discontinued four years later. As noted above, it was relaunched under different circumstances at the end of 1969 and in a much more professional manner, with the title *TH Information*. It was intended to serve as a guide within and for the entire corporate group.

With the advent of the dishwasher, the last element missing from the "complete kitchen" as it was understood at the time had become available. The thus completed Therma kitchen celebrated its premiere at the 1972 Muba, promoted as a *Wunschküche* (dream kitchen), and caused something of a stir among the public and experts. *TH Information* reported on this to the group's workforce under the cheerful title "Muba Report 1972" and with a contemporary twist. "Dream kitchen: The dream kitchen – with which Therma's Household Goods Division aimed to present trends and developments, housewives' wishes and dreams – was never as empty during the trade fair as in this photo. It was besieged all day long by housewives, architects, kitchen manufacturers and amateur chefs. It made a significant contribution to setting straight the image conveyed by Therma's Household Goods Division."[24]

The in-house newspaper described the complexity of a development project like the new household kitchen by listing the comprehensive specifications that justified the epithet of "complete kitchen":[25] [→ B] "most rational production," "simple storage," "accelerated assembly." The remarkable point here is the emphasis on economic factors related to production. There had been repeated laments over the years about Therma products proving unprofitable despite strong demand. The redesign aimed to change that and finally achieve good business results again.

Reports on public reactions were also addressed to the workforce. They established a link between daily factory work, where the workpieces were on display, and how the products were received by the target group, the fascinated general public, how visitors and impressed competitors laid siege to the appliances at the fair.[26] [→ C] A double-door larder unit mentioned in this connection was an obvious solution to keep spices, provisions and other ingredients neatly organized. The refrigerator door with its internal compartments was in a sense retranslated here into folded-out cupboard compartments reminiscent of an altar's opened wings. A convincing idea like this was not patentable, but was immediately grasped and appreciated

[←C]

"The new Therma dishwasher was immediately the talk of the town – especially among our competitors. Time and again, representatives from competing companies were spotted inspecting the appliance and examining the arguments put forward by Therma staff. [...] In addition to the other new products, the Therma dream kitchen was the number one attraction. The dream kitchen in stained mahogany was practically besieged with visitors throughout the trade fair. The double-door larder unit with hinged interior racks repeatedly prompted compliments and exclamations of appreciation from visitors to the Therma kitchen manufacturers. However the glass ceramic hob was also attractive enough to inspire housewives, amateur cooks, architects and kitchen manufacturers. [...] The press, in particular several editors of well-known women's magazines, were also welcomed and informed. And even Federal Councilor Tschudi was warmly greeted by his friend G. Roth at the Therma stand with the words 'Hi there, Hanspeter.'" (27)

by the public – perhaps also because its obviousness was tinged with reminiscences of an old, forgotten solution to a problem?

Group President Wimmer described the 1972 show to the Board of Directors as a "resounding success," in particular because of the new kitchen (the "dream kitchen") and the dishwasher.[27] The new cooking stove had a glass-ceramic surface and a self-cleaning oven that used the catalytic or – in the more expensive models – pyrolytic method. Production of the dishwasher began in late summer of 1972 and there was great demand, also for the extractor hood. As overall customer preference continued to shift from metal to wood, Therma decided to start manufacturing wooden kitchens in a recently vacated factory in Rupperswil, Aargau, in May 1972. The design and manufacturing were based on chipboard with a plastic coating (with a wood-style look or plain green or white), held together by a screw connection recently developed by designer Oswald Zangerle. This economical construction principle did not require any expensive equipment, just a relatively small number of new machines, such as circular saws and presses for the coating. Its lower production costs and the high degree of public acceptance increased profit margins. Metal kitchens continued to be manufactured in Schwanden, as did the essential appliances (stoves, fridges, boilers, extractor hoods) for them, along with custom-made variants in wood.

The less profitable range of small appliances was significantly reduced, with only the coffee machine (now with an automatic warming function), the hotplate and the hotplate set remaining in the production program.[28] Irons were no longer manufactured; however, Therma purchased two iron models (with or without steam) in the GDR and marketed them under the Therma brand without disclosing their origin. (→ 6.19a)

Halpern was still the agency that conjured up the visuals for Therma's advertising during this decade – until around 1973 – but those visuals had changed. Pre-1970, the brochures and catalogs still stuck to a hallmark landscape format of 21 cm × 26.5 cm with precisely positioned typography; in 1971, that switched to A4 in portrait format. References to the Halpern agency no longer appeared.[29] The controlled profile, cultivated for years under Hilfiker, became rather less rigorous and the seemingly ascetic, yet appealing, discipline evaporated. The erstwhile "Japanese" lucidity gave way to naturalism; the predominance of black and white, interspersed with sparse color highlights, was replaced by continuous four-color printing; the arrangement of the typography turned symmetrical; the always deliberately stylized color composition capitulated to the depiction of reality; the printing colors corresponded to the objects' actual colors; the once meticulously controlled visual direction, incorporating sharpness and blurring, stillness and movement, had had its day. The A 3000 stove appears in the image as I see it when cooking, diagonally from above, as does the frying pan with the veal shanks ready to be served and the vegetable pan to the left (when the brochure is unfolded). If you think you hear a touch of regret in these lines about this shift into the realm of the prosaic, you would not be mistaken. And if you suspect the influence of marketing behind this categorical change of course, you are probably not mistaken either. However, it is only fair to note that the canonical visual language of the cultural advertising elite had its own expiry date. Visual design as presented in the Swiss journal *New Graphic Design* thrived to a large extent because it stood out from the mainstream. When the extraordinary becomes a stylistic model, it contains the seed of rigidity within it.

Over and above the visual material, it is also remarkable to see how the language per se, including the vocabulary, shifted, for example in the meaning of the term "trend," as utilized above in the phrase "the emerging trend." That was a new addition to Therma's vocabulary, as was the willingness to acknowledge the phenomenon: the trend as a driving force in the market,

6.17

demanding to be listened to and demanding a response. With his confidence in progress, Hilfiker had paid little attention to trends; in this context he viewed his role, if at all, in setting trends, rather than in passively following them. During the trajectory that led to the kitchen's modernization, he had 27.5-cm-wide (1/2 module) enameled wall cladding panels developed for the area between the worktop and the wall units; originally only available in white, in 1972 they were also offered in red and orange, two trendy colors typical of the period around 1970.[30] They remained in the range for some time. From year to year, however, the general public increasingly began to prefer brown-toned ceramic wall tiles decorated in farmhouse-pottery style. The brochure for the pull-out extractor hood from 1972 already shows these tiles, which convey a completely different message to the sheet steel elements. (→6.21) That was the seventies vibe: back to the cozy and solid. There was a tendency at the time to make designs generally chunkier and that became the defining trait of the decade, whether one thinks of goblets, seating, or the tableware selected for Therma's advertising. That more robust look was supposed to signify something like authenticity. As already mentioned, the company newspaper reported that the dream kitchen has thus "made a significant contribution to setting straight the image conveyed by Therma's Household Goods Division."[31] That photograph of the Therma kitchen at the 1972 Mustermesse was not just a random snap, but the key image of the time in brand recognition terms.

Throughout Therma's history, the kitchen had been a place where technical progress was immediately apparent. In 1960, Hilfiker saw the kitchen as a stage on the path to comprehensive modernization of the living room and the entire home, which he described to customers as a highly desirable development. At this point, however, there was what could be termed a backlash on the part of the cozy front rooms, with the self-cleaning oven, extractor hood, large freezer compartment, dishwasher and sink all adopting a retro look – although for the time being appliances such as the stove, refrigerator and dishwasher remained metallic white. Sophisticated technology appeared in a familiar guise. As mentioned above, the design and manufacturing foundation for this look was screw-fixed chipboard with a plastic coating in a what today would be called a "wood-style look." The wood variants available were "bog oak" and "walnut," complemented by green, combined with white edging, in a mix emblematic of the furnishing style fashionable at the time. It might seem like a rather lighthearted consideration: With the first successful moon landing by the American Apollo 11 mission in summer 1969, a fascinating goal of progress had been achieved; after that it was no longer quite so clear what "progress" could mean. "Coziness revisited" was one option for a broader audience. A glaring example of this "revisiting" of the past was on display at the Domotechnica trade fair in Cologne in 1977, when Therma subsidiary Hergensweiler staged a wooden kitchen with a "cabinet door relief" (the in-house term for the baroque-style scrollwork on the cupboard doors) for the traditionalists among the German public.[32]

Economically, the early 1970s were characterized by a tight labor market, rising wages and intense competition for orders. Demand for complete kitchens was strong. Seeking to counteract the staff shortage in Schwanden, Therma opened a crèche, which was expected to attract ten to fifteen additional employees, in 1970. "The number of women working part-time is constantly increasing," the 1970/71 annual report noted. As in the early days of Therma, orders were again placed for work to be carried out at home: assembly of components or small appliances, mainly by women and in sheltered workshops in neighboring villages such as Haslen, Luchsingen or on the Urnerboden alp. Producing entire kitchens was space-intensive and the available premises in Schwanden were far too small for efficient production. In May 1972, Therma therefore began to manufacture kitchens in wood with new components in a recently vacated factory in Rupperswil, Aargau, where

6.17 Brochure for the top-notch 3000 cooking stove model, 1971: The angle from which the shot is taken corresponds to the gaze of the person cooking. Naturalism took the place of programmatic abstraction during the Hilfiker era.

6.18

6.19a

6.19b

6.20

Therma-Auszugsentlüfter

Formschön, frontbündig, funktionstüchtig, leicht einzubauen

Das sind vier Vorzüge des Auszugsentlüfters
von Therma

6.21

6.22

6.18   The 1974 Muba presentation and the
        swirly pop-style stand design.
6.19a   Flyer with the steam iron and the iron
        with regulator switch.
6.19b   The 6/12 filter coffee machine was
        available in red, the quintessential flair
        of the early 1970s, and, as here, in
        brushed chromium steel to chime with
        refined, dark-toned surroundings. This
        kind of adaptability in addressing various
        customer segments was growing ever
        more advisable in the light of the emerg-
        ing market saturation.
6.20   Kitchen setup with built-in hotplates
        in chromium steel accompanied by
        a hyperactive background intended
        to convey forceful vitality, 1970.
6.21   A contrast to 6.20: Page from a brochure
        with an extractor hood and tiles in a style
        reminiscent of peasant ceramics, 1974.
6.22   Further upping the ante, the sentimental
        relief frontage of Therma Hergensweiler
        (Baden-Württemberg), shown at Domo-
        technica in Cologne in 1977.

it had rented a substantial 7,500 m² space. By way of comparison, the total production area in Schwanden was around 25,000 m², the floor space of the production hall with the sawtooth roof only a tenth of that. The order books for 1972/73 were even healthier than in the previous year, so Therma confidently rented a further 5,000 m² in fall 1973.[33] Shortly afterwards, it emerged that this was an inopportune moment to expand, for in late 1973 OPEC's oil production policy triggered the first acute global recession since the 1930s. Although there was a time lag before it affected sales of complete kitchen sets, the impact was all the more severe; however, in the 1973/74 financial year, sales of complete kitchens, kitchen ensembles and boilers continued to grow.

Compared to the previous year, 1973 was less spectacular in terms of new products. The latest dishwasher received good ratings in test reports and sold well.[34] In spring 1974, Therma considered discontinuing refrigerator production but that idea was later abandoned.[35] The Administrative Committee noted that developing what was dubbed the "wet room," a combi-nation of kitchen and bathroom, would depend on cooperation with the construction industry and was viewed as a long-term task.[36] However, that project was never implemented as Therma also experienced a sharp drop in orders in fall 1974, which led to job cuts and curtailed working hours. There was a nasty sting in the tail for Therma, as this occurred just a few months after the aforementioned 5,000 m² additional space in Rupperswil was rented. Household Goods was the division most affected by the down-turn.[37] Once again, as in 1967/1968, Therma was surprised to see how the market developed. Group Chairman Robert G. Wimmer, who now held the title of General Manager, mentioned "organizational problems in gradually separating kitchen construction from appliance manufacturing" and re-ferred to the heavy workload he faced due to his responsibilities throughout the group. On the Board of Directors, the mood concerning Wimmer shift-ed. Group Chair H. R. Niggli (representing Elektrowatt) commented that Wimmer "had long since had the opportunity to implement the measures he was now proposing and/or that we had requested" and demanded that he should move his place of work to Schwanden and "ensure everything is in order" there. However, Wimmer handed in his resignation just days later.[38] In view of the situation, the Administrative Committee discussed whether Therma should seek to involve an outside company, but decided against it for the time being.[39] The issue had already been briefly mentioned in 1967. The fundamental decision in 1975 to discontinue kitchen production, thus resolving the old conflict with the other kitchen manufacturers, was painful, but unavoidable. The intention was to revive the business with ready-to-install appliances. Only twenty-five percent of production capac-ity was utilized in the 1975/76 financial year. However, kitchen production was not entirely terminated until April 1, 1979.

The idea of cooperating with an outside company arose again and again over the years. After the 1974 crisis, in June 1975 the main shareholder, Elektrowatt, announced its intentions to sell its Therma shareholding to Bauknecht (group management in Stuttgart, a branch in Hort); the name Electrolux was also mentioned by the Hefti Group.[40] At this point, a differ-ence of opinion emerged between President Hefti and the group's Vice President, Director Hans Bergmaier from Elektrowatt. Quite apart from the general economic situation, Bergmaier viewed Therma and Schwanden as the crux of the problem and was inclined to seek affiliation with Bauknecht, a proposal for which Hefti could not work up any enthusiasm at all. Hefti considered the preparatory negotiations with Bauknecht, which collapsed rapidly, to be damaging to the company's reputation and at this point favored a collaboration with Electrolux, but not a takeover – although he was aware that there was not yet an entrepreneurial concept for such collaboration. While the vertical restructuring of 1969 had entailed auda-ciously plucking potentially useful instruments out of the toolbox, the dis-

[→ D]

"There was a remarkable change in kitchen and appliance construction. Up to this point, white appliances had been predominant, but it became increasingly clear that colored appliances would soon have their day. Stylists and designers from kitchen manufacturers, the furniture industry and also purchasers seemed increasingly to agree that color was needed in the kitchen. This change was another important reason to create new kitchen appliances." (47)

6.23   Ludwig Walser, production-ready design for the Alpha model of the 77 cooking stove series, 1977.

6.24   Ludwig Walser, production-ready design for the Gamma model of the 77 cooking stove series, 1977. The mocha brown color tone was not derived from the RAL color system but was instead chosen by the designer.

6.25   The Therma structural design team for the new cooking stoves in the 77 series, from left to right: Head of Development Oswald Zangerle, Rudolf Tschudi, Paul Combet, René Blesi. In contrast to the previous series, the 77 focused more on a stable form, including prior to the units being built into the kitchen, and were much more solidly built.

cussions about establishing a connection to an international firm went more in the direction of self-medicating. In late summer 1975, Friedrich Zweifel, previously Director of Elcalor, was appointed as the new Group Manager with the title of General Manager.[41] In his acceptance speech, Zweifel stalwartly outlined the broad compass of all the issues he was entrusted with addressing. Over and above the most urgent issue of sales problems, this remit included "internal rationalization, streamlining work processes, more stringent management, simplification of appliance types, improving quality and working on the problem of new products, possibly also on a licensing basis. He noted that he was aware that the focus is on the Schwanden Household Goods division."[42] In 1976, the Board of Directors appointed Ernest Hösli, who had a doctorate in business administration and was born in Schwanden in 1924, as the new director of the Schwanden plant; he was the last operational manager of what was then still the independent headquarters who had local ties to Therma's birthplace.[43] The 1975 financial year brought a twenty percent drop in orders for the entire industry in Switzerland. When developing new models, it had long been a requirement to reduce the number of variants to allow for more economical production. A new series would combine more models than ever before.[44]

This was achieved alongside other important objectives in the case of the new BR 77 household cooking stove (BR stands for *Baureihe*, meaning series). Its basic features and numerous details were more solidly constructed and more finely formed than in its predecessors, giving it an overall higher-quality appearance. Its improved design concept was tangible when you opened the oven door or rapped your knuckles on the metal paneling. The ready-to-install cooking stove had a sturdy frame made of angled profiles, which clearly set it apart from the less stable structural designs in the previous series, which had been made of flat bar.[45] A clear, uncluttered design was chosen for the front-facing surface with the switches. Development of the BR 77 had taken over two years. Its most striking feature was the mocha brown color scheme of the superior comfort categories, which chimed subtly with other details; the Alpha model was only available in white.[46] [→ D] The stove exuded a sense of careful design and manufacturing thanks to the narrow aluminum frames around the switch front and the lower part of the oven door and appliance drawer. This appearance was largely created by industrial designer Ludwig Walser. In the company magazine, he was only mentioned in passing in connection with the demanding development process: "Mr. L. Walser, freelance 'industrial designer,' finally explained the difficult design challenge that he had to resolve."[47] Unfortunately there is no record of what Walser said when the new cooking stove series was first presented. Very few of those reading the information sheet will have understood the demands that the profession of industrial designer entails, in particular that it is not limited to visual appearance but also includes seeking out user-friendly and production-oriented structural design; Walser, however, did get that message across to his audience. One person involved at the time reports that Walser always came to the meetings with models and clear ideas – including proposals for the color scheme.[48] The use of mocha brown (not a standardized RAL color) was also inspired by a proposal from Walser. It was one of the color options for the dishwasher, too, and was defined to be compatible with the color palette used by kitchen manufacturers at the time. The four comfort categories available for the stove, for which Therma reverted to the earlier names Alpha, Beta, Gamma and Delta (for the deluxe model), were developed with a view to reducing the number of variants. The prestige model, Delta, boasted an impressive set of sophisticated details: an entirely glass front, illuminated rings around the switches, a meat thermometer and a heated drawer, as well as a timer with a chiming sound and programming functions.

At this point in the late 1970s, after a period of crisis, Therma's appliances were once again offering convincing quality – once the Household Goods

6.23

6.24a

6.24b

6.25

Die neue Therma Linie:
damit in Ihrer Küche wirklich eins zum andern passt.

In einem warmen Bronzebraun präsentiert sich die neue Therma Linie. Eine Farbe, die der Natur nachempfunden wurde. So fügen sich alle Geräte natürlich in Ihre Küche ein. Besonders bei modernen Küchenfarben und bei Holz.

Auch das Design ist so durchdacht, dass eine ruhige Harmonie entsteht. Keine überflüssigen Verzierungen. Dafür eine klare Flächenaufteilung. Und zweckentsprechende Formen. Das zeigt sich deutlich an den übersichtlichen Bedienungs-Elementen und den griffigen Schaltern.

6.26

6.27

6.28

6.26   In the late 1970s, Adolf Wirz AG, which had by then taken charge of Therma advertising, tapped into the slogan "Back to Nature"; brochure for the 1978 manufacturing program.

6.27   A view of the trick photography workshop used to produce the previous photo: the gesture of "naturalness" is produced as an ultra-analog image involving considerable staging efforts.

6.28   Just out: the new cooking stove. A faint echo of the 1961 advertising idea (cf. 5.31). But however much you love nature – why unpack the cooking stove in freshly fallen snow?

Division had freed itself of competition-related problems for complete kitchens and could concentrate instead on the appliance categories of stoves, dishwashers and extractor hoods. This made Therma an attractive choice for an affiliation with the Swedish Electrolux Group. For a time, Therma Haushalt (Household Goods) was labeled as "sick" by the Board of Directors and Administrative Committee. However, the company managed to consolidate its position thanks to the new high-quality appliances and, after lengthy discussions to clarify various questions, was in much better shape when it joined the Electrolux Group at the turn of 1978/1979.

The plant in Schwanden thus became a production plant for Electrolux. The logo of the new group that now owned the site was set above the entrance to the administration building; it was no longer the corporate headquarters, just one of several bases. Refrigerator production was discontinued in 1979. The other appliances – cooking stoves, dishwashers and extractor hoods – continued to be manufactured in Schwanden, with the Therma brand remaining active until 2004. New models were developed at Electrolux in Zurich in the 1980s, but in the early 1990s development was moved back to Schwanden along with the specialist staff for the cooking/baking units. Appliances were still produced there for Electrolux until 2015. The plant consistently operated profitably within the Electrolux Group throughout the thirty-seven years following the end of Therma's independence. Today, all of Therma's key buildings in Schwanden have been preserved and are used comprehensively. Being easily accessible has helped them avoid the fate of other industrial sites in the area that are still abandoned.

1 Hans Hilfiker, "Therma und Therma-Konzern. Bericht an den Verwaltungsausschuss der Therma AG" (typescript, 49 pages), October 31, 1959, p. 2. – Hefti Family Fonds, Dr. Hans Hefti-Haab Estate, Schwanden (Glarus South) [hereinafter: Hefti Family Fonds], "Organisatorisches" file.

2 File note by Peter Hefti on the meeting of the consortium members at Therma AG on September 27, 1967 in the meeting room of Elektrowatt in Zurich, p. 3. – Hefti Family Fonds, "Analysen F+E"

3 Ibid.

4 Letter from Peter Hefti to ICME/Stettbacher, July 6, 1968. – Hefti Family Fonds, "Analysen F+E"

5 W. Lindecker, "Untersuchung über Therma AG und ihre Tochtergesellschaften," August 1, 1968, pp. 1–2. – Hefti Family Fonds, "Analysen F+E"

6 Ibid., p. 2.

7 VR-Protokoll [Minutes of Board of Directors meeting] 407, June 5, 1970, p. 11. – Hefti Family Fonds

8 GWA Elux K 4–1/1

9 *TH – In Richtung Zukunft. Information der Therma-Gruppe*, November 1970, p. 12. – GWA Elux K 4–1/1

10 Peter Hefti, "Bemerkungen zum Bericht ICME vom Juli 1969 'Europäischer und Schweizerischer Markt für gewisse Haushaltprodukte,'" October 20, 1969. – Hefti Family Fonds, "Analysen F+E"

11 Large housing estates built by Ernst Göhner AG: Adlikon, Benglen, Greifensee, Volketswil (all Zurich Canton), Neuenhof (Aargau Canton).

12 The plug-in principle was a contagiously popular idea in the 1960s and 1970s as a central facet of industrially produced architecture. Prefabricated technical modules consisting of one or very few units would be brought to the building site ready for connection and only needed to be plugged in. The "wet room" theme should be seen in this context.

13 The group management office was located at Wilfriedstrasse 6 in Zurich-Hottingen.

14 CH patent no. 538249: "Backofen mit Sichtfenster," filed on October 13, 1972. CH patent no. 575580: "Abzugshaube," filed on November 29, 1974.

15 VR-Protokoll 398, March 4, 1969, p. 2. – GWA Elux B 2-1/3

16 Peter Hefti, "betr. Funktionsbeschreibungen Leiter der Gruppe bzw. Leiter der PC [profit center]," letter to ICME, September 9 1969, pp. 2–3. – Hefti Family Fonds, "Analysen F+E"

17 Klaus Schlensog, "Das neue Sortiment der Therma-Herde und -Backöfen," in: *TH Information*, no. 2, late 1969, p. 7. – GWA Elux K 4–1/1

18 Brochure for the cooking stove program, April 1970, illustration by Christa Zelinsky / Erwin Halpern advertising agency.

19 "Die 'totale' Küche von Therma," in: *TH Information*, June 1972, p. 6. – GWA Elux K 4–1/1

20 *TH Information*, June 1972, p. 4. – GWA Elux K 4–1/1

21 CH patent 423120: "Geschirrspülmaschine," filed on April 21, 1965.

22 Minutes from the Administrative Committee, no. 1, January 29, 1971, p. 2. – Hefti Family Fonds

23 VR-Protokoll 390, November 24, 1967, p. 4. – GWA Elux B 2-1/3

24 *TH Information,* June 1972, p. 7. – GWA Elux K 4–1/1

25 "Die 'totale' Küche von Therma," in: *TH Information*, June 1972, p. 6. – GWA Elux K 4–1/1

26 *TH Information*, July 1972, pp. 6–7. – GWA Elux K 4–1/1

27 VR-Protokoll 421, April 20, 1972, p. 2. – Hefti Family Fonds

28 66. Jahresbericht, 1972/73. – GWA Elux B 4–1/2

29 Archive documents from the Erwin Halpern agency made available to the author contain printed matter relating to Therma up to around 1975 (privately owned, Zurich). On this basis, it can be concluded that these specimen copies originated from the Halpern advertising agency.

30 CH patent 424185: "Wandverkleidung zu Küchenkombination," filed on June 18, 1965.

31 *TH Information*, July 1972, p. 7. – GWA Elux K 4–1/1

32 Illustration in *TH Information*, April 1977, p. 3. – GWA Elux K 4–1/1

33 See the annual reports from 1970/71 to 1975/76. – GWA Elux B 4–1/2

34 67. Jahresbericht, 1973/74. – GWA Elux B 4–1/2

35 Protokoll des Verwaltungsausschusses [Minutes from the Administrative Committee], no. 2, March 21, 1974, p. 2. – Hefti Family Fonds

36 Ibid., p. 5.

37 68. Jahresbericht, 1974/75. – GWA Elux B 4–1/2

38 VR-Protokoll 436, September 13, 1974, p. 1. – Hefti Family Fonds

39 Protokoll des Verwaltungsausschusses, no. 5, September 5, 1974, pp. 1–2. – Hefti Family Fonds

40 VR-Protokoll 439, June 20, 1975, p. 2. – Hefti Family Fonds. Elektrowatt was not prepared to raise further capital for a share capital increase of 2.5 million CHF.

41 VR-Protokoll 440, September 18, 1975, pp. 3–4. – Hefti Family Fonds

42 Ibid.

43 Both Zweifel and Hösli only stayed on until the takeover of Therma by Electrolux, which took legal effect with an extraordinary general meeting on January 4, 1979.

44 Cf. VR-Protokoll 407, June 5, 1970, p. 3. – Hefti Family Fonds

45 Interview with René Blesi, then a structural design office employee, February 2025.

46 H. J. Gredig and H. P. Lips, "Die neuen Therma-Herde BR 77," in: *TH Information*, May 1978, p. 6. – GWA Elux K 4–1/1

47 Ibid.

48 Interview with René Blesi, February 2025.

6.29

6.29 The testing carousel for technical
approval of each cooking stove, here
the Alpha model, 1978.

Remarks on a Mutually Dependent Relationship: Therma and Schwanden Power Station

August Berlinger

Samuel Blumer's name first appeared in connection with the Schwanden electricity company (EWS) as a supplier, recorded in the firm's 1904 annual accounts as "S. Blumer, mechanic, for electric oven including plug, cooking stove and serpentine plug – 164.90 CHF." In 1905, he was already listed in an EWS invoice "for irons and electric stoves" to the tune of around 130 CHF, compared with 155 CHF paid to his competitor "Elektra Wädenswil, for cast-iron table-top hotplate, stove hotplates, tailor's irons and repairs." In 1906, "Sam. Blumer, Fabrik elektr. Heiz- und Kochapparate" can be found in an entry for 130 CHF for the budget item "Installation revenue" in EWS' annual accounts and, again, this time on the revenue side, in the operating account under the heading "power supply" (electricity to drive motors), in this case with 170 CHF indicated.[1]

This was still the order of magnitude to be expected for a small trader and craftsman, almost twice as much as the 90 CHF paid by the tinsmith, less than the 200 CHF for each of the butchers' refrigeration compressors. The sums were a far cry from the approximately 3,500 CHF bill for the local brewery or the 14,400 CHF that the neighboring spinning mill paid the electricity company. After Therma's first factory building was constructed in 1907, the EWS bill in 1910 showed power consumption of 13 hp (10 kW), a tenth of the power that Textil AG had signed up for. In the wake of the initial expansions at the Schwanden site in 1916, that figure rose to 45 hp (33 kW). In 1919, Therma secured 140 kW by contract, although the recession that set in after the First World War meant that only 85 hp (63 kW) was de facto utilized in 1920.[2] In those days, the power-equivalent units for electricity consumed were expressed in horsepower (hp), drawing our attention to this pre-industrial unit of measurement, which has survived to this day in common parlance.

The 1919 supply contract between the electricity company and Therma stipulated that the energy supplied could be used to drive engines, for lighting and for other technical purposes. It was "three-phase alternating current of 3,000 volts, 50 Hertz frequency" and it was "guaranteed that the voltage and frequency are subject only to the usual fluctuations." Therma also had to stump up for cable feed-in from the Plattenau transformer station to its own transformer station.[3]

By 1923, the economic context had improved and the EWS power plant at Niederenbach had increased its output significantly. For that reason, the new supply contract did not only include "125 kW of electrical energy for any use for its own purposes in its business operations," but also stipulated that "over and above this connected load, Therma AG shall purchase all the energy it requires from EWS, provided that EWS is in a position to fully cover Therma AG's demand for energy." However, Therma's electricity consumption did not outstrip EWS output until 1926.[4]

After further expansions to Therma's premises, the electricity to be supplied was set at a maximum of 220 kW in 1927, "for which Therma AG guaranteed EWS a minimum income of 17,600 CHF." It was also stipulated that "in addition to the contract of January 2, 1923, EWS shall supply Therma AG with up to 80 kW of electricity at night." In 1928 an enameling furnace had just been installed in the production hall that extended the factory to the east and plans for a new large-scale electricity power plant on the Sernf and Niederenbach watercourses were in the pipeline; against this backdrop, an additional contract was signed for supply of a further 120 kW "to be utilized for heating-related, electrolytic and electrochemical purposes."

This marked the start of an era of parallel contracts determined by the intended use. That distinction was vital, as electricity supply for heating purposes was organized with specific delivery times and tariff models, which meant that purchases and billing had to be carried out separately.

It was therefore agreed that "Therma AG shall install facilities in the relevant buildings in a manner that precludes transfer of this electrical energy to other premises." This was to ensure that cheaper electricity intended for heating could not be used for other purposes, which would have been in breach of the contract.[5]

Calorific electricity, i.e. electricity for heating, is generally provided at night, when demand for other purposes is lower. This power is therefore offered at particularly low rates. Through these contractual conditions, the parties prepared to make the most of the Sernf-Niederenbach power plant's future potential. A further aspect of this was EWS' decision to install a higher capacity cable supply line directly from its "In der Herren" switching station to Therma's second transformer station in 1929. This became necessary because EWS did not have the technical capacity to supply the quantity of energy that Therma now required from its own power plant, nor could it offer the requisite prices. However, invoicing was nonetheless through EWS as the Sernf-Niederenbach power plant was not authorized to supply end customers for political and legal reasons. The energy was now supplied at 8,000 volts. These developments meant that Therma became EWS' largest electricity customer.[6]

During the crisis-stricken early 1930s, industrial energy purchases fell noticeably, leading electricity suppliers to seek further sales outlets. Competition broke out between the gas and electricity companies to power kitchen appliances in homes and thus to win the hearts of housewives. That of course had a direct impact on Therma. In the first instance, prices for heating energy were lowered and subsequently demonstrations with electric stoves were offered. Vaunted as "cooking displays," these shows sparked an immediate retort from competitors in the form of similar demonstrations for gas stoves. The electricity suppliers countered by offering free installation and reduced appliance prices. That was only possible with support from appliance suppliers and in turn large electricity producers also subsidized advertising campaigns and sales of electrical appliances. Therma also ensured its business appeared in the local media in addition to "standard" advertising campaigns throughout Switzerland – independently, in association with local appliance suppliers or municipal electricity utilities, as well as in conjunction with electricity generators.

Construction of the new gas pipeline network in the Glarus hinterland in 1910/1911 already constituted a commercial challenge for the electricity company and for Therma. As an initial reaction, EWS slashed the summertime tariff for cooking with electricity by thirty percent in 1911 and redoubled its efforts the following year, running a sales campaign for household appliances in cooperation with Therma. An illustrated flyer, directed "to the housewives of our esteemed subscribers!" announced that "Schwanden's electricity company has taken up the challenge of putting electricity at the service of housewives, too. One useful application is the electric iron." In prime advertising style, the leaflet went on to list the drawbacks of gasoline-powered or conventional coal-powered irons, before pronouncing that "all these advantages make the electric iron indispensable for domestic use." It concluded with the announcement that "in order to accommodate the less well-off, Schwanden electricity company is prepared to offer a significant reduction in both the annual fee for electricity and installation costs, including the iron." The same applied to the express cookers. Furthermore, "we provide a one-year guarantee for all appliances, i.e. we will bear the costs of all repairs during this period caused by poor materials. Finally, we should like to inform you that the Schwanden electricity company will provide both irons and stoves free of charge for a fourteen-day trial period."[7]

Fears of a coal shortage during the Second World War led Therma to secure a third contractual supply line in 1939. Years earlier, the Glarus textile industry had already begun to generate the hot water and steam needed for its production processes using night-time electricity from its own small-scale power plants or from major suppliers, with the coal-fired boilers continuing to operate in parallel if required. Therma contractually secured 250 kW for its heating system, followed by an additional 500 kW in 1940. In 1941, joint contractual provisions for the two sums were stipulated as follows: "Supply of electrical energy required for hot water production comprises subscription to a maximum of 700 kW. The subscriber undertakes not to exceed the specified power offtake." If overruns were urgently required, Therma had to consult with EWS and the Sernf-Niederenbach power plant.

The other contractual clauses reveal that the suppliers had the upper hand at this point. "Energy shall only be supplied to the extent permitted by the available capacity of EWS and/or Kraftwerke Sernf-Niederenbach AG. However, they are not obliged to supply such energy. EWS may interrupt a supply of electricity that has been initiated at any time after giving four hours' notice." Furthermore, "if the subscriber's central heating system is in operation and EWS and/or Kraftwerke Sernf-Niederenbach AG are in a position to offer energy, the subscriber undertakes to offtake this energy and to switch from fuel-fired operation to electrical operation within a maximum period of twelve hours." EWS declared that it was not liable to pay compensation for any of these restrictions and interruptions in electricity supply. When setting prices, a figure dubbed the "coal equivalent" was applied, i.e. one kilowatt-hour was calculated to correspond to 165 grams of Ruhr coke.[8]

In 1944, the basic supply contract was adapted to the new circumstances. "The electricity to be supplied comprises a subscription for 500 kW," now with the more flexible condition that "the energy supplied to Therma shall be made available for any use for its own purposes in its own factory operations." As the end of the war was in sight and there were widespread fears of a recession akin to the one after the First World War, EWS secured its position as best it could: "Therma guarantees EWS minimum annual income of 500 × 75 CHF = 37,500 CHF for this supply of electricity, with a maximum volume of 500 kilowatts. It undertakes to pay for any shortfall at the end of the contractual year if this volume is not consumed in full." The electricity company also reserved the right to demand appropriate reimbursement from Therma if the federal government or the canton imposed an unforeseen levy on the power plant.[9]

However, the recession did not materialize and Therma continued to thrive. In 1948, when the Erlenhof welfare center began to operate, the contractual agreement with the electricity producer stated that "the electricity to be supplied comprises a subscription for 40 kW. This can be exceeded after prior agreement with EWS management. However, unless the contract has been amended in advance, EWS is under no obligation of any kind to supply more than 80 kW. Therma expressly declares that the energy supplied will only be used for operation of the factory canteen and will not be transmitted to third parties." In this case, too, there was a latent fear that Therma was "optimizing" its purchases at the expense of EWS. Not without good reason: in 1951, following an inspection of the transformer stations, EWS insisted that Therma must put a stop to connections in breach of contract as well as eliminating the option to switch between the two Therma transformation stations. In addition, EWS demanded that the firm's electricity consumption be billed correctly – energy purchased illegally that year amounted to two thirds of the amount purchased in compliance with the contract! That same year, Therma's second switching station received an upgraded connection, as did Therma's first switching station in 1953, opening up the prospect of supplying them with 16 kV in the future.[10]

Expanded production meant the basic supply contract was increased from 500 to 700 kW in 1956. In view of EWS' plans to raise the grid voltage to

16,000 volts, Therma pledged to "equip any new high-voltage installations to be built or converted with series 20 materials (i.e. 16-kV-compatible) and to design the premises in such a way that the requisite clearances for the increased voltage are available." The latter point was necessary to help prevent electric arcs (flashovers) between the power cables.

In 1957, the energy contract for the enameling furnaces was also revised and the power to be supplied was set at 500 kW. As had been the case since 1931, the electricity was de facto supplied directly from the Sernf-Niederenbach power plant. In 1960, the contract for the power needed for the heating system also had to be amended, as Therma switched from coal to heating oil as a parallel energy source. The energy to be supplied was raised by another 500 kW. At the same time, 1 kWh was computed as being equivalent to 0.115 or 0.117 kg of heating oil (depending on the type). In 1970, energy supplies were uniformly subject to the EWS' industrial tariff and the power under contract was 2,000 kW.

The relationship between Therma and EWS was not limited to the dusty, somewhat abstract world of energy contracts. Power shortages when water was scarce posed very real challenges for electricity generators and consumers alike. In 1920, for example, an "electricity shortage" forced EWS and the Linthal power plant to restrict or displace the supply periods for industry in their catchment area of Glarus Grosstal (the main valley). In the worst case scenario, half of the large consumers would be supplied from 4 a.m. to 1 p.m. and the other half would receive electricity from 1 p.m. to 10:30 p.m. Particularly energy-intensive work was shifted entirely to nighttime hours. School lessons also had to adapt to this regime. In spring 1944, the drought was so severe that the federal government ordered electricity-saving measures. That was again the case in 1947, but the situation was even more severe, as the dry period lasted into the fall that year. There was also a significant reduction in the water available in the winters of 1948/1949 and 1955/1956.[11]

Unless otherwise indicated, the minutes and files referred to are in the Glarus State Archives, the archives of Technische Betriebe Glarus Süd, Elektrizitätswerk Schwanden (EWS) department and the Glarus Local Business Archives (GWA), Therma department, or are taken from: August Berlinger, *Strom fürs Glarnerland. Die Entwicklung der Stromversorger in den Glarner Gemeinden 1890–2010* (Näfels: Technische Betriebe Glarus Nord, 2022).

1   EWS Annual Accounts for 1904–1906.
2   EWS Annual Accounts for 1906–1920.
3   Purchase/supply contract dated March 31, 1919.
4   Purchase/supply contract dated January 2, 1923; EWS Annual Accounts for 1926.
5   Purchase/delivery contracts dated July 20, 1927 and August 1, 1928.
6   Purchase/supply contract dated December 1, 1931; EWS Annual Accounts for 1929 and 1931; plan with line outlets from the In der Herren EWS switching station, approx. 1930.
7   EWS Annual Accounts for 1934; EWS household appliance campaign 1912, advertising leaflet and registration card as well as subscriber information 1930; Bilten electricity supply: Annual Accounts for 1932; advertisements in the local press (*Glarner Nachrichten*, *Neue Glarner Zeitung*, *Glarner Volksblatt*), 1932–1934; *Strom fürs Glarnerland*, p. 243.
8   Purchase/supply contract dated May 15, 1941; EWS Annual Accounts for 1939 and 1940.
9   Purchase/supply contract dated July 10, 1944.
10 Purchase/supply contract dated June 16, 1948; EWS Annual Accounts for 1951 and 1953; EWS letters to Therma dated May 21 and November 15, 1951; *Strom fürs Glarnerland*, pp. 249–250.
11 Purchase/supply contracts dated October 10, 1956, November 1, 1957, June 14, 1960; EWS annual invoices for 1951, 1953, 1956 and 1957; EWS information letter to Therma, September 4, 1975; *Strom fürs Glarnerland*, pp. 244 ff.

7.1   "Cooking with electricity – a demonstration": advertisement in the regional press for a display intended to convince the audience of the advantages of cooking with electricity. Glarus, April 1932.
7.2   Renowned chef A. Niederhauser with two assistants standing next to Therma household cooking stoves. The photo must date from after 1935, as the successor model from 1935 is already visible alongside the popular *Siedlungsherd* (four of the latter shown here).
7.3   The transformer station in the Therma factory, photographed in 1927 before the large-scale expansion of the plant the following year; from an extensive album to commemorate Therma's twentieth anniversary with photos taken by the Schönwetter photographer dynasty in Glarus.
7.4   The enameling plant and a view into one of the four furnaces for porcelain enameling of the sheet-metal-formed components. The photo epitomizes the thirst for electric power, which the electrical plants were designed to satisfy.

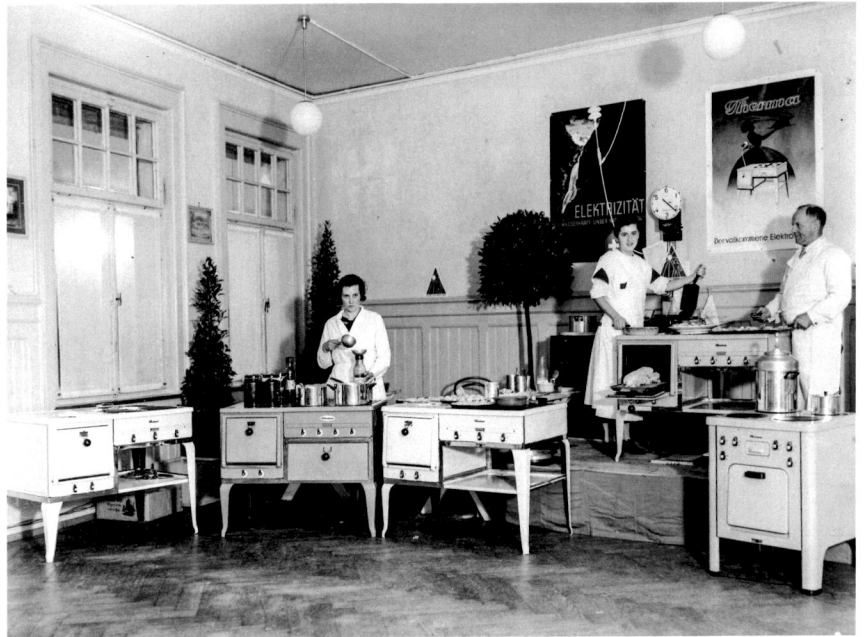

7.1

7.2

7.3

7.4

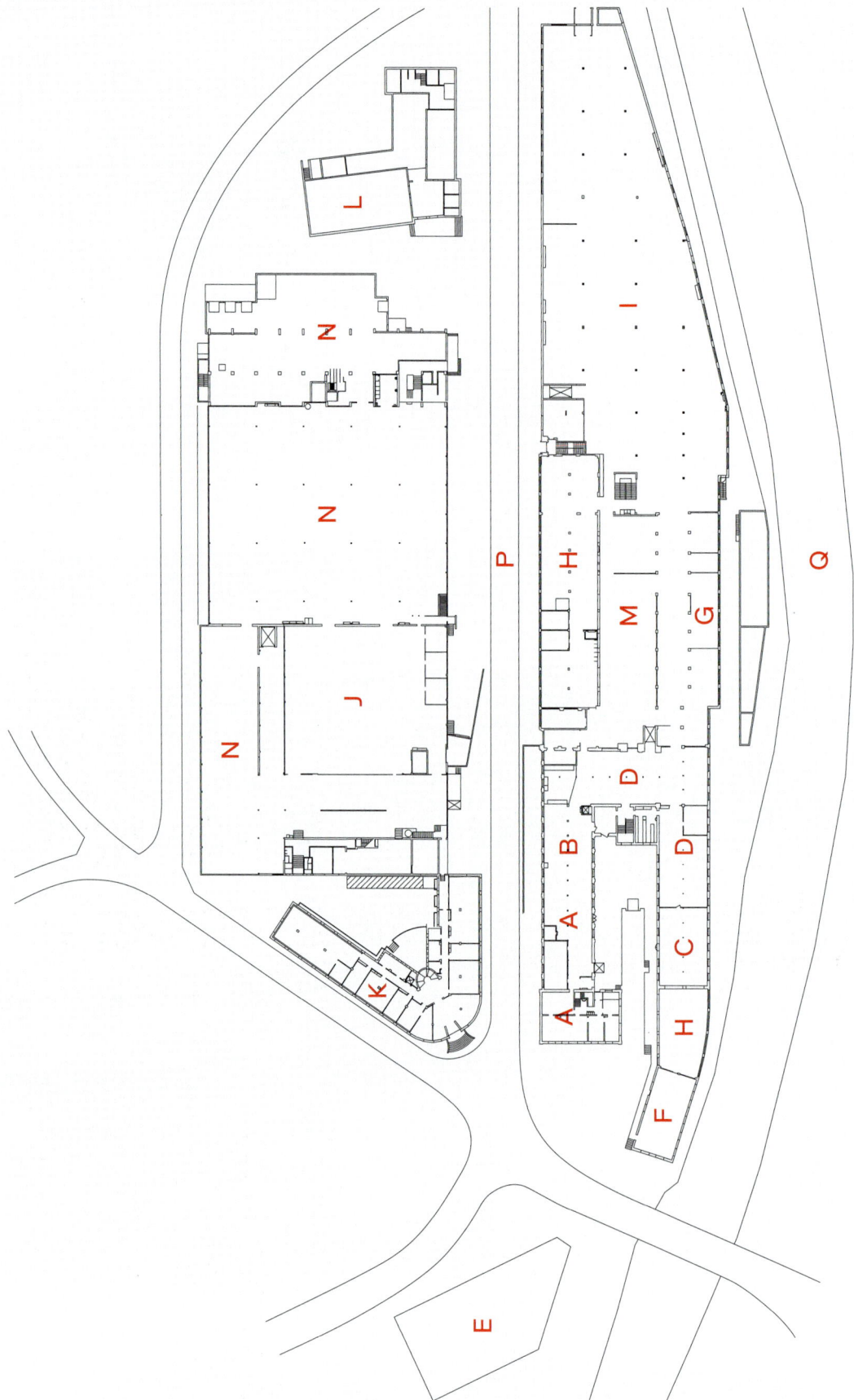

L

N

N

N

J

K

P

H

M

G

I

A

B

D

D

A

C

H

F

Q

E

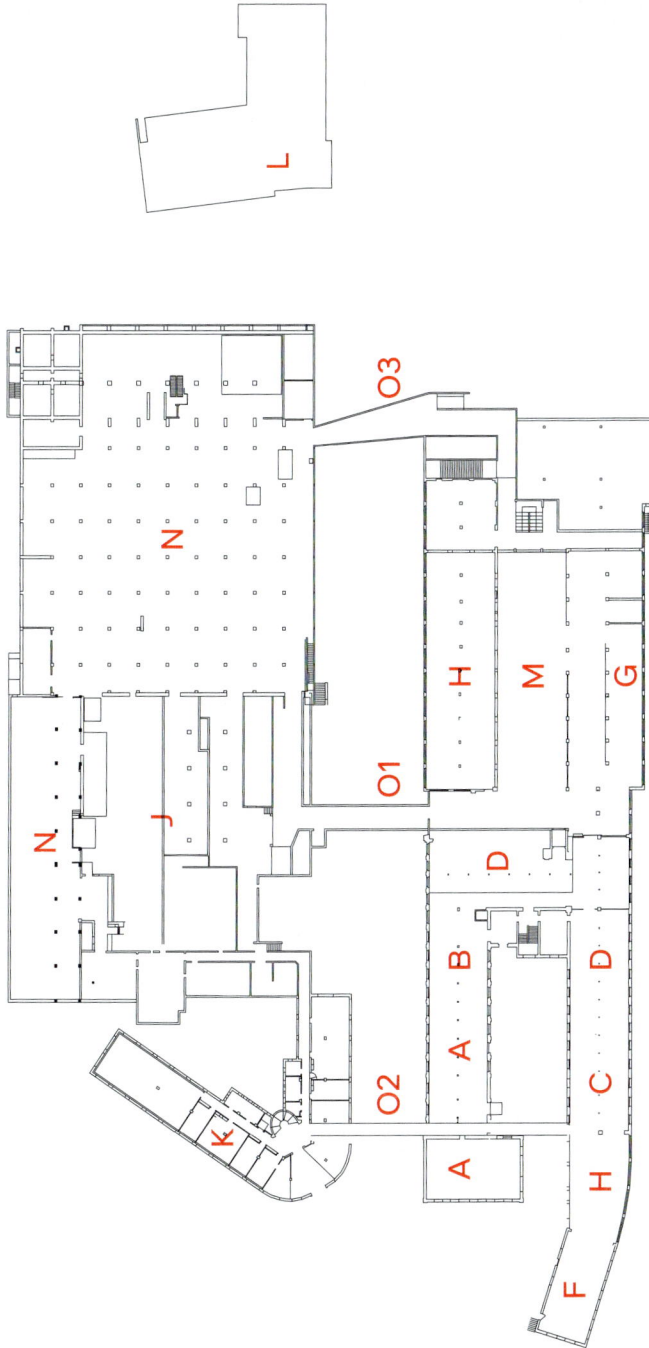

Therma Site, Schwanden
Overview Plan of the Structural Development

Floor plans, scale 1:1250, as of ca. 2010:
232   First floor
233   Basement

A   1907
B   1912 (extended 1918)
C   1914
D   1916 (extended 1918)
E   1918 dispatch building (demolished 1983)
F   1924
G   1925
H   1926 (extended 1928)
I   1928 hall for production of parts
J   1931 enameling plant
K   1941–1942 administration building
L   1947–1948 Erlenhof (welfare center)
M   1955 development of the east yard
N   1962–1963 sawtooth-roof hall/four-story building
O1   Underpass (1931)
O2   Underpass (1941)
O3   Underpass (1962)
P   Sernftalstrasse
Q   Sernf (direction of flow is to the left)

1904 Founding of the firm S. Blumer, Schwanden, Fabrik elektrischer Heiz- und Kochapparate (July 1); first product: heating pads for medical applications; recognition from doctors for this innovation.

1906 Design and production of a simplified iron, price war with competitor Elektra in Wädenswil; gold medals in Paris and Milan for S. Blumer; project: to found a stock corporation and construct a factory.

1907 The stock corporation is founded: share capital 250,000 CHF; the firm's name is registered as: Therma, Fabrik für elektrische Heizung A.G., formerly S. Blumer, Schwanden; plans for the factory drawn up by Séquin & Knobel, architects specialized in industrial buildings; start of construction in March 1907, commissioning in October.

1911 First pioneering use in Switzerland of robust nichrome wire, a material developed in the USA, for heating elements.

1912 Founding of the Electrotechnical Institute at the Swiss Federal Polytechnic (today: ETH Zurich): Therma's early days reflect the state of play in the natural sciences at the time.

1912–18 Several extensions to the factory in rapid succession; in 1912, five new bays extend the length of the production hall, further extensions in 1914 and 1916, floors added in 1918.

1913 First mention of commercial appliances: roasting and baking oven for the zero-alcohol café run by Zurich Women's Association for Temperance and National Welfare.

1913/14 Share capital increased to 312,500 CHF, 93-strong workforce.

1913/14 Development of hotplates with a heating element in a spiral-shaped recess beneath the cooking surface (grooved hotplate); household cooking stoves with a remarkable functional design.

1914 Gold medal at the National Exhibition in Bern.

1915 After the outbreak of the First World War, pronounced increase in demand for electric household appliances due to fuel shortages; share capital 375,000 CHF.

1917 Further increase in capital to 750,000 CHF; establishment of an in-house workers' assistance fund; 208-strong workforce.

1917 Textile dealer and Glarus politician Heinrich Jenny-Schuler (1861–1937) is appointed President of the Board of Directors (to 1936); from 1915 to 1935 he is also a member of the National Council in Bern.

1918 Construction of the dispatch building at the western end of the Schwanden site.

1919 The letterhead mentions a "Permanent Exhibition at Zurich Main Station"; share capital 1.5 million CHF; the workforce numbers 276 workers and employees.

1920 Construction of Rüteli residential estate with six detached and semi-detached houses for employees' families; purchase of Hotel Bahnhof and fitting out of the common room as a dining hall for non-local workers; workforce numbers around 350 workers and employees.

1921/22 Economic crisis; workforce cut to 200.

1924 The firm advertises in October proclaiming its success, "Appareils électriques THERMA / de toute première qualité / Plus d'un million en usage dans le monde entier" ["THERMA electrical appliances / top quality / Over a million in use worldwide"]; ads and brochures from this period testify to Therma's impressive international reach, extending far beyond Europe (Argentina, Mexico, Maghreb, South Africa).

1925 Purchase and decommissioning of competitor Elektra in Wädenswil, founded in 1898 by Friedrich Wilhelm Schindler-Jenny; engineer Hans Dietler becomes Technical Director of Therma; opening of first sales office in a Swiss city: Zurich, Seefeldstrasse 9.

1925/26 Factory extended to the southeast, initially one story, additional floors added in 1928.

1926/27 Vigorous support through promotional campaigns by various power plants in Switzerland to encourage use of electric energy, inter alia through cooking demonstrations.

1927 Introduction of the new long-standing wordmark (in use until 1958, designer unknown); sales office in Bern, Monbijoustrasse 47.

1927 Special Prize at the Swiss Hotel and Catering Exhibition in Zurich (ZÜGA).

1928 Samuel Blumer resigns as Director and Delegate Representative to the Board of Directors as of July 1 and is succeeded by Hans Dietler; another large-scale extension of the factory on the eastern side for component production: single-story hall with skylights, installation of a large deep-drawing press.

1929/30 Intensive period for exhibitions and trade shows: Barcelona International Prize (Grand Prize for the electric heating sector – Therma had 20 sales outlets in Spain alone); Sample Fair in Basel and in Milan; ZIKA (Zurich International Culinary Show) where the firm was awarded 2 Grand Prizes with a gold medal ranking; Basel Housing Exhibition with the new cooking stove range (Siedlungsherd). Designer Wilhelm Kienzle is involved for the first time in developing new products.

1931 Construction of the enameling plant: commissioned on December 20 after only five months of construction work; 70% of electrical household appliances in Switzerland are made by Therma; domestic sales rise dramatically, but exports sink by a third; 780-strong workforce.

1932 The economic crisis hits Switzerland hard, too; redesigns in the interest of more rational manufacturing; Saturday is no longer a working day; launch of refrigerator production, cooling units initially from Kelvinator in Detroit, USA; 25th anniversary; since 1907 Therma has produced 3 million appliances.

1933 At Mustermesse Basel (Basel Sample Fair) Therma announces: 80,000 Therma boilers and 180,000 Therma cooking stoves in operation; sales office in Lausanne, Rue Pichard 13.

1934 Production launch for stainless steel sinks; in-house production of compressors due to USA trade barriers; new share capital 1.7 million CHF.

1935 Crisis, 3 to 6% wage cuts for workers; state subsidies for exports, including to the Netherlands.

1936 30% devaluation of the Swiss franc in September helps export business and thus also Therma.

1936 Purchase of Maxim AG, Aarau.

1937 Death of Heinrich Jenny-Schuler, lawyer Hans Hefti-Haab (1886–1964) is appointed new President of Board of Directors.

1937 Acquisition of "Guggach" building in Zurich (Hofwiesenstrasse) from Zurich municipal electricity utility and conversion to assembly and repair workshop (from 1942: "Refrigeration Office"); this step also taken to avoid being categorized as a non-local firm on the Zurich market; new share capital of 2.2 million CHF.

1938 Relaunch of the existing assistance fund foundation as a Therma savings and life insurance fund; one of the first pension funds in Switzerland.

1939 National Exhibition in Zurich (colloquially shortened to "Landi"); strong Therma presence in 10 commercial kitchens, inter alia at: Kongresshaus, Turmrestaurant, Belvoirpark, Fischerstube, Musterhotel, Veska-Klinik; September 1: German invasion of Poland, subsequently general mobilization, 60% of the Therma workforce join the military.

1941 Agreement with the firm Kummler & Matter, Aarau, in July: transfer of its appliance production to the newly founded Elcalor AG, Aarau; Therma provides 100% of the capital; severe shortage of metal raw materials; in light of the supply situation, the national government orders "the strictest frugality with raw materials and foodstuffs"; in July architect Hans Leuzinger is contracted to design a new administration building, start of construction in October.

1942 Inauguration of administration building on December 4.

1943 Share capital increased to 3.5 million CHF.

1944 Opening of a sales office in Geneva, Passage du Terraillet; construction of houses for employees in "Güetli," Schwanden.

1945 Workforce in Schwanden: over 1,000.

1947 Sales office in Zurich now on first floor at Claridenhof, at the time the largest department store complex in Switzerland, Beethovenstrasse 20; Therma becomes majority shareholder in Sursee-Werke (commercial kitchen appliances).

1947/48 Hans Leuzinger is contracted to design the Erlenhof welfare center: a dining room for workers and one for employees; ambitious technical amenities, such as floor heating with a heat pump; inauguration on September 30, 1948; establishment of a sales office in Basel: Aeschenvorstadt 24. Share capital is 5 million CHF.

1949 The easy-clean stove or Rinnenherd is a huge attraction at the Mustermesse Basel.

1952 Years of difficulties in obtaining materials draw to a close, paving the way for development and production of kitchen ensembles ("in a single block"); market launch of the new filter coffee machine and rapid heater, both "in appealing designs."

1953 Therma joins the Swiss Market Research Association.

1954 Director Hans Dietler resigns, engineer Oskar Steiger becomes new Technical Director; formally, Dietler remains a member of the Board of Directors for "special tasks" but there is no evidence of his continued involvement; Elektrowatt AG (with a long-standing connection to Schweizerische Kreditanstalt) purchases a large number of Therma shares.

1955 Therma appliances are now also sold in department stores; the Board of Directors has to overcome concerns in its ranks about resistance from installation companies concerning this decision; striking shift in demand away from individual appliances and toward ensembles.

1957 Development of the "installation frame" by Karl Keller, head of the structural engineering office; objective: interchangeable sub-units; October 18: large official 50th anniversary celebration.

1958 In spring, production of standardized ensembles with inter-changeable sub-units begins; lawyer R. Peter Hefti-Spoerry (1922–2012, Hans Hefti's son) becomes new President of Board of Directors and new Group President; introduction of a 46-hour week on full pay as of May 1; engineer Hans Hilfiker starts work in his newly created role as Delegate Representative of the Administrative Council (July 1); Oskar Steiger heads the newly created Research and Development unit; "Responsible Design": lecture by Hilfiker to the Swiss Commercial Association in Zurich (September); at the end of the year the new wordmark designed by Carlo L. Vivarelli is introduced.

1959 Death of founder Samuel Blumer on January 15; reorganization of the group: merger between Sursee-Werke and Elcalor in Aarau; exchange of product range between Therma and Elcalor-Sursee: production of commercial appliances and boilers by Elcalor-Sursee, household cooking stoves and kitchen ensembles by Therma; in April: Mustermesse Basel, presentation of compact cooking stove on legs, in fall: (Comptoir Lausanne, Olma St. Gallen) presentation of Butterfly heating stove (seven colors); redesign of showrooms in Basel and Zurich.

1960 Purchase of new service vehicles, introduction of 48-hour repair service; Oskar Steiger resigns in March; Mustermesse Basel: 31 modular components to be configured freely as ensembles, introduction of plastic finishes, further development of compact cooking stove on legs; 45-hour week on full pay as of May 1.

1961 Systematic "cooking stove campaign" for the new stove program by Erwin Halpern advertising agency; new refrigerator concept: modular chilled compartments; Hans Neuburg presents Therma's new visual identity for the first time in issue 9 of the journal New Graphic Design, published in Zurich (March).

1962 Elektrowatt becomes the Therma Group's majority shareholder; Hilfiker develops the project for an extension between the administration building and the Erlenhof: conversion of the enameling plant, a sawtooth-roof hall for assembly of kitchen ensembles and a four-story building; fitting out of the new production line with a view to genuine industrial production.

1963 Inauguration and commissioning of the new buildings in late summer; reduction of the working week to 44 hours; issue 15 of the journal New Graphic Design includes a detailed presentation of the new visual advertising language and product culture; First Prize in the "Most Beautiful Swiss Posters" competition for the three-sheet poster for refrigerators – format 128 × 273 cm – designed by Hans Heinrich Pidoux from the Halpern agency.

1964 Showroom kitchen at Expo 64 (National Exhibition): innovative sink with additional components, fold-out cooktop; visit to Expo 64 with entire workforce (May 22, specially chartered train); project to group together the commercial kitchens production of the firms Elcalor, Sursee and Therma as Therma Grossküchen [Therma Commercial Kitchens]; search for an appropriate location; strong demand for Therma's economical complete household kitchens; an additional hall to produce these has to be rented in Glarus.

1965 Introduction of television advertising in Switzerland: 30-second advertising films in German, French and Italian for the oven and the refrigerators; International Group Catering Trade Fair in Basel: presentation of the Therma rotating frying pan for commercial kitchens.

1966 Opening of the "Therma Commercial Kitchens" Center in Schlieren near Zurich (April); joint development, planning, structural engineering and sales organization of Therma, Elcalor and Sursee for the center; at the end of 1966 it has a 76-strong workforce; the group's total workforce is 1,108.

1967 Drop-off in construction activity due to countercyclical economic measures by the national government; rising costs, falling sales prices; initial consideration of the momentous question: Should Therma merge with another firm?

1968 Hans Hilfiker resigns effective October 1.

1969 Reorganization of the corporate group by management consultancy ICME, Zurich; vertical organization of the group with four business divisions: Household Goods, Cooling, Commercial Kitchens and Heating/Industry; engineer Robert G. Wimmer appointed Group Director; 1,000-strong workforce in Schwanden.

1970 Spin-off of production of cooking stoves and kitchen ensembles from Elcalor to Therma Schwanden; opening of a child daycare center in Schwanden as a measure to combat staff shortages.

1971 Fitting out of commercial kitchen at the United Nations in Geneva.

1972 Successful presentation at Basel: the "dream kitchen" as an evocative project flanked by the contemporary "complete kitchen"; market launch of the Therma dishwasher; first presentation of a glass-ceramic cooktop; Robert G. Wimmer receives the title "Director-General."

1973 Complete kitchens are produced primarily in Rupperswil in Aargau, the associated appliances in Schwanden; plastic-coated wooden cabinet doors and surfaces replace their white spray-coated metal counterparts; head count for the whole Therma Group is around 2,000.

1974 Economic downturn: sharp decline in orders and pronounced drop in sales across all corporate divisions, most notably in Household Goods; production of complete kitchens abandoned for competition-related reasons (quasi-boycott by previous purchasers of Therma appliances); Director-General Robert G. Wimmer resigns.

1975 Friedrich Zweifel (previously Director of Elcalor) becomes new Group Director-General.

1976 Refrigeration Office in Zurich closed, with its activities transferred to Elcalor in Aarau; Ernest Hösli, a native of Schwanden, becomes Director of Therma Household Goods.

1977 Development of 77-series cooking stove program headed by independent industrial designer Ludwig Walser; leading to significant improvements in structural design and better value for money, the program is a commercial success.

1978 Serious financial crisis, Electrolux Schweiz takes over the Therma Group and the shares of Therma AG (Therma Schwanden, Therma Sursee, Elcalor Aarau, Volta Bregenz); A. Pestalozzi is appointed President; the Schwanden district hopes for a corporate policy for their site that will show responsibility towards the local populace; that hope is largely fulfilled; in 1980 there is still a roughly 270-strong workforce in the plant in Schwanden in 1980; production of cooking stoves and cooktops for the Electrolux Group is terminated in 2015.

Image Credits

Claude Lichtenstein (b. 1949) published his first texts after completing his degree in architecture at ETH Zurich; 1985–2001 architecture and design curator for the Museum für Gestaltung Zürich (inter alia for the overall concept for the Design Collection), subsequently taught design studies and architectural history at various Swiss universities and technical colleges. Works published by Lars Müller Publishers: *Hannes Meyer Architekt. Schriften der zwanziger Jahre im Reprint* (1990, with Martin Kieren); *Streamlined: A Metaphor for Progress* (1992, with Franz Engler); *Air Made Visible / Far vedere l'aria: A Visual Reader on Bruno Munari* (1995, with Alfredo W. Häberli, Museum für Gestaltung Zürich); *Your Private Sky: R. Buckminster Fuller* (2 vols., 1999/2001, with Joachim Krausse); *As Found: The Discovery of the Ordinary* (2001, with Thomas Schregenberger); *Jacques Schader, Architect Freudenberg 1959: A Masterpiece of European Architecture* (2003, book and DVD, with Marc Schwarz); *Playfully Rigid: Swiss Architecture, Graphic Design, Product Design, 1950–2006* (2007). His most recent book was *Die Schwerkraft von Ideen. Eine Designgeschichte* (2 vols., Basel/Berlin: Birkhäuser Verlag, 2021). Lives in Zurich.

August Berlinger (b. 1953), self-employed master upholsterer and decorator with a keen interest in history, particularly regional industrial and energy-related history. Guest papers and lectures on these topics in various publications and fora. Selected publications: *Strom fürs Glarnerland. Die Entwicklung der Stromversorger in den Glarner Gemeinden 1890–2010* (Näfels: Technische Betriebe Glarus Nord, 2022); *Seit 100 Jahren Strom im Glarner Mittelland* (Glarus: Werkbetriebe, 2008); "Glarus," in *Schweizer Städtebilder. Urbane Ikonographien (15.–20. Jahrhundert)* (Zurich: Chronos, 2013); "Protokollbuch des Hülfskomités," in *Glarus 1861. Der Brand und seine Bewältigung* (Näfels: Historischer Verein des Kanton Glarus, 2011). Lives in Glarus.

My gratitude goes to:

Thomas Schätti, president of gukum (society for the history and culture of Schwanden and environs), for his trusting confidence, the extensive information he has shared and his constant helpfulness;
Dr. Madlaina Brugger, head of GWA, for all the many ways she has provided assistance and for her collegial support;
Andreas Iten, archivist at GWA, for being so reliable and consistently diligent in providing data about the images;
Dr. iur. Thomas Hefti for entrusting us with documents on Therma's history from the estates of his father, Dr. R. Peter Hefti, and his grandfather, Dr. Hans Hefti;
Hester van den Bold for her painstaking supervision of the project on behalf of Lars Müller Publishers;
Markus Zehentbauer for his attentive copyediting;
Helen Ferguson for her meticulous work translating the text into English;
Dimitri Bruni (NORM) for his enthusiasm in designing this publication, as well as for his inspired creativity and great precision.

I should like to thank the following people for their information, advice and help:

Hans Aebli
Dr. Hans Berger
August Berlinger
René Blesi
Giampiero Bosoni
Ruth Brechot-Störi
Jürg Brühlmann
Alf and Barbara Dietrich-Hilfiker
Fredi Ehrat
Jürg Erni
Reto Gugg
Emanuel Halpern
Dorothee Huber
Claudia Jenny
Dora Jenny-Dietler
Prof. Peter Jenny
Barbara Junod
Marcel Just
Dr. Rolf Kamm
Heidi Keller van der Kooy
Claudio Leibacher
Christina Reble
Dr. Bettina Richter
Daniel Schlensog
Ruggero Tropeano
Verein Glarner Industrieweg
Thomas Walser
Oswald Zangerle-Wagnière

C. L.

239

Colophon

Therma
Swiss Pioneer of Electric Appliances 1904–1978

Author: Claude Lichtenstein
Contribution by: August Berlinger
Translations: Helen Ferguson
Proofreading: Michael Pilewski
Project coordination: Hester van den Bold
Design and production: Norm, Zurich
Lithography, printing and binding: DZA Druckerei zu Altenburg, Germany
Papers: Dacostern, 135 g/m^2; Wibalin Natural White, 120 g/m^2
Typeface: LL Riforma

Lars Müller Publishers is supported by the Swiss Federal Office of Culture with a structural contribution for the years 2021–2025.

Lars Müller Publishers
Pfingstweidstrasse 6
8005 Zurich, Switzerland
+41 44 274 37 40
info@lars-mueller-publishers.com
www.lars-mueller-publishers.com

Product safety
Producer: Lars Müller Publishers GmbH
Responsible person in accordance with
EU Regulation 2023/988 (GPSR):
Michael Klein, sales representative,
Hub 1, DE-84149 Velden
+49 8742 964 552 2
gpsr@lars-mueller-publishers.com

ISBN 978-3-03778-792-2

Distributed in North America, Latin America and the Caribbean by ARTBOOK | D.A.P.
www.artbook.com

Printed in Germany

This publication was made possible thanks to the support of

STIFTUNG PRO SCHWANDEN

GLARNER HEIMATSCHUTZ

kanton glarus   Kulturförderung SWISSLOS

SCHÄTTI

ERNST GÖHNER STIFTUNG

CONRAD PEYER

VRENI + ROLF HÜRLIMANN

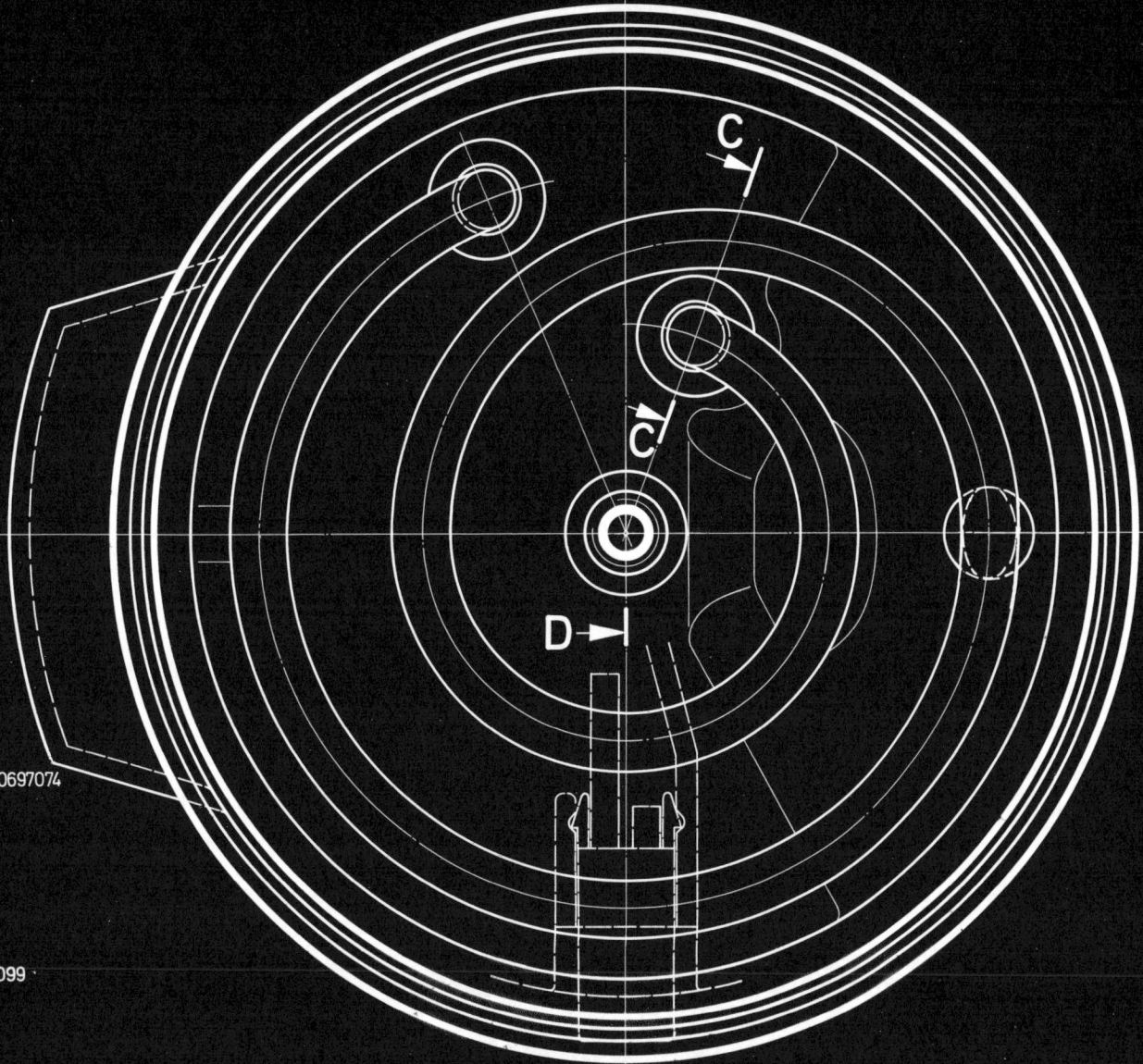

Schnitt B-B

C

C

D →

D →

Ansicht A, Sockel weggelassen

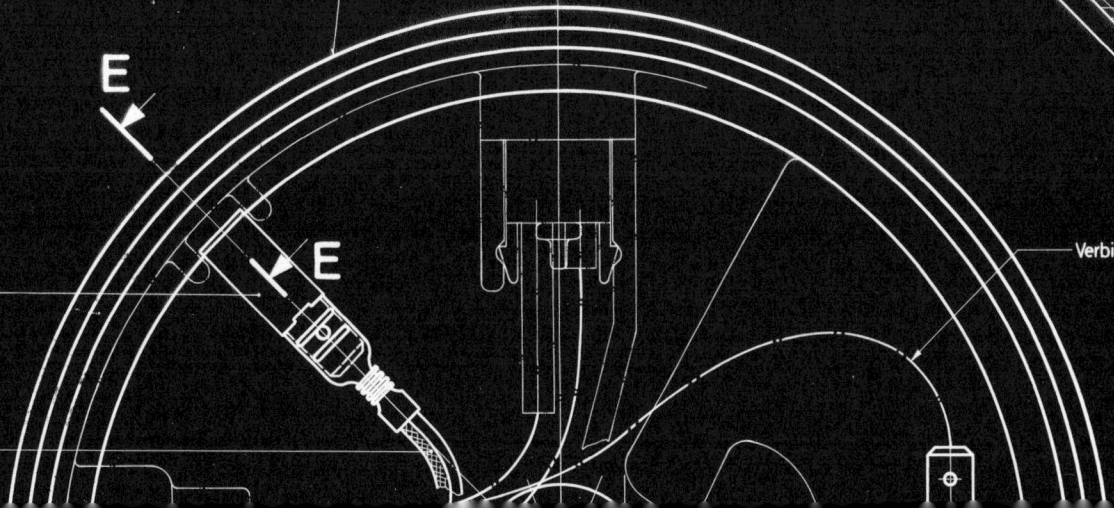

E

E

stift „Prim"
×10

Griff kompl.0697074
5

kompl.06 97099
0

06

063

06 3269

0697080

Verbindunge

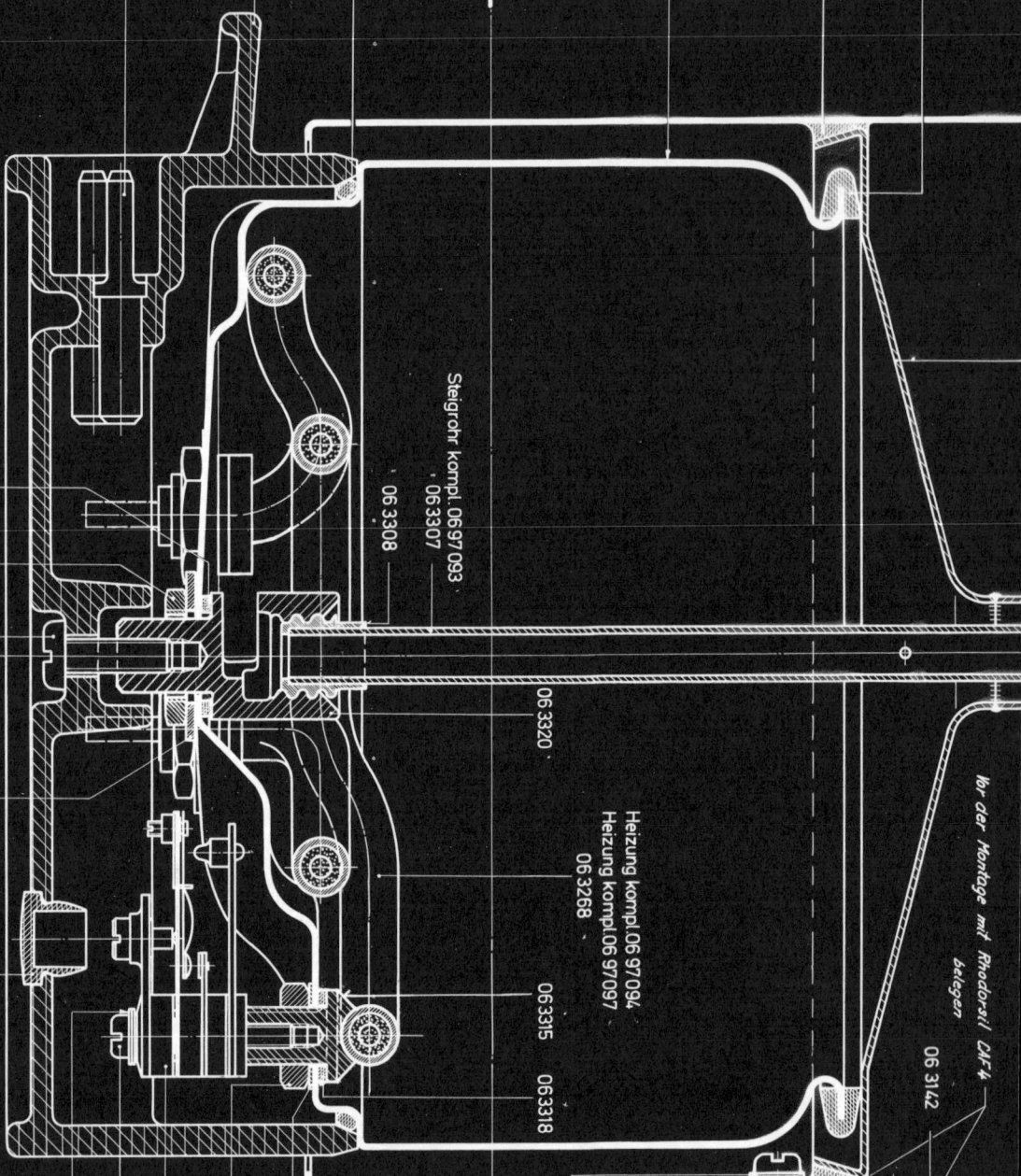

063325 ·

063323 ·

A ◄

Pan-Head-Schraube
M5×16 VSM 13304 ·

Federscheibe
B 12 DIN 137

063277

Steigrohr kompl. 06 97 093
· 063307

063308

063320 ·

Heizung kompl.06 97094
Heizung kompl.06 97097
063268

063315

063318

063329

063292 ·

Spannscheibe ⌀ 4×8 VSM 12 745

Vor der Montage mit Rhodorsil CAF 4
belegen

063142

063326

063278

063280

⌀4,/8 VSM 12745
Spannscheibe

M3,5×25 VSM 13 300
Zyl.Schraube

Flache Sechskantmutter
M8 DIN 439

Federscheibe A8,4 DIN137

▼ B

Schnitt D-D

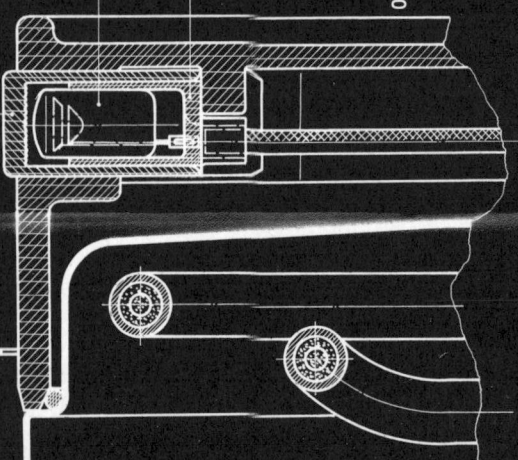

063223

063160

063333

063267
063331

063266

063 3141

0697094

06 3268

Zylinderschr.
M4×12 VSM13300

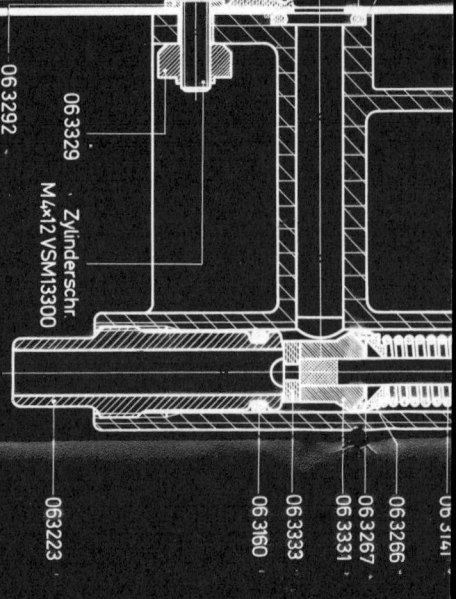